A Travel Guide to Leadership

How to Use Positive Psychology, the New Physics, and Spirituality to Transform Yourself, Your Relationships, and Your Career

Alan A. Mikolaj, MA

Lædan Enterprises, LLC
Colorado Springs, Colorado ♦ Houston, Texas
www.alanmikolaj.com

Lædan Enterprises, LLC
9850 Pagewood Lane, Ste 808
Houston, TX 77042

A TRAVEL GUIDE TO LEADERSHIP: HOW TO USE POSITIVE PSYCHOLOGY, THE NEW PHYSICS, AND SPIRITUALITY TO TRANSFORM YOURSELF, YOUR RELATIONSHIPS, AND YOUR CAREER

Copyright © 2012 by Lædan Enterprises, LLC and Alan A. Mikolaj. All rights reserved.

All rights reserved, including the right of reproduction in whole or in part in any form whatsoever without the prior written permission of Laedan Enterprises, LLC, except where permitted by law.

Scripture quotations taken from the Amplified® Bible, Copyright © 1954, 1958, 1962, 1964, 1965, 1987 by The Lockman Foundation Used by permission. (www.Lockman.org)

Limit of Liability /Disclaimer of Warranty: While the publisher and author have used their best efforts in preparing this book, they make no representation or warranties with respect to the accuracy or completeness of the contents of this book and specifically disclaim any implied warranties of merchantability or fitness for a particular purpose. No warranty may be created or extended by sales representatives or written sales materials. The advice and strategies contained herein may not be suitable for your situation. You should consult with a professional where appropriate. Neither the publisher nor author shall be liable for any loss of profit or any other commercial damages, including but not limited to special, incidental, consequential, or other damages.

ISBN: 978-0-9852286-1-3 (paperback)

Library of Congress Control Number: 2012903999

Printed in the United States

It is with great respect, admiration, gratitude, and love that this book is dedicated to:

My three beautiful children, Benjamin Raymond, Joseph Eric, and Jessica Lynn. You taught me how to be a father and a better leader.

And, to Bernadette Marie and Benjamin Abraham Mikolaj, my mother and father.

You are my first and best teachers and leaders.

A Father's Prayer

Build me a son, O Lord, who will be strong enough to know when he is weak,
And brave enough to face himself when he is afraid;
One who will be proud and unbending in honest defeat,
And humble and gentle in victory.

Build me a son whose wishes will not take the place of deeds;
A son who will know thee…
And that to know himself is the foundation stone of knowledge.

Lead him, I pray, not in the path of ease and comfort,
But under the stress and spur of difficulties and challenge.
Here, let him learn to stand up in the storm;
Here, let him learn compassion for those who fail.

Build me a son whose heart will be clear,
Whose goal will be high;
A son who will master himself before he seeks to master other men;
One who will reach into the future,
Yet never forget the past.

And after all these things are his,
Add, I pray, enough of a sense of humor so that he may always be serious,
Yet never take himself too seriously.
Give him humility, so that he may always remember the simplicity of true greatness,
The open mind of true wisdom,
And the meekness of true strength.

~ Benjamin Abraham Mikolaj
circa 1978

Also by Alan A. Mikolaj

*Drug Dosage Calculations for the Emergency Care Provider**

*Stress Management for the Emergency Care Provider**

*Available from Brady/Prentice Hall

A Travel Guide to Leadership

How to Use Positive Psychology, the New Physics, and Spirituality to Transform Yourself, Your Relationships, and Your Career

Alan A. Mikolaj, MA

Acknowledgements

My deepest gratitude and love to my lovely wife and senior editor, **Priscilla Leah Borbon-Mikolaj**, Educator, Pasadena Independent School District. Without your dedication, tireless hours of reading and editing, patience, inspiration, support, and love; this book would not be possible. You are a true leader and a leader of leaders. I am so proud, honored, and grateful to call you my wife and partner. I've finally found someone!

To my editors I offer my sincerest gratitude for your amazing ideas and stories, courageous feedback, keen editing suggestions, support, prayers, and love. I owe my deepest gratitude and love to: **Glenn Seehausen**, President and CEO, ACAD Plus, Inc.; **Renee Seehausen**, Homemaker, Pianist, Educator, and Vocalist; **Rebecca Mikolaj-Shirley**, Director of Real Estate, Greystar; **Charles Shirley**, CEO, Aidan Capital Management, LLC; **Jack Williams**, Patient Services Manager, Quest Diagnostics and Minister at Bro Jack Ministries; and, **Barbara Nance**, Patient Services Area Manager, Quest Diagnostics. Thank you for your hard work with this project, inspiration, and for allowing me to grow. Truly, this book would not be what it is without you! You exemplify the New Millennial Leaders!

Special thanks to **Reginald Coachman**, Regional Director,

Franchise Operations, Schlotzsky's Franchise LLC and president-elect, Greater Houston Restaurant Association; **Darlene Coachman**, District Manager, Five Guys and Fries; **Bertha Evans**, Educator, Pasadena Independent School District; and, **Rev. Eric Pitre**, Pastor, Immaculate Conception Catholic Church, Sealy, Texas for your input on cover design, editing ideas, and constructive feedback.

There are some angel guides/New Millennial Leaders out there who may not realize what an inspiration they have been to me. They have my admiration, respect, and deep gratitude.

- **Stacey Robyn** (www.gogratitude.com)
- **Wes Hopper** (www.dailygratitude.com)
- **Mike Dooley** (www.tut.com)
- **Martin "Marty" Seligman, PhD** (www.authentichappiness.sas.upenn.edu)
- **Doug Parks**, Spirit2000, and the Science for Life weekly radio show (http://scienceforlife.net)
- **Marci Shimoff** (www.happyfornoreason.com)
- **Stephen R. Covey** (www.stephencovey.com)
- **Lynne McTaggart** (www.lynnemctaggart.com)
- **Robert Holden, PhD** (www.robertholden.org)
- **Bruce Lipton, PhD** (www.brucelipton.com)
- **Paul Hoffman** (http://successsongs.com)
- **Daniel Nahmod** (www.danielnahmod.com)
- **Danish Ahmed** (www.ordinarywords.com)
- **Peggy McColl** (www.destinies.com)
- **Louise Hay** (www.louisehay.com/)
- And all of the researchers who work so diligently to bring us the answers to some of life's most complex questions.

There is one angel guide/New Millennial Leader to whom I owe the deepest of admiration, respect, and gratitude:

- **Wayne Dyer, PhD** (www.drwaynedyer.com).

Your life's work, transformation, inspiration, and being inspire me and have helped shape who I am. Thank you!

Thank you to All Free Clipart (www1.free-clipart.net) for the free clipart of the covered bridge used in the book.

A huge hug and thanks to all of you who have allowed me to serve you as care provider, friend, leader, learner, teacher, or servant, whether it was formally, in the classroom, by the nature of life's circumstances, or by Divine guidance. You have blessed and honored me.

Děkuji ti, Bohů! Salamat sa iyo, Diyos! Thank you, God!

Contents

INTRODUCTION

Leadership is a Journey

Leaders don't force people to follow – they invite them on a journey.
~ Charles Lauer ~

After I left the seminary in 1982, I embarked on a rather prolonged and sometimes haphazard, but progressive journey of study and amazing life experiences. Even though I did not complete my formal theological studies in the seminary, an appreciation of theology and a deeper experience of spirituality would be a part of me for the rest of my life. I soon began studying medicine and the miraculous nature of how the body works. I began to appreciate how science was systematically trying to understand our human experience and help improve it. Whether I was learning about cellular structures or how to manage someone in cardiac arrest; the more I learned, the more the discoveries of science amazed me. For example, in my lifetime I have witnessed the transformation from manual typewriters to electric typewriters to personal computers, the internet, laptops, smart phones, and eBook readers.

Science offers a precise methodology that tests its findings with observation and experience. It *changes* based on what is learned and offers new understandings, interventions, processes, technologies, and visions of the universe and our part in it. The words of the renowned Ervin Laszlo resonate well for me, "It [science] matters not only because it is a source of the new technologies that are shaping our lives and everything around us, but also because it suggests a trustworthy way of looking at the world – and at ourselves in the world." Seeing it in practice as a combat medic and practical nurse in the Army, a 911 civilian paramedic, university instructor, small business owner, author, husband, father, and organizational leader only whet my appetite to learn and experience more. I began to hunger for the most reliable answers to life's deepest questions.

My focus shifted from theology and medicine to the philosophy of science and psychology. When I completed my Master of Arts in Clinical Psychology, however, I felt as though a fragmented, reductionist picture had been presented that didn't give me a coherent and complete understanding – and still left me wondering. Then I began to read about the latest findings in a new school of psychology, positive psychology, and a new science, the New Science of modern quantum physics. It dawned on me that they might very well be the missing links that bridge us closer to a complete Theory of Everything (or TOE). What modern psychologists and quantum physicists were saying sounded like ancient mystics with a scientific twist. My journey had brought me almost full-circle. These new sciences provide connections between philosophy, classic psychology, science, theology, spirituality, and yes, leadership development, too.

Then I entered the corporate world conducting training, project development and deployment, and leadership development, among other duties. I began to enjoy some of the best by motivational and inspirational authors both past and present along the way. Common themes from both formal and informal lessons and life experience began to emerge. I knew I had to start writing them down. This book is the culmination of what I have discovered thus far on my journey. And, although I do not claim to have all of the answers nor is my journey complete, I offer you the most important and fundamental lessons that when put into practice have the power to transform you, your relationships, and your career.

Travel Guide

I love word origins. I usually learn something meaningful – and sometimes even life changing – when I look up a word and reflect on what it means and how it was originally used. When I looked up the origins of the word *leadership*, I was amazed! The word *lead* originates from the Old English, *lædan*, meaning "cause to go with one" or "to travel." To be a leader is to be a travel guide of sorts – to lead and be on a journey with others. Indeed, as Charles Lauer so famously tells us in the opening quote to this chapter, leadership is a journey.

Equally amazing is the origin of the word *success*. It comes from the Latin *succēdere*, which means "to go." That may be why the late author and psychologist, Ben Sweetland, wrote, "Success is not a destination – it is a journey." Both leadership and success are journeys. This book will help you navigate your journeys of leadership, happiness, and success. It will challenge you to reflect on the awesome responsibility you chose to accept when you chose to become a leader.

What is Leadership?

It is important to understand what leadership is and what it is not. First, I distinguish differences between leadership and management. Internationally acclaimed author and speaker, James Hunter, wrote in his powerful book, *The Servant: A Simple Story About the True*

If both leadership and success are journeys, where are you going?

Essence of Leadership, (emphasis in the original), "You manage *things*, you *lead* people." As a leader, you manage many resources: budgets and money, time and schedules, materials and supplies, intellectual capital, emails, and the like. I've often heard business leaders say, "Our people are our most valuable resource." The *position* a person fills is a resource – something you manage; the person is a fellow human being – someone you lead.

This is not merely a play on semantics. Looking at the origin of the word *manage* provides a clearer understanding. It originates from the Latin *manus* or 'hand' and was originally used in regards to horse-handling and training. Referring to your people as a 'resource' risks dehumanizing them, even if on a subtle level. Your direct reports, management team, little league team, church choir members, and family – all of the people you lead – are people worthy of respect and concern. They are not things, nor are they resources in the strictest sense. Now the position that someone fills *is* a resource that you manage. The schedule, work assignments, compensation and benefits, required skills and knowledge, and the results produced are the resources. The person, however, is someone very much like you who has dreams, wants to be happy, desires to contribute meaningfully to the world, and wants to love and be loved. And just like you, they can be inspired by great leadership or be demoralized by the inept or callous. I realize that there are those who use the words *manage* and *management* when referring to people, however, for the purposes of this text, *management* and *leadership* are distinguished as two and distinct constructs. With that differentiation in mind, this is not a book on management, although it will help you manage. So if leadership is not management and is more closely aligned with its word-origin as a journey, what is the essence of leadership?

Influence, Change, Creating Value, and Relationships

Remember the last time you returned home from a trip or journey? When you returned, you probably felt different somehow. Your life was going to be different now – maybe even in a profound way – because of the experience. You had a new, slightly broadened view of the world. Something had changed in you and your life. Journeys have that kind of power – the power to transform our lives and the lives of others. In his best-selling book *The Power of Infinite Love and Gratitude*, Dr. Darren Weissman wrote, "Emotions transform energy; energy creates movement; movement is change; and change is the essence of life."

This book is about change – the essence of life – and arguably the essence of leadership, as well. And though, you may think about the change you want to bring to the world, that cannot happen optimally until *you* change. This book will challenge you. It will challenge how you think and how you feel. You will learn powerful, new ways of being – as a leader *and* as a person. This book will provide you with fundamental strategies and steps that will foster positive, meaningful, and healthy change so that you can be the most effective leader you can be.

Creating and fostering positive, meaningful, and healthy change allows you and those you lead to grow – to move ahead on your journey. Robert E. Quinn, Professor at the University of Michigan School of Business and author wrote about your change as a leader, "One key to successful leadership is continuous personal change. Personal change is a reflection of our inner growth and empowerment." When you experience positive personal change, it lifts you up and fosters your ability to influence

> Journeys have the power to transform our lives and the lives of others.

change in others, thus affecting systems, organizations, and the world. But as the leader, you are the key ingredient.

Influencing others requires a keen awareness of self, others, communication, and relationship dynamics. *A Travel Guide to Leadership* will help you on your journey of personal and professional transformation increasing your ability to influence others and lead. James Hunter defines leadership as "The skill of influencing people to work enthusiastically toward goals identified as being for the common good." In order to influence others, your relationships become a central concern – if you want to be the most effective leader.

The New Millennial Leader

In 2004, Doc Childre, founder of the Institute of HeartMath (IHM), and Bruce Cryer wrote in their groundbreaking book, *From Chaos to Coherence: The Power to Change Performance*, "A study at Cornell University's Johnson Graduate School of Management found that compassion and building teamwork will be two of the most important characteristics business leaders will need for success a decade from now." That decade is upon us. This book will help you respond positively to the leadership challenges of this decade and the new millennium. When you do, you will be what I call a New Millennial Leader or NML.

At the heart of the NML and leadership is moving towards and meeting goals, influencing positive change, and creating value in the world. This can only be accomplished *with others*. How you relate to others, your ability to build teams and community, exercising gratitude, compassion, and love, goes hand in hand with influence, change, and creating value – with great leadership. That journey begins with you. This book highlights nine characteristics of New Millennial Leaders that will empower you to become the best leader you can be:

1. **Thinking, Awareness, and Choice:** These three elements are the most important affair for any leader. Learn why and all about them in Chapter 1, The Most Important Affair.
2. **Clearing out Automatic Negative Thoughts:** ANTs or automatic negative thoughts can sabotage even the best of intentions. In Chapter 2, you will learn how to conduct your own personal Baggage Check and rid yourself of these nasty pests.
3. **Life Mission Statement:** Having a vision leads you and you lead others. Without a vision, mission, and purpose a leader is like a ship's captain without a map or GPS. In Chapter 3, GPS for Leaders, you will learn how to create a powerful Life Mission Statement and the Four Rules of Contemplation.
4. **Happiness:** In Chapter 4, The Highway of Happiness, you will learn why cultivating happiness for yourself and others is critical to success. You will also learn some surprising things about employee engagement.
5. **Love:** You may be wondering what love's got to do with leadership. You're in good company. But, you don't want to miss the secrets revealed in Chapter 5, A Path of Love.
6. **Gratitude:** In Chapter 6, The Bridge of Gratitude, you will discover one of the most powerful tools for not only your own success and happiness, but your team's, as well.
7. **Relationships:** It's no surprise that some aspect of relationships is now an MBO for most leaders. You cannot influence change outside of relationships. In Chapter 7, Relationship Road, you will learn how to use powerful tools that will nurture your relationships and teams.

8. **Trust and Integrity:** In Chapter 8, you will embark on the Trust Trek. Find out why and how trust can make or break you as a leader.
9. **Living in the Now:** In Chapter 9, You Are Here, learn how to free your mind from regret about the past and worry about the future so you can lead more effectively.

NML as Learner

These nine characteristics of the New Millennial Leader (NML) could be further complemented by one more characteristic that is not included in the main chapters: the NML as a learner. Ursula G. Lohmann, PhD, the former Dean of Academics at the Army Management Staff College, wrote that a "Leader is or ought to be synonymous with *learner.*" I agree. The best leaders always seem to be hungry for new knowledge, skills, and a deeper awareness of themselves and the world. Why? Learning is a form of change and growth and as mentioned above, change is arguably the essence of leadership.

The best leaders are on a continual journey of learning, whether that is formally or informally. That is what you are doing by reading this book. This continual learning process either begins with or leads to an inner journey of self-discovery. Knowing your strengths and areas of needed growth, how you deal with crises and disappointments, having a personal vision, being aware of your beliefs, thinking patterns, and emotional reactions, and other areas of personal development are your greatest source of power as a leader.

It is from a personal journey of discovery that the most effective leaders learn the best, and the worst, about themselves. With that awareness, they learn to wield and cultivate their best and work on improving the worst. This heightened sense of awareness of self opens up whole new ways of relating to and influencing others. Inspired by their own expanding awareness and abilities, they are then empowered to enable and challenge others to learn and grow, too.

The best leaders always seem to be hungry for new knowledge, skills, and a deeper awareness of themselves and the world.

We Are All Leaders

The leadership journey is a special kind of journey. It is interwoven with our life journey. Leaders are in every avenue of life and have many names: captain, coach, counselor, director, doctor, friend, grandparent, group lead, manager, parent, pastor, president, role model, sergeant, spouse, student, supervisor, teacher, volunteer, and so on. We are all leaders in some role or capacity. As Bruce Schneider, Master Certified Coach, author, and founder of iPEC Coaching wrote (emphasis in the original), "*Everyone is a leader either by choice or default.* If you don't think of yourself as a leader, then you're limited in your thinking. Leading is the way we help move people into action, including ourselves. The question is not whether you *are* a leader, *but how well you lead*."

Our leadership journey or leadership development is integrated into who we are. It is both personal *and* professional. You cannot have integrity at work and then suddenly not have it at home. You cannot be nurturing at home and then put on a hat of neglect at work – at least not without negative consequences. The leadership journey is analogous to what Abraham Maslow defined as *self-actualization*; what Leo Buscaglia described as *becoming;* Wayne Dyer calls the *fully-functioning person* and *your higher self;* and, what Robert Holden refers to as *authentic success* or the *Unconditioned Self.* It is no coincidence that common themes recur from different traditions, perspectives, and people. Wisdom traditions have reiterated common themes throughout the ages. So whatever name you give it, the self-actualized leader, the fully-functioning leader, or the New Millennial Leader; leadership is about the whole person – not just your work or role or title. Your body, thoughts, emotions, spirit, and relationships working in harmonious synergy help bring you closer to your highest self and affect how you "help move people into action," including yourself.

Leadership Occurs in the Now

It is critical for you to decide what type of journey you want to have. Are you on a journey "to leadership," "to success," and "to happiness" or are you on a journey "*of* leadership," "*of* success," and "*of* happiness?" This is not just a play on words; the difference in perspective makes a real difference.

As we will later see, personal happiness has been shown to positively affect leaders, work groups, and business outcomes in almost every way. Therefore, nurturing your personal happiness and the happiness of those you serve is one of the most powerful tools you have. All too often, leaders view their leadership, success, and happiness as something "out there," some yet-to-come future goal, event, or MBO. This future-focused orientation leads us to what Marci Shimoff calls the 'Myth of I'll-Be-Happy-When' in her bestseller, *Happy For No Reason*. She wrote, "When you're caught up in the 'I'll-be-happy-when,' happiness is always off in the future, while in truth, the only time you can actually experience happiness is right here in this moment." Everyone seems to be chasing some future 'it' that never quite seems to arrive. Robert Holden, PhD, echoes a similar thought in his book, *Success Intelligence*, "All their energy is invested in a ticket that will get them to a land called 'there.' But life isn't about 'getting there;' it is also about 'being here' and enjoying your journey."

When we see our leadership, success, and happiness as something yet to be gained – as 'out there' somewhere – then our focus shifts from the here and now to the future and 'out there' never seems to get *here*. While always looking to the future, we never seem satisfied and risk creating worry, anxiety, and fear. We often confuse the early American saying, "the pursuit of happiness," as if we are pursuing something 'out there' to be gained or caught – like a rabbit on a trail. However, the 'pursuit' of something in the 1700 and 1800s was predominantly understood as the *perfecting practice* of something – such as when one pursues a hobby or career. "I pursue golf," or "I pursue philosophy," or "I pursue needlepoint." You already do it – and you might even already be doing it well – but like a great athlete, you never give up on improving your game. It is powerful to keep in mind that your leadership is both a process occurring in the now *and* a quality to develop and nurture over time.

It is powerful to keep in mind that your leadership is both a process occurring in the now *and* a quality to develop and nurture over time.

When looked at this way, the pursuit of happiness is not something yet to be gained or captured at some future point, but something you possess ***now*** and that you are working on ***now*** in order to improve. As a leader, when you nurture happiness in yourself and in those you serve; you breed success. I'm not talking about a fleeting happiness like when your team wins the Super Bowl, but a deeper joy and fulfillment in one's life – a happiness based on purpose, service, and gratitude. And although it involves a deeper commitment and effort, it is worth it, both from a business perspective *and* a personal perspective.

The Never-Ending Journey

I have had the good fortune to travel to both Korea and the Philippines. Before each journey, I bought at least one travel guide to help me plan my trip and guide me during my journey. You know what? Although the guides were excellent resources, once I actually began my trip, I only occasionally referred to them. Sure, they were great tools to help me prepare and find my way, but no travel guide can take the place of the actual experience of a journey. So many wonderful, powerful, and unique experiences occurred on those journeys that no travel guide could foretell. For example, the differences between reading about the beaches of Boracay Island and Tagaytay Volcano in the Philippines or of the beauty of Kojedo Island and the Buddhist Pomosa Temple in Korea and actually *being* there experiencing the beauty and awe and sharing the experiences with real people are so profound that words become elusive. They are one of those 'you had to be there to know what I mean' kinds of things.

With that in mind, this travel guide is offered as just that – a guide. It is my intention that this book will be a great reference source for you and that it can assist you on your own personal leadership journey. It contains ideas, techniques, lessons, and references that have helped many people. Each of our journeys are animated and empowered by our own unique gifts, environments, and by those who we meet and accompany us along the way. This book is not designed to be a final exposé for your personal and professional leadership development, but rather, as one tool among many which you can use to supplement your own toolbox and supplies while on your own personal leadership journey.

The leadership journey is a never-ending journey.

The leadership journey is a never-ending journey. While there may be many milestones along the path, the best leaders are on a continuous road of self-improvement and growth. Therefore, the best leaders have a commitment to becoming – formally, informally, and through analysis of experience. In the words of the great pioneer in leadership studies, Warren Bennis, "No leader sets out to become a leader. People set out to live their lives, expressing themselves fully. When that expression is of value, they become leaders. So the point is not to become a leader. The point is to become yourself, to use yourself completely – all your skills, gifts, and energies – in order to make your vision manifest. You must withhold nothing. You must, in sum, become the person you started out to be and enjoy the process of becoming."

Leadership is not just what you do, it is about who you *are*.

Leadership is not just what you do, it is about who you *are*. Don't worry about what the TV or tabloids say you should be or have in order to be successful and happy. Nurture your deeper, passion-driven purpose with service and gratitude, and happiness and success will be with you no matter where you journey. As a result, you will also become the best leader you can be. This book will provide you with proven techniques and tools to do just that.

Since we are all leaders and we are all on a leadership journey of one sort or other, different travelers may require different travel tips at different points along their path. This travel guide was written with a specific sequential organization in mind and is best read from beginning to end. In Part I, Getting Outfitted for the Journey, we prepare for the leadership journey. Before you begin any journey, it is important to know what is most important, pack wisely, and plan the journey. Part I will get you ready for your leadership journey, and if you're already on one, give you the tools to re-evaluate your journey from a unique perspective. Part II, then, takes the best lessons from positive psychology, the New Thought Movement, the New Science, and spiritual traditions and explains them to you systematically so that you can apply them to your leadership journey.

Although competencies, such as time management or professional writing skills, are critically important to any leader, they are not the focus of this book and there are already plenty of excellent materials to guide you with those types of skills. This book focuses on a deeper level of who you are as a person and as a leader. In the words of Six Sigma, we'll get to 'root cause.' The lessons in this book have the power to change your life, to help you become happier, more successful, and to become the best leader that you can be. It is my intention that this book will offer you simple but powerful travel tips that will assist you so that you will have an awe-inspiring and amazing leadership journey.

~ **Alan A. Mikolaj**
Houston, Texas

Leadership Travel Tips Introduction: Leadership is a Journey

- Both leadership and success are journeys that have the power to transform our lives and the lives of others. It is a process of moving towards and meeting goals, influencing positive change, and creating value in the world.
- We are all leaders and we are all on a leadership journey.
- Leadership is both a process occurring in the now and a quality to develop and nurture over time.
- Take the perspective that your pursuit of excellence as a leader, happiness, and success are qualities you already possess and that you are continuously developing them.
- Commit to learning and growth for yourself and those you lead.
- Leadership is not about what you do, it is about who you are.

Part I

Being Outfitted for the Journey

And you get there, not by asking for it, because you don't – and this is really important... this is what The Secret missed talking about the Law of Attraction – you do not attract into your life what you want, you attract into your life what you are... what you <u>are</u>.

~ Wayne Dyer, PhD ~

CHAPTER 1

The Most Important Affair

Your thoughts are either faithful servants or tyrannical masters – just as you allow them to be. You have the say about it; take your choice.
~ William Walker Atkinson ~

My wife Leah and I were sitting outside after having one of those 'heated discussion' over something so trivial, I don't even remember what it was all about now. You know the kind. It's the end of the day, everyone's tired, someone says something to try to push your buttons, and things start to get tense. You can feel in your gut or your chest that this has the potential to go down the wrong path and ruin everyone's evening – and maybe even tomorrow, too.

Quite to my surprise, it all ended quite well. We didn't go down the wrong path. We ended up in a very good place. Was I ever pleasantly surprised! So, with us being in a good place and feeling stronger as a couple and as partners, we decided to go sit outside on our balcony and enjoy the evening together. The whole thing could have just as easily gone south pretty quick. But it didn't, and I was taking in the beautiful Texas live oaks and nature and feeling like we had just averted a hostile takeover. Just resting there quietly was a relief.

Then, one of the most amazing and memorable things in my life happened. She turned to me and very sweetly said, "You're the most patient man I have ever known." Now, you might be thinking that I'm going to gloat about that. But seriously, and I mean *seriously*, tears came to my eyes. It was the first time in my life that I heard anyone in an intimate relationship with me say anything like that. For example, if we could rewind about ten years earlier and witness a similar exchange between my ex-wife and I; the outcome would have been very different and she would have said just the opposite about me – that I was the most *impatient* man – and probably more! Something dramatic had changed.

Let's pretend for a moment that the 'heated discussion' between Leah and I had been recorded and a group of experts sits down to analyze it. Some of them might say that we used effective conflict management skills. Others, that it was the empathic listening techniques. Others still, that we were able to focus on our love and commitment to one another – and all of those observations may or may not be true. However, the most important element that influenced such a positive outcome could not be seen on a video. I had changed *how* and *what* I think.

The reason for my tears, tears of joy? I had been consistently and methodically working on my thoughts (and my patience) for several years, and in that moment when Leah told me that I was the most patient man she knew, I realized I had successfully manifested something into reality – something that I could only dream about some ten years earlier. This change produced amazing success in my personal life and my relationships – especially with my wife. But it wasn't only showing up in my personal life, it was also showing up at

Then, one of the most amazing and memorable things in my life happened.

work and in my income, too. In that moment, sitting on our balcony and looking at my lovely wife, I felt like the wide receiver who had just caught the game-winning touchdown pass and was dancing in the end zone.

A common thread among success stories like mine is simple – not necessarily easy – just simple. One of the most important affairs for any leader being outfitted for the leadership journey is the awareness of your own thoughts. One of the most important lessons on our leadership journey, if not *the* most important lesson, is to realize that we must take control of our mind and our thoughts in order to reach our goals, add value to others and the world, be happy, successful, increase our influence, and become more effective leaders. As William Atkinson, lawyer, businessman, and one of the truly 'greats' among the New Thought Movement, said in the opening quote of this chapter, we get to choose whether our thoughts will be our faithful servants or our tyrannical master. Why is this the most important affair? Because thoughts become things.

One of the most important affairs for any leader being outfitted for the leadership journey is the awareness of your own thoughts.

Thoughts Become Things

In his book, *Leveraging the Universe,* Mike Dooley wrote, "Your *thoughts become things.* They always have, and they always will. This is your divine inheritance. This is how you can change your life. It's *the* answer. It's the solution. It's *the* salvation of all who discover it." He is right. It may have taken me over forty years to discover it for myself; but when I did, my whole life began to transform.

Let's try a simple experiment. Get yourself a scratch piece of

You have possession of one of the most amazing gifts of evolution: you can be self-aware.

paper and something to write with. Really. Now, I want you to draw a circle on the scratch piece of paper. Draw a really nice circle that you can be proud of. Got it? Great.

Now look at what you've created. What had to happen in order for you to draw that circle? Like all of us, you first had to decide whether you would draw a circle. I mean, heck, you just started reading this book on leadership, and I'm asking you to draw a silly circle? If you just kept reading up to here and thought that, stop. Put the book down and draw a circle. This really makes more sense when you draw the circle and can hold it in your hands and look at it.

Okay. You made a decision to draw a circle and you're looking at it. Then, after you made a decision to draw a circle, you had to think (maybe rather subconsciously or automatically) about circles and memories of drawing previous circles, call on motor neurons in the habit of drawing circles, and then actually put pen or pencil to paper and draw. Maybe you weren't satisfied with the first circle you drew and tried again. You thought a little differently, maybe focused a little harder, and drew a better circle. Either way, your thoughts became some *thing*. It changed the world in a small way. There is now something in the universe that wasn't here just a few moments ago.

This lesson, that thoughts become things, is what the great masters have been teaching since recorded history and most likely before that. But, that in and of itself, is not the most important affair. It is crucial, but it is not *the* most important affair. What then, *is* the most important affair? That you know that you know it.

You have possession of one of the most amazing gifts of evolution: you can be self-aware. You can know that you know something – most importantly here, that you know that your thoughts become things and you can choose your thoughts. You can reflect on your thoughts and experiences, and make choices based on that. The consequences of this realization are immense. The visionary theologian, evolutionary theorist, Jesuit priest, and co-discoverer of the 'Peking Man' fossils, Pierre Teilhard de Chardin, wrote of this, "The being who is the object of his own reflection, in consequence of that very doubling back upon himself, becomes in a flash able to raise himself into a new sphere. In reality, another world is born." You have the ability to raise yourself to a new sphere, to birth a new world for yourself and others through your awareness of yourself – of your thoughts. It's what psychologists call *metacognition.* You can think about thinking. The most important affair, then, is really three critical elements rolled up into one:

- Thoughts become things.
- Metacognition: You can become aware of and reflect on your own thoughts, raise your consciousness, and know what you know.
- You can choose what you think.

In his first book, *Your Erroneous Zones*, Wayne Dyer agrees, "Taking charge of yourself begins with awareness." Taking charge of yourself is where your true power as a leader lies. Your true power as a leader begins with your ability to be aware of what and how you think, that your thoughts become things, and that you have a choice to master your thoughts and thus,

The most important affair, then, is really three critical elements rolled up into one.

yourself. When you do that, you begin the journey of transformation. You become more effective. You gain true power. As Lao-tzu wrote over 25 centuries ago:

Knowing others is intelligence;
Knowing yourself is true wisdom.
Mastering others is strength;
Mastering yourself is true power.
33rd Verse of the Tao Te Ching

Everything is Energy

Your body is composed of many organs. Those organs are composed of somewhere between 50-100 trillion cells. Those cells are composed of around 7 octillion molecules or 7×10^{27} molecules – that's a 7 followed by 27 zeros! Peculiarly, those molecules are composed of about 7 octillion atoms. What's most amazing about those atoms – and all of the atoms in the universe – is that each one of them is almost entirely empty space. They are composed of quanta (plural). A quantum (singular) is energy. Over the last century, quantum physicists have discovered that underlying the entire known universe, including all of that so-called 'empty' space, is an energy field. We can all recite Albert Einstein's famous discovery that $E = mc^2$. Everything is energy, including you and me… and our thoughts.

What we consider 'normal' matter only constitutes four percent of the total energy in the universe. Physicists have calculated that in every cubic centimeter of so-called 'empty' space there exists *more energy than the total energy of all matter in the known universe*. This is just simply amazing. Wouldn't you like to tap into that?

When a vacuum is created, taking away all matter, and it is brought to absolute zero, we were taught that there shouldn't be anything there – but there is! Scientists have named that 'something' the Zero-Point

Field (ZPF) or simply, the field, as it is informally called. This energy field permeates the universe. We are in it and we *are* it. When you read and listen to what the scientists have to say about it, you would think they were talking about God – and some of them are.

All of the so-called 'empty space' between subatomic particles, like electrons and protons, is actually teeming with random energy and the very stability of atoms, and therefore all of material reality, is due to interaction with the ZPF. Nineteenth century physicists called it the *luminiferous ether*. Others have called it the *unified vacuum*. Albert Einstein referred to it as the *cosmological constant* and others, as *dark energy*. Einstein's protégé, David Bohm, concluded that the universe is one gigantic and detailed hologram. Max Planck, considered by many to be the father of quantum physics, called it a *matrix* and bestselling author, Gregg Braden, refers to it as the *Divine Matrix*. The best explanation of the ZPF I've found comes from world-renowned astrophysicist and author, Bernard Haisch, PhD, in his thoughtful book, *The God Theory*:

> To understand the zero-point field, consider an old-fashioned grandfather clock with its pendulum swinging back and forth. If you don't wind the clock, friction will, sooner or later, bring the pendulum to a halt. Now imagine a pendulum that gets smaller and smaller – so small that it ultimately becomes atomic in size and subject to the laws of quantum physics. There is a rule in quantum physics called the Heisenberg Uncertainty Principle that states (with certainty, as it happens) that no quantum object, such as a microscopic pendulum, can ever be brought completely to rest. Any microscopic object will always possess a residual random jiggle, thanks to quantum fluctuations... And if you add up all these ceaseless fluctuations, you get a background sea of light whose total energy is enormous. This is the electromagnetic zero-point field.

Max Planck, the father of quantum physics, came to the conclusion that underlying all of this energy and vibration is *mind.* He said, “As a man who has devoted his whole life to the most clear headed science, to the study of matter, I can tell you as a result of my research about atoms this much: There is no matter as such. All matter originates and exists only by virtue of a force which brings the particle of an atom to vibration and holds this most minute solar system of the atom together. We must assume behind this force the existence of a conscious and intelligent mind. This mind is the matrix of all matter.” Movie buffs must be reminded of the famous character, Obi-Wan Kenobi, played by Alec Guinness in *Star Wars*, “The Force is what gives a Jedi his power. It's an energy field created by all living things. It surrounds us and penetrates us. It binds the galaxy together.” If you’ll pardon the pun, even Hollywood is in on the act.

Everything is vibrating energy and underlying that is mind or thought. Thought is a force, an energy, a vibration, a wave. Hungarian philosopher of science, systems and integral theorist, author of over 70 books, and classical pianist, Ervin Laszlo wrote, “It turns out that life itself depends crucially on interactions with the vacuum.” Similar to Planck, Laszlo further postulates that the Zero Point Field (ZPF) and other wave field theories have not taken the paradigm far enough. He proposes that underlying all of reality is an ‘in-formation’ field that he calls the Akashic Field (from Indian-Hindu philosophical origins) or A-field. Just as invisible and mysterious as a gravitational field, the A-field is the connecting field of

Everything is vibrating energy and underlying that is mind or thought. Thought is a force, an energy, a vibration, a wave.

the universe – connecting all energy, matter, time, space, memory, and information. He said of our thoughts, perceptions, and feelings:

> All we experience in our lifetime – all our perceptions, feelings, and thought processes – have cerebral functions associated with them. These functions have wave-form equivalents, since our brain, like other things in space and time, creates information-carrying vortices – it "makes waves." The waves propagate in the vacuum and interfere with the waves created by the bodies and brains of other people giving rise to complex holograms.

Laszlo, from a scientific perspective, contends that all things – subatomic particles, atoms, molecules, cells, organisms, the galaxies, and even human thoughts – and the A-field or ZPF interact with each other and persist beyond space and time in an ever 'in-forming' evolution of metaverses.

I was sitting by the pool with Leah, one morning, watching the morning light beam through the small waves being created by the water return nozzles strategically placed around the edge of the pool just below the water line. The waves radiated a beautiful luminiferous pattern as they met and crisscrossed. I walked over to the edge of the pool mesmerized by the diamond-shaped pattern that seemed to have a life of its own. Suddenly, I plunged my fist into the water. A new, larger wave began to move out and become part of the mosaic, mixing with and amplifying the existing wave pattern. A new and even more beautiful pattern began to form. Our thoughts are like that; moving out from our mind and interacting with other waves in the universe.

The wavelike patterns of our thoughts, like the ripples in the pool I saw, are now believed to either be a part of and/or create a larger holographic brain and universe. In *The Holographic Universe*, Michael

Talbot also describes the wavelike properties of thought:

> It was known that the electrical communications that take place between the brain's nerve cells, or neurons, do not occur alone. Neurons possess branches like little trees, and when an electrical message reaches the end of one of these branches it radiates outward as does the ripple in a pond. Because neurons are packed together so densely, these expanding ripples of electricity – also a wavelike phenomenon – are constantly crisscrossing one another. When Pribram [Karl Pribram, professor of neuropsychology and author of the Holonomic Brain Theory] remembered this he realized that they were most assuredly creating an almost endless kaleidoscopic array of interference patterns, and these in turn might be what give the brain its holographic properties.

This new understanding of the universe and particularly our thoughts and belief systems challenges what we may have learned in school and from our culture. What we think may be controlling more than we think – if you'll pardon the play on words. After years of researching cellular biology and environmental influences on genes, protein receptors, cells, and the person as a whole, Bruce Lipton, PhD, the famous cellular biologist, researcher, professor, and best-selling author, concludes, "It is not gene-directed hormones and neurotransmitters that control our bodies and our minds; our beliefs control our bodies, our minds, and thus our lives…" Thoughts become things – even our very selves. You've heard the old adage, "You are what you eat." We can now take that a step father and solemnly declare, "You are what you think."

These ideas are not new – just new science. Over 100 years ago, Charles Haanel wrote in his classic instructional guide, *The Master Key System*, "Thought is energy. Active thought is active energy; concentrated thought is a concentrated energy. Thought concentrated on a definite purpose becomes power." These types of ideas began to flourish in the late 19th and early 20th centuries and became known as the New Thought Movement (NTM) or Mental Science. While the NTM is considered a spiritual movement or even a religion, its adherents also included businessmen and entrepreneurs such as Charles Haanel, Earl Nightingale, author of *The Strangest Secret*, and Wallace D. Wattles, author of *The Science of Getting Rich.* Business leaders and spiritualists of the late 19th and early 20th centuries foreshadowed what modern science is saying today.

Where Do Beliefs Come From?

Brain waves are classified by their EEG frequency – the cycles per second or Hertz (Hz) – *by their energy waves.* Throughout infancy and toddlerhood, brainwaves predominantly oscillate as delta waves, the lowest frequency. As a child enters early childhood, the brain begins to oscillate at a bit of a higher frequency known as theta waves. It is interesting to note that when someone is hypnotized, brainwaves are brought down to the theta and delta wavelengths because it is at these wavelengths that the human brain is in a state that is more open and receptive to suggestion and deeper programming. When we were children, we were basically walking around in a hypnotic state absorbing everything around us. See Table 1, below for a breakdown of brainwaves and their associations.

In his best seller, *The Biology of Belief*, Bruce Lipton wrote, "This gives us an important clue as to how children, whose brains are mostly operating at these same frequencies between birth and six years of age, can download the incredible volume of information they need to thrive in their environment." This is how our parents' behaviors and beliefs and the social mores of our childhood become so rapidly and deeply ingrained into our subconscious.

Table 1.

Brainwave Frequencies		
Frequency Name	**Hertz**	**Associated With**
Beta Waves	14 - 30 Hz	Focused, fully awake, and alert states. Occur when engaged in any form of activity. High beta without alpha is associated with stress, anxiety, and high blood pressure.
Alpha Waves	8 - 13 Hz	Relaxed, but alert states. Sometimes described as the 'daydream' state.
Theta Waves	4 - 8 Hz	Occur mainly in children ages 2–5 years old. In adults, associated with drowsiness, the first stage of sleep, hypnotic and deeply relaxed states of consciousness, lucid dreams, and even emotional stress.
Delta Waves	0.5 – 4 Hz	Occur mainly in infants, sleeping adults (deep, dreamless sleep), or adults with brain tumors. Known for triggering the release of growth hormone, which provides healing.

Adapted from *Frequency of Brain Waves* (Charles, 2004) and *EEG and Your Brainwaves-Binaural Beats* (Anthony, 2002).

Automatic Processing and the Subconscious Mind

Many compare subconscious processes with an analogy to computer 'programs.' Some of those 'programs' are unpleasant, negative, or self-defeating. These programs originate from the messages that we received when we were very young and they were internalized into our subconscious. Beliefs are handed down through families, come from trusted persons, groups, from religious writings and practices, and/or they evolve through culture. Little or no verifiable evidence is required; beliefs from childhood, especially early childhood, are based in an innocent, blind acceptance –primarily due to the hypnotic thought frequencies and the influence of those passing the beliefs on.

Concepts and ideas about the self and the world and 'what it's all about' are simply accepted and downloaded into the mind partly because of the brain frequencies of the child, partly because the beliefs are often touted as inspired or self-evident, and/or because of their strong emotional elements and repetition. Imbedded in these beliefs are unspoken rules that guide a variety of behavior. These beliefs and unspoken rules can be positive or negative, self-enhancing or self-defeating and unless we uncover and work on them (the negative, self-defeating ones); we have little control over them. They become our "tyrannical masters."

In psychology, this is referred to as *automatic processing.* Automatic processing and beliefs are powerful. In a landmark 2001 report, the Institute of HeartMath noted, "Thus, subconscious emotional memories and associated physiological patterns underlie and affect our perceptions, emotional reactions, thought processes, and behavior." Our thoughts and beliefs, especially subconscious, automatic ones, create who we are.

Doug Parks interviewed Rob Williams, originator of PSYCH-K, on his weekly radio show, *Science for Life.* During the interview, Rob said, "For the listeners that don't know about the latest research about the subconscious mind, there's a powerful, powerful revelation that's come out of that neuroscience community that 95-99% of the time – let me repeat that – 95-99% of our behaviors and views are orchestrated from the subconscious level of the mind – that means the automatic part of the mind. That means most of the time we're running our lives on autopilot." Less than five percent of our daily thoughts are anything new or under our direct, conscious control. That's monumental.

Our thoughts and beliefs, especially subconscious, automatic ones, create who we are.

How we think, especially subconscious thinking, may be one of the

Not only does the subconscious mind process and attend to more data, it does so much faster than the conscious mind.

most important things we do. Thinking positively has now become more than just a feel-good, pop-psychology fad; it's real mainstream science. However, nurturing happiness and change that leads to success may require much more than simply thinking positively. Although the mind is incredibly powerful, we are wise to bring some caution to any positive thinking panacea. Why? Lipton warns us, "You need more than just 'positive thinking' to harness control of your body and your life. It *is* important for our health and well-being to shift our mind's energy toward positive, life-generating thoughts and eliminate ever-present, energy-draining, and debilitating negative thoughts. But, and I mean that in the biggest sense of 'BUT,' the mere thinking of positive thoughts will not necessarily have any impact on our lives at all!" He further explains, similar to Rob Williams, that the power of the subconscious mind is "millions of times more powerful than the conscious mind."

According to Lipton and other scientists, the subconscious mind can process 20,000,000 – that's *20 million* – environmental stimuli or bits *per second*! Compare that to the conscious mind's ability to process between 40-2,000 environmental stimuli or bits per second. Greg Braden and Gary Schmid, PhD both independently calculate that this means that the subconscious mind is 500,000 times faster than the conscious mind. Not only does the subconscious mind process and attend to more data, it does so much faster than the conscious mind.

When I was interviewing the CEO and owner of a multi-million dollar AutoCAD and document management software company about this, he brought up golf. He knew I wasn't a golfer and proceeded to explain. If there's a water hazard between you and the green, even if it's a relatively easy shot, inevitably you hit the water. Why? Even though your conscious mind is doing everything it can to compensate for the water, your subconscious mind just can't seem to shake that dang water hazard – and your body follows your mind. On the other hand, when you find yourself in an almost identical shot without a water hazard, you more consistently make the shot. The subconscious mind overrides your conscious desire and efforts to make the shot – and it works that very same way in situations with much more important consequences than bragging rights at the nineteenth hole.

The power of the subconscious mind can be a great thing when adjusting heart rate, blood pressure, or in an emergency, but oftentimes we are subconsciously reactive with programming from the past that is no longer realistic, healthy, or functional to current life-situations – it is negative and self-defeating. Our thoughts and beliefs can even change our physiology.

The Placebo Effect

We've all heard or read about studies where a control group receives a sugar pill believing it to be an actual treatment and it turns out to be as effective as the actual drug being administered for whatever the illness is. A recent meta-analysis in *The Journal of the American Medical Association* on antidepressant medications, for example, clearly demonstrated that except for the very severely depressed, antidepressant medications are no better than placebos for treating mild, moderate, or even severe depressive symptoms. If you're taking Prozac, odds are that you might as well be eating M&Ms, as long as you believe it is therapeutic.

Throughout the literature, the placebo response has been reported to be as low as twenty percent and as high as eighty percent, depending on the condition and types of people being studied. Generally, for most situations and conditions, placebos contribute 30-40% to the benefit of a treatment or intervention. Our thoughts and beliefs are more powerful than we've been led to believe.

These effects don't just happen with sugar pills. One of the most amazing and recent reports of the placebo effect was reported in the *New England Journal of Medicine* in 2002 and was featured on ABC news. The researchers didn't even intend to test the placebo response. While trying to discover which part of a two-part knee surgery performed over 650,000 times a year worked best, Dr. Bruce Moseley and colleagues discovered it was… neither! In the study, patients with osteoarthritis of the knee were assigned to one of three conditions: 1) arthroscopic surgical debridement, 2) arthroscopic surgical lavage, or; 3) a placebo surgical procedure – a fake or sham surgery complete with IV sedation and three 1-centimeter incisions and manipulations as if the surgery was actually being performed. The participants were followed for two years.

The results were simply amazing! All three groups did equally well. The 'real' surgeries proved to be no better than the placebo surgical procedure. Those who had the placebo surgery reported just as much pain relief, increase in mobility, and even did equally well on an objective 100-foot walk and stair-climbing measure. The authors went so far as to say, "If the efficacy of arthroscopic lavage or debridement in patients with osteoarthritis of the knee is no greater than that of placebo surgery, the billions of dollars

Our thoughts and beliefs are more powerful than we've been led to believe.

spent on such procedures annually might be put to better use." Similar results have been found in pacemaker implantation studies, beta-blockers, cardiac resynchronization devices, and catheter ablation.

But what about thoughts and beliefs, themselves? Can merely changing our thoughts and what we believe to be true – our perception about something – change our physiology? Researchers Alia Crum and Ellen Langer from Harvard University wanted to find out. In an ingenious study design, they studied hotel room attendants (hotel maids), their perceptions, and their health.

Hotel room attendants clean about fifteen rooms a day. It takes them between twenty and thirty minutes to clean each room. Their daily work activities are physically exerting – walking, bending, pushing, lifting, and carrying almost all day long. By simply doing their jobs, hotel maids meet or exceed the Surgeon General's and CDCs recommendations of a healthy, active lifestyle of 30 minutes of exercise per day – and yet most of them didn't *think* they were. At baseline, almost seventy percent of the hotel room attendants in the study did not think they exercised regularly and nearly forty percent thought they didn't get any exercise at all – and their health measures reflected that perception. Whether they measured blood pressure, body mass index (BMI), percentage of body fat, or waist to hip ratios (WHR) – the hotel room attendants' measurements at baseline measurement were considered to be "at risk."

The hotel room attendants from seven hotels were divided into two groups. The control group was told that the researchers were interested in gathering information on their health and in return for helping; they would receive information about health and happiness. An "informed group," however, received detailed information about how their work met or exceeded the CDCs recommendations for an active, healthy lifestyle both

By simply changing their perception about their physical activity, they became healthier.

in a verbal presentation and in handouts and posters that were posted in break rooms and lounges. For example, they were told that exercise does not have to be painful or difficult to be good for one's health and details about the number of calories burned during individual work tasks (e.g., vacuuming, changing linens, etc.). Then, they just let them simply go about their normal lives for a month.

After only one month, the informed group lost, on average, two pounds, lowered systolic blood pressure by 10 points, and were "significantly healthier as measured by body-fat percentage, BMI, and WHR" compared to the control group. They did this without any changes in workload and reported *not* getting any additional exercise outside of work. In addition, they reported that their dietary habits had not changed over the past month. They still reported eating the same amount of sugary foods or vegetables, for example, and drinking the same amount of caffeine, alcohol, and water that they ate and drank before the study. By simply changing their perception about their physical activity, they became healthier. The authors concluded, "It is clear that health is significantly affected by mind-set."

The Nocebo Effect

Just as positive effects can stem from perception, so too can negative effects or symptoms – even death. The phenomenon known as *voodoo death* or *hex death*, has been reported scientifically since at least 1942. A famous example of the nocebo effect in medicine was the observation during the Framingham Heart Study that women who believed they were prone to heart disease had a four times higher risk of death than women with the same risk factors who did not believe they were prone to heart disease. Even healthy people will have adverse effects – or the nocebo effect – to a placebos about 15-28% of the time. Our thoughts, beliefs, and perceptions are powerful forces that can affect our physiology. But does it stop there? Can the effect our thoughts, beliefs, perceptions, and feelings have extend beyond our own internal world?

The Participatory Universe

The American physicist who coined such terms as *black hole* and *wormhole*, John Wheeler, once said, "We are participators in bringing into being not only the near and here but the far away and long ago." Many scientists now postulate that not only do our thoughts create who we are, but also by observing reality, we actually participate in the creation of that reality.

American author, Michael Talbot, and award-winning journalist and author, Lynne McTaggart, both independently describe in some detail, a series of studies of the observer affect at Princeton University's Princeton Engineering Anomalies Research program or PEAR that began in the 1970s. Princeton engineering professor and dean, Robert Jahn, and his colleague, Brenda Dunne, a developmental psychologist, took the investigation of what had been called *the observer effect* to an entirely new level. In a series of experiments spanning nearly 20 years, they uncovered some of the most remarkable findings of our times. They report clear and conclusive evidence that the mind can psychically interact with physical reality outside of ourselves at the subatomic level.

Modern research in quantum physics is saying that thoughts actually influence the subatomic field of energy! They have concluded that when two or more people focus on the same thought or desire, the effect increases. When those two or more people are related, such as spouses or close friends or family members, the effect can become quite profound. I can't help but be reminded of what Jesus of Nazareth said, "Again I tell you, if two of you on earth agree (harmonize together, make a symphony together) about whatever [anything and everything] they may ask, it will come to pass and be done for them by My Father in heaven. For wherever two or three are gathered (drawn together as My followers) in (into) My name, there I AM in the midst of them" (Matthew 18:19-20).

The idea that our thoughts, and most powerfully our subconscious thoughts, can shift the subatomic field, transforms the old paradigm that we are simply passive observers of a universe who have no effect on what we are observing into one in which we are co-creators of an amazing, participatory universe. As Gregg Braden so famously wrote, "They [the words of Max Planck, father of quantum physics] imply that we're much more than simply the 'observers' that scientists have described, passing through a brief moment of time in a creation that already exists. Through the connection that joins all things, the experiments have now shown that we directly affect the waves and particles of the universe. In short, the universe responds to our beliefs."

Personal Responsibility

The final piece of this understanding of our thoughts and beliefs is that of personal responsibility. If we are in a participatory, creative universe as the physicist working in the New Science, New Thought adherents, and others point us toward, then we are, at least partly if not wholly, responsible for our lives, each other, the planet, and the universe. Gregg Braden in *The Spontaneous Healing of Belief* adds impetus, "In other words, the discoveries [of quantum physics] reveal that we are active contributors to everything that we see in the world around us, precisely as the spiritual traditions of the past have said that we are."

That personal responsibility derives from our minds and how we think. As Charles Haanel wrote almost 100 years ago, "The great fact is, that the source of all life and all power is from within." This understanding of thought and belief mirrors the teachings of Jesus of Nazareth, "For behold, the kingdom of God is within you [in your hearts] and among you [surrounding you]" (Luke 17:21). Spiritualists, psychologists, and scientists are all saying we have the power to create our life and our world. It also means that we share responsibility for our lives – or at the very least, our response to it.

Religious and Philosophical Traditions

Religious traditions have handed down this same message since recorded history. Hinduism's roots date as far back as 5500 BCE, making it one of the oldest surviving religions. Laszlo's A-field mentioned above is named after the Sanskrit word *Akasha*. In Hinduism, Akasha is the primary element and underlying "aether" of all things and becomes all things. Explaining it, the famous Hindu monk, Swami Vivekananda said,

> The whole of this universe, according to the Hindu philosophers, can be resolved into one material, which they call Akasha. Everything that we see around us, feel, touch, taste, is simply a differentiated manifestation of this Akasha. It is all-pervading, fine. All that we call solids, liquids, or gases, figures, forms, or bodies, the earth, sun, moon, and stars – everything is composed of this Akasha.

Buddhists also speak of Akasha or the space of the universe; a universal medium in which every single thing is surrounded, contained, and touched by. The Buddha said around 500 BCE, "All that we are is the result of what we have thought. The mind is everything. What we think we become." Some 600 years later, the venerable Roman stoic philosopher, Epictetus, said, "As you think, so you become." Jesus of Nazareth instructed:

> Have faith in God [constantly]. Truly I tell you, whoever says to this mountain, 'Be lifted up and thrown into the sea!' and does not doubt at all in his heart but believes that what he says will take place, it will be done for him. For this reason I am telling you, whatever you ask for in prayer, believe (trust and be confident) that it is granted to you, and you will [get it]. (Mark 11: 22-24)

Thoughts are primary to and generative of reality – including the person and leader who you are. So, our thoughts and beliefs are essential in manifesting the type of person and leader we want to be and the kind of world we wish to create and participate in. Before action, before things, must first come thought – especially thought empowered with positive emotion. And that emotive thought, like the waves in a pool, moves out in all directions interacting with the medium and other waves moving through the universe.

The New Thought Movement adherents, quantum physicists, neuropsychologist, cellular physiologists, and others are all telling us that our emotions, thoughts, and beliefs are a waveform of energy that affects whatever the underlying fundamental nature of reality is. Religious and philosophical traditions mirror these ideas. Thoughts are energy. Thoughts become things. You can be aware of your thoughts – your energy, your state of being. You can also choose your thoughts. In other words, you participate in the creation of who you are and your world. When you know this, you become very careful about what you think. If we don't get hold of our thoughts and beliefs, they will become our "tyrannical masters." In the chapters ahead, you will learn how to make them your "faithful servants."

Leadership Travel Tips Chapter 1: The Most Important Affair

- Thoughts become things.
- You can become aware of and reflect on your own thoughts, raise your consciousness, and know what you know. You possess the ability of metacognition. You can be self-aware.
- You can choose what you think.
- Thoughts are energy.
- Everything else is energy, too.
- You participate in the creation of who you are.
- You participate in the creation of your world.
- Become very careful what you think about.

CHAPTER 2

Baggage Check

Don't believe everything you think!
~ Wayne Dyer ~

First, get out your ID and boarding pass and have it ready to be visible – and if you really want to shave a few extra seconds, you'll have them both in a holder dangling from around your neck so your hands are free. After ID and boarding pass check, walk as briskly as possible to what you hope will be the fastest lane (you've already been scanning the line ahead of you and conducting your own security checkpoint personality profiling). Take off your shoes (slip-ons, of course) and put them in a plastic tray. They go first so that they are the first out on the other side of the x-ray machine. Next goes the laptop into a separate plastic tray. You'll need a third plastic tray for your '3-1-1' bag, cell phone, keys, belt, and what little jewelry you've got on (you're wearing very little because you just know better). Finally, the carry-on bag with a layer of clothes at the bottom, personal electronics on top of that which are neatly spread out and organized to avoid looking like a bomb, and any heavier clothes on top of all that to hold it all in place goes in your last plastic tray. That's how you get through a Transportation Security Administration's (TSA) security checkpoint line faster, right? Well-prepared, light, and lean.

Why does there always seem to be someone who can't believe she can't take the entire 8.5-ounce hairspray bottle through? Or the guy who doesn't remove his belt that's hidden under a pullover shirt and keeps going back through the metal detector over and over until he is finally scanned with the wand to find it? What's even more truly astonishing is that as of October 2011 – more than ten years after September 11 – the TSA has already found over 800 guns trying to be brought on board airplanes in the US (usually accidentally)! Baggage check today just ain't what it used to be.

The process of getting through an airport security check successfully and expeditiously is a microcosm of being outfitted for the leadership journey. It may not be the most fun or exciting part of a journey, but if we don't go through it, we risk being sidetracked and/or weighed-down with self-destructive things in our baggage or even worse, derailing the journey altogether. To illustrate:

1. You must first know who you are and where you're going. Like having your ID and boarding pass ready and visible, great leaders have a clear and powerful vision, mission, and purpose. We'll examine how you can develop your own, personal and powerful mission statement in Chapter 4.
2. Second, pack only what serves you on your journey (the thoughts, beliefs, perceptions, emotions, and skills that you need) and discard or never pack something that might slow you down, sidetrack you, get you arrested, or totally derail your journey (such as self-defeating, negative thoughts, beliefs, habits, and emotions). In the pages ahead, this book

will show you how to clear out the stuff you don't need and more importantly, in later chapters, will guide you through packing the most powerful tools for you to take on your leadership journey.

3. Finally, just like going through an airport security check successfully and expeditiously, you can only take the step right in front of you, right now. Don't be overly concerned with what happened a few minutes ago back in the line behind you or with what might happen in an hour or you'll lose focus. Focus on what you're doing now and you'll get through this just fine and be on your way in no time.

Could you be carrying something around in your mental baggage that is self-defeating or even sabotaging your leadership journey? Knowing yourself, your environment, and your relationship to it are crucial to being outfitted for the journey. When you realize and hold in your awareness that thoughts are energy, that thoughts become things, that you can be aware of your thoughts, your energy – your state of being – and that you can choose your thoughts; you not only become very careful about what you think, you stop and conduct a baggage check.

The Power of Your State of Being

Our thoughts and beliefs are powerful. They create our feelings. Together, our thoughts, beliefs, and feelings create our energy state or our *state of being*. Our state of being drives our choices and actions; it affects our physiology; and, it creates our habits – all for better or worse. Cumulatively, over time, this is who we

Together, our thoughts, beliefs, and feelings create our energy state or our *state of being*.

become – it is who we are. Think about where you are right now in your life – your health, the education you have, the job you hold, where you live, the state of your relationships, your religion and/or spirituality – all are in some way due to the thoughts, beliefs, emotions, and decisions you had or were given to you at some point in the past. Your state of being also defines who you are as a leader.

Since our thoughts and beliefs are mostly subconscious or automatic, without some guidance, we may find it difficult to get at some of the ones we want to change. For example, you may want a fulfilling, romantic relationship in your life. However, deep down, you have feelings of doubt and unworthiness – maybe even low self-esteem. Simply having a tiny smear of positive or wishful thinking that is actually covering deeper negative, doubting, unworthy, or self-defeating thoughts and automatic processes from childhood won't bring about much change. The power of the deeper negative emotions triggered by those subconscious thoughts is stronger than any meager attempt at positive thinking –and that deeper, more powerful negativity is what ends up manifesting. Ever wonder why we always seem to end up repeating the same tragic love story over and over – just with someone different? Let's rewrite these old programs or conditioning in our subconscious mind and replace them with feelings, beliefs, and thought patterns that generate courage, confidence, abundance, love, and meaningful contributions to life.

If you want to change the way you think in order to create for yourself and others a better world, you will also have to change the way you feel.

Beliefs are interwoven with feelings, oftentimes strong ones. If you doubt that, ask yourself or anyone else to share his or her feelings about modern social issues that are part of our beliefs, like abortion, the death penalty, whether creationism or evolution should be taught in schools, their political party, and so on. Discussions about these social issues and the beliefs that underpin them are usually intense with emotion because they are deep-rooted and wrapped up in a person's identity. If you want to change the way you think in order to create for yourself and others a better world, you will also have to change the way you feel. You will also have to deal with the deep-rooted feelings and beliefs of those you lead. Changing thoughts, thought-patterns, and beliefs also means changing emotions.

Treasures of the Heart

As the new millennium was about to dawn, I began studying, teaching, writing, and helping people with stress through my work as an Emergency Medical Services adjunct faculty at the University of Texas Health Science Center in San Antonio and through various critical incident stress management organizations. Science had long contended that the brain and the nervous system controlled stress, and all other bodily functions. My old anatomy textbook captures well what science taught for a very long time, "The nervous system is the master controlling and communicating system of the body; every thought, action, and emotion reflects its activity." I even wrote in my own text on stress for emergency care providers, "The brain takes in the information, processes it in various locations, and if a threat is perceived, the stress response is activated." While the brain is still considered the 'master system,' groundbreaking studies by the Institute of HeartMath (IHM), an internationally recognized nonprofit research and educational organization on the heart and emotions, has revealed that the heart itself is a "little brain." A 2001 IHM report describes the research of Dr. J. Andrew Armour:

> The heart's brain is an intricate network of several types of neurons, neurotransmitters, proteins, and support cells like those found in the brain proper. Its elaborate circuitry enables it to act independently of the cranial brain – to learn, remember, and even feel and sense.

The IHM reports that the heart has its own nervous system with nearly 40,000 neurons. They pick up information from circulating blood and communicate this information to the brain, even to "the higher centers of the brain, where they may influence perception, decision making, and other cognitive processes." The heart also secretes hormones, similar to the brain, most notably oxytocin, or the "love" or "bonding" hormone. Surprisingly, there are more neural connections going from the heart-feeling systems to the brain-thinking systems than the other way around. Our heart and emotions are a powerful force in our lives – for better or worse.

Studies have demonstrated that negative emotions such as self-pity, despair, anxiety, and hopelessness, can overwhelm our concentration or what psychologists call 'working memory.' There's only so much your brain can handle at one time. When you're consumed with negative emotions, the effectiveness of working memory is impaired and you can't think straight. Negative emotions and impaired thinking can then lead to mistakes, misperceptions, and a downward spiral towards disaster. On the other hand, when you're full of positive emotions, like enthusiasm, happiness, love, and gratitude, you're energized and motivated. The IHM report said that, "This goes some way to explain the tremendous power of emotions, in contrast to thought alone. Once an emotion is experienced, it becomes a powerful motivator of future behaviors, affecting moment-to-moment actions, attitudes, and long-term achievements." The IHM is not alone. Peter Salovey and his colleagues report that the neurological research suggests that we cannot make good decisions without emotions. Emotions, when properly harnessed, have the power to positively influence almost every aspect of our lives.

How is this so? Let's look at how we can measure the heart's power. As a young paramedic student, I remember being trained to read and interpret the ECG or electrocardiogram tracings of patients' hearts. Quickly being able to understand what a patient's heart is doing during an emergency can lead to lifesaving interventions. Little did I know at the time that the heart is the most powerful generator of electromagnetic energy in the body.

According to the IHM, the heart's electrical field is 60 times greater in amplitude than the electrical activity of the brain and the magnetic field of the heart is more than 5,000 times stronger than the brain's magnetic field! The electromagnetic field of the heart can be detected for several feet in all directions around a person.

Figure 1. Electromagnetic Field of the Heart

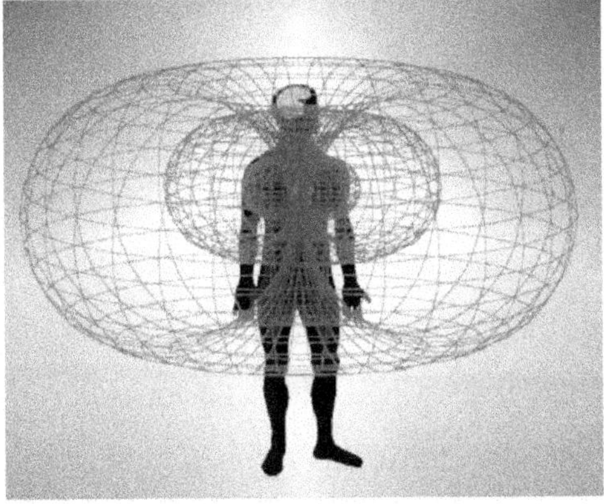

McCraty, R., Atkinson, M., & Tomasino, D. (2001). Science of the Heart: Exploring the Role of the Heart in Human Performance. Page 20. Boulder Creek: Institute of HeartMath. Used with permission.

There is an interplay between our thoughts and feelings – both affecting the other. Studies demonstrate that successfully integrating the cognitive or thinking centers of the brain and the affective or emotional feeling centers of the heart results in improved awareness, vision, listening abilities, reaction times, mental clarity, and feeling states.

The Institute of HeartMath uses a surprising term when describing this integration: *coherence.* Coherence is the same term that physicists use to describe the non-locality or entanglement effects of subatomic particles. *Psychophysiological coherence*, as the Institute of HeartMath (IHM) calls the state of heart-brain synchronization, "is associated with high performance, reduced stress, increased emotional stability, and numerous health benefits." IHM researchers measured heart rate variability in several studies. They discovered that when a person is feeling negative emotions, such as frustration, the heart rate variability becomes scattered and disordered, or what they termed *incoherent.* However, when a person feels positive feelings, such as appreciation or gratitude, the heart rate variability becomes harmonious and ordered. They called this cardiac or *heart coherence.* Several studies investigating heart coherence report amazing findings:

- Heart-focused positive feeling states, such as gratitude and love, can bring the brain into synchronization or entrainment with the heart.
- Heart coherence resulting from these heart-focused positive feeling states enhances brain alpha waves (relaxed but alert states) and improve cognitive performance.
- A person's heartbeat signal can be picked up by another person's brainwaves by touching or simply being in close proximity.
- When a person generates positive feeling states, such as gratitude and love, and those feelings results in heart

> coherence, that person's brainwaves can synchronize with someone else sitting just a few feet away – a biological empathy of sorts.

One of the key places to find treasures on your leadership journey is right in your own heart.

Emotional Intelligence

These and other findings in the literature have increasingly pointed to the notion that our emotions are crucial to effective learning, decision-making, problem-solving, and action – all crucial to effective leadership. In his groundbreaking book, *Emotional Intelligence*, Daniel Goleman, PhD, argues that a healthy awareness and the use of our emotions are more important than mental IQ or pure rationality. He points out that people who have high emotional intelligence most successfully meet life's challenges. He elucidates,

> As we all know from experience, when it comes to shaping our decisions and our actions, feeling counts every bit as much – and often more – than thought. We have gone too far in emphasizing the value and import of the purely rational – of what IQ measures – in human life.
>
> What seems to set apart those at the very top of competitive pursuits from others of roughly equal ability is the degree to which, beginning early in life, they can pursue an arduous practice routine for years and years. And that doggedness depends on emotional traits – enthusiasm and persistence in the face of setbacks – above all else.

So what is emotional intelligence? Since the 1980s, Peter Salovey, who coined the term *emotional intelligence*, and his colleagues have developed and tested a Four Branch Model of Emotional Intelligence.

They define emotional intelligence "as involving both the capacity to reason about emotions and to use emotions to assist reasoning." In other words, it's a two-way street. Thoughts and beliefs affect emotions and emotions affect our thoughts and beliefs. Thoughts empowered with emotions – *emotive thought* – especially strong emotions, trigger the subconscious, and you, into action. Even small steps acted upon by emotive thought create powerful waves of energy or a powerful state of being. Napoleon Hill said of this, "The emotions, or the 'feeling' portion of thoughts, are the factors which give thoughts vitality, life, and action."

The four branches comprise a hierarchy that begins with the most fundamental level and moves upward to more advanced skills. The four branches are:

1. **Perceiving Emotions:** This basic level of emotional intelligence involves the ability to register, attend to, and decipher emotions in others through their facial expressions, tone of voice, and body language. It also includes the ability to accurately and verbally express your own emotions and related needs.
2. **Using Emotions to Facilitate Thought:** Moving to the second branch involves the skills of being able to prioritize thoughts based on feelings, the ability to generate emotions to further performance, and capitalize on mood changes in order to appreciate multiple points of view. This branch is unique in that it uses emotions to enhance reasoning, rather than the other way around (reasoning about emotions).
3. **Understanding Emotions:** The emotionally intelligent individual at this branch recognizes that emotions are arranged into families or 'fuzzy' groups and appreciates the causes and

consequences of different emotions. They further understand transitions among emotions. For example, they understand how a simple trigger can cause annoyance that leads to irritation, frustration, anger, and even rage if the trigger is not removed or positively managed.

4. **Managing Emotions:** The fourth and highest branch of emotional intelligence involves the ability to manage emotions in a way that enhances personal growth and social relations. This requires the abilities to monitor and reflect on emotions, being receptive to both pleasant and unpleasant emotions, and the ability to engage, prolong, or detach from an emotional state. It also includes the ability to manage emotions in others, particularly "helping others feel better and by contributing to their joy."

Salovey's model and research have huge implications for leaders in all arenas. Those with high emotional intelligence are seen by their peers as better able to develop visionary goals – a key characteristic of leaders. They are more likely to have satisfying social interactions and elicit social support from others. In addition, related studies suggest that high emotional intelligence predicts customer satisfaction, annual salary raises, and total compensation. The benefits of being able to perceive feelings and show empathy were revealed by tests with thousands of people from all over the world. They include being more emotionally adjusted, more popular, more outgoing, and more sensitive.

The meaning of the word *emotion* comes from the Latin "to move." And remember, the essence of leadership is the ability to influence and change – in other words, to move. Those you lead experience emotions at work, at home, on the ball field, in the classroom – wherever

Your thoughts, beliefs, and feelings – your state of being – and of those you lead, have great power.

you lead them. According to theorists Neal Ashkanasy and Catherine Daus, these emotions (whether positive or negative) either will lead directly to emotionally driven behaviors or indirectly to judgment-driven behaviors via the attitudes derived from those emotions. In other words, the emotions and the emotional climate experienced by those you lead are at the core of their attitude formation and behaviors – their performance. This led them to caution, "Emotions in organizational settings and the events that cause them are not to be ignored, even if they appear to be relatively minor." Developing emotional intelligence is key to your success as a leader.

Your thoughts, beliefs, and feelings – your state of being – and of those you lead, have great power. Nothing you do is possible without emotive thought – whether conscious or unconscious. Your decision to read the words on this page, for example, is the result of your thoughts and emotional state. After reading the words, you may think new or different thoughts and have different feelings that then affect what you do. The quantity, quality, and focus of your emotive thoughts and beliefs will determine, whether to a greater or lesser degree, the quality of your life.

So how do we conduct a mental and emotional baggage check so we can be more focused, effective, and better outfitted for the leadership journey?

The Subconscious Mind and ANTs

As we learned earlier, our thoughts and beliefs are like programs that originated from the messages that we received when we were very young and they were internalized into our subconscious. Here are some common examples of negative or self-defeating thoughts or beliefs that we may have heard or picked up on and internalized:

"You're a bad boy (or girl)."

"It's too difficult for you."

"You'll never amount to anything."

"You're worthless."

"We can't afford that."

"You're not smart enough."

"You're fat."

"It (being some challenge or characteristic) just runs in the family. You can't change it. That's just the way you are."

"You're just like your mother (or your father) and she..." followed by some negative judgment.

"It's all your fault."

"You can't do anything right."

We oftentimes find ourselves repeating the same old self-defeating stories with ourselves, our relationships, our careers, and our lives – and this may be the result of our subconscious or automatic processing, habits, and the attachment styles ingrained into us by others when we were very young. Automatic processing/thinking that is negative or self-defeating is known as *automatic negative thoughts* or ANTs.

They happen automatically and we barely notice them or don't notice them at all. Have you ever had someone cut you off while driving and immediately yelled, "Jerk!" or some other obscenity? That's an ANT. Have you ever received a call from your boss and he asks, "I need to talk to you about [insert your latest project or report]. Can you come to my office, right now?" As you're walking over you can't help but wonder what you screwed up, why he may be upset, and you begin to feel nervous or even guilty and you don't even know why, yet. That's an ANT. It happens in our intimate relationships, too. The love of your life asks, "Why didn't you [insert some chore or task]?" and you immediately get defensive thinking, "She's *always* on my back!" Another ANT. Automatic negative thoughts or ANTs, bite! When we have a disagreement or problem with a loved one, direct report, or our boss and we are trying to work it out or resolve it in the best way possible, relying on subconscious reactions or ANTs often escalates the problem and just gets us into deeper trouble.

Keep in mind that our thoughts and emotions are energy that is also composed of quanta. Dr. Darren Weissman said, "Emotions transform energy; energy creates movement; movement is change; and change is the essence of life." So, when we can change, retrain, or reprogram our subconscious mind into automatic thoughts such as:

"I am good."

"It will be easy."

"I am worthy, valuable, and lovable."

"I am smart enough."

"I am empowered to grow and change."

"I deserve to be loved and love others in meaningful and powerful ways."

"I can make a meaningful difference."

we may be mobilizing an enormous force that can affect every part of our being *and* the subatomic energy field of the universe. That has great empowerment and helps us to change our lives and the lives of those we lead. The question is "How?"

Stamping Out ANTs

From time to time, we all get out of alignment when ANTs come storming out of our subconscious. You can notice this when you are feeling less productive emotions such as fear, anxiety, lack of confidence, jealousy, anger, etc. There are multiple techniques, that when used together, can stamp out the ANTs in your subconscious mind and the feelings they produce so that you can replace them with empowering thoughts and feelings.

Be Defined and Aligned. In the next chapter, we will examine the empowering effects of a Life Mission Statement for leaders from any walk of life. Many personal and professional success writers and coaches use the metaphor of a ship's voyage to describe the journey towards happiness and success. That's because it helps us to visualize our personal and professional journeys and the obstacles that we face. A ship leaves the port to sail to its destination. Along the voyage, it has to deal with winds and ocean currents, storms, icebergs, other ships, and supply vessels – the analogy to ANTs and diversions (some of which are necessary). What we thought would be a straight path turns into a zigzag course and the ship is constantly making adjustments in order to arrive at its final destination. If we don't have a clear purpose and vision, we are like a ship without a map, passage plan, or GPS. A beautiful poem written by Ella Wheeler Wilcox in 1919 captures this so eloquently:

THE WINDS OF FATE

One ship drives east and another drives west,
With the self-same winds that blow,
'Tis the set of the sails
And not the gales
That tell them the way to go.
Like the winds of the sea are the winds of fate,
As we voyage along through life,
'Tis the set of the soul
That decides its goal
And not the calm or the strife.

Almost every book I've read or motivational speech I've heard about personal and professional growth and success at some level addresses knowing your purpose, vision, or life mission. It's about having our lives defined and aligned. In our analogy to the TSA's security check, it's about knowing who you are and where you're going. It's your personal answer to "What's my purpose in life?" When ANTs begin to show themselves, having a Life Mission statement with guiding principles to contemplate gives us the guidance and direction to redirect ourselves on our journey and toward our final destination.

If you ever feel something negative towards yourself or someone you love, serve, or lead – which we all do from time to time – and you want to change that so you can harness the positive, ask yourself or the Divine something I heard Dr. Wayne Dyer recommend, "What's my purpose in this moment?"

Take my wife, who teaches fourth grade, for an example. She was recently challenged by a student with ADHD and his mother who was sitting in on the class. The boy was being particularly challenging and the mother wasn't helping the situation. Negative thoughts and emotions swelled inside my wife. Right on the spot, she privately took a deep breath, reminded herself of her life mission of serving students and parents as a teacher, and asked God for help. Suddenly, everything shifted – her emotions, her thoughts about what she was doing, and what she needed to do next. In just a few minutes, everything turned around and the lesson continued with success and because of the outcome, the mother accepted the school's offer for a further, more in-depth intervention that she had been resisting for several years. Because my wife was able to shift back to her life mission and become defined and aligned, this student not only got the help he needed in the moment, but for the long term, as well.

It's about having our lives defined and aligned.

By taking a time-out and asking

this question, you shift away from self-serving, self-defeating, and negative energy and towards thoughts and feelings that are more aligned with your vision, mission, and purpose and guiding principles. "What is my purpose in this moment?" helps you shift to higher-level focus and response. In the coming chapters, we will learn how to contemplate and how to develop a powerful Life Mission Statement.

What is my purpose in this moment?

Replace the ANT using the Sedona Method. A terrific technique for letting go of negative emotions is the Sedona Method. The first thing to remember is not to push away or bury negative emotions arising from ANTs. Simply let them be for a moment, examine them, wonder about where they come from, and think about what kind of thinking produced them. Most importantly, *feel* the emotion. Then ask yourself the following four questions:

Could I allow myself to welcome this feeling the best I can?
Could I allow myself to let it go?
Would I let it go?
When?

Continue this process until you begin to feel like you are able to let go of at least some – or all – of what you are feeling. I highly recommend that you read *The Sedona Method* by Hale Dwoskin for a magnificent and in-depth explanation of the method. I'd like to share with you a twist on the Sedona Method that I've found adds some real *oomph*! Just as soon as I'm starting to feel some relief from the negative feeling while using the Sedona Method, I immediately replace it with as close to a polar opposite feeling. For example, if I'm feeling nervous before a talk or presentation, I'll go through the questions above about the nervous feelings several times. When I start to feel some relief, I turn it around like this:

Could I allow myself to welcome the feeling of confidence the best I can?
Could I allow myself to feel confident?
Would I allow myself to feel confident?
When?

Again, I continue to repeat it over and over until confidence (or whatever positive feeling I'm trying to nurture) begins to take hold.

Similar to this technique, you can simply ask yourself, "How will feeling [insert negative, self-defeating emotion] serve me or help me in *any* way?" "Do I *want* to feel this way or something more positive and productive?" The key to these techniques is to repeat them until you feel a shift.

Freeze-Frame. Another technique to shift away from negative emotions is known as the Freeze-Frame technique. It was developed by the Institute of HeartMath. People who are taught to consistently disengage from negative emotional and mental reactions and shift their attention to the area around their heart and generate sincere positive feelings such as gratitude or love experience greater autonomic nervous system balance, increased immune function, improved psychological well-being, adopt healthier strategies for resolving interpersonal conflict, and significantly increase mental clarity and productivity.

You place a hand over your heart, take a few slow, deep breaths and imagine something or someone positive in your life or about the issue, and quietly repeat, "Love and gratitude." You can alter this a bit by repeating positive affirmations or asking, "What's my purpose in *this* moment?"

Reframing. ANTs and negative emotions often show up as cognitive distortions. Cognitive distortions have been well researched in psychology and reframing is widely used in therapy. Here are some common cognitive distortions that sabotage our success and happiness:

Dichotomous or all-or-nothing thoughts. Black and white thinking that only sees two extremes and no middle ground is a common ANT.

Examples:

"There's no way I'll ever get this done so I might as well not even start."

"Look at this mistake. I'm a total failure."

The negative mental filter. When someone picks out a single negative event or part of an event and discounts the positive and then views the entire event, self, relationship, or even life as negative or defeated, this is a negative filter.

Examples:

"I know my boss said she liked the presentation... but she said there's room for improvement. She must think I'm a disappointment and a failure."

"He didn't put the toilet lid down. I guess he just doesn't love me."

Overgeneralization. Whenever you hear words like "always" or "never" coming out of your mouth, you can bet this ugly ANT is around.

Examples:

"You never listen to me."

"He always does that!"

Catastrophizing or magnification. Expecting the absolute worst or intolerable outcomes of a situation characterize this type of ANT. Also called *the fortuneteller error*, this ANT anticipates that a prediction is an established fact and often become self-fulfilling prophecies because we react to them as if they are true.

Examples:

"I've always been this way. I'll never change."

"He's looking at that woman. I guess he's going to have an affair and destroy our marriage."

"This project will never work. We just can't do it that way."

Personalization. Whenever we take personal responsibility for someone else's actions, this ANT is crawling around.

Examples:

"He didn't even say 'good morning' back. He must not like me."

"The boss is in a really foul mood. It must be something I said or did."

Emotional reasoning. Whenever we assume our emotional state reflects the way things really are, this ANT is lurking around the corner.

Examples:

"I feel like a failure, therefore I am a failure."

"I feel rejected, therefore I am rejected."

Mind reading. If we're making conclusions that someone is reacting negatively to us without checking it out, that's an ANT.

Examples:

"I can tell she thinks I was bossy in the meeting."

"My boss talks to Bob all the time. She must like him better than me."

When these ANTs come around, cognitive psychology provides us with a simple, three-step process. First, simply say, "Stop!" Recognize the ANT. Then, label the ANT. Finally, purposefully and methodically, reframe the thoughts behind the negative emotion. Some psychologists recommend that you do this in written format using three columns, at first. By doing this, you transform ANTs into what is called *controlled processing* – you bring the subconscious, conscious. You are using the magnificent gift of the most important affair: higher, self-awareness. However, in order to be effective, you must *want* to change the ANT and make the time to reframe them regularly.

For example, if you hear yourself say, "You never listen to me," write it down. Name it as overgeneralization. Then, remember a time when the person *did* listen to you and find an explanation for why they may not be listening now. Maybe they're preoccupied in thought or very busy.

ANT	TYPE	REFRAME
You never listen to me.	Overgeneralization	Yesterday he listened to me when I shared about my day. Maybe he's busy or preoccupied in thought.

The 100% Test. One of my favorite techniques comes from Dr. Wayne Dyer's bestselling book, *Excuses Be Gone*. He points out that our excuses, or what we've been calling ANTs, are simply justifications that may or may not be true. If a thought we have is actually preventing us from growing or getting what we want or moving forward effectively, then why hang on to it?

For example, a top excuse he points out that people often use is: "It will be difficult." If I go around thinking that "it" (the new strategy, program, losing weight, being calm and confident – whatever) is going to be difficult, then guess what? It more than likely *will* be difficult and thinking that thought (consciously or unconsciously) will stand in the way of my achieving what I want. But here's the rub. That thought, "This is going to be difficult" might not even be true! So thinking a possibly untrue thought, "It will be difficult," keeps me from achieving my goal.

He advises that we ask a simple question about our excuses or what we've been calling ANTs: "Can you be one hundred percent certain that this thought is true?" And, of course, we can't be one

If a thought we have is actually preventing us from growing or getting what we want or moving forward effectively, then why hang on to it?

hundred percent certain that *any* thought, especially an ANT, is true. It *could* be false. It's just a thought. If I consider that the thought "It will be difficult" could possibly be true or untrue then the opposite thought, "It will be easy" could also possibly be true or untrue. Which thought will actually help me achieve what I want? Choose, affirm, and regularly contemplate the one that *will* help, "It will be easy." You can apply this technique to any thought process, excuse, or ANT that is keeping you from getting what you want or who you want to be or what you want to achieve. Pick up his book and discover more insights into this powerful technique. I highly recommend it.

Binaural Entrainment. Binaural sounds played through headphones or ear buds have been shown to help entrain brainwaves to certain wavelengths – like the alpha, beta, theta, or delta frequencies describe earlier. Two sounds or impulses, one to each ear, are received by the brain. The brain then processes the phase differences between the two frequencies as they wax and wane producing the desired third frequency. They are often called *binaural beats*, because the frequencies produce a unique, rhythmic sound.

When the brain is entrained to theta and delta wavelength levels, you can use this as a form of self-hypnosis to help you re-write old, negative, or self-defeating beliefs and instill positive, new ones and refresh your state of being.

You can re-write old, negative, or self-defeating beliefs and instill positive, new ones and refresh your state of being.

Brain cells reset their sodium and potassium ratios when the brain is in theta state, usually when you're sleeping. These electrolyte levels are involved in osmosis – the chemical process that transports chemicals into and out of your cells. After an extended period in the alert, beta state, the ratio between potassium and sodium gets out of balance. This is what causes that common feeling of mental fatigue. Spending between 5-15 minutes in a theta state can restore the ratio to normal, resulting in mental refreshment. Others use alpha binaural clips to relax and beta waves to increase concentration.

Spending between 5-15 minutes in a theta state can restore the ratio to normal, resulting in mental refreshment.

Many varieties are available on CDs and MP3s online. There are "raw" binaural audio clips with just the two frequencies. I like these, but some people prefer to listen to binaural clips that have nature sounds, white noise, or meditative music mixed in. Sample some online to find out which ones you like best. Remember, you must use headphones or ear buds for them to work. Here's what you do:

Take a 5-15 minute break. Play a binaural audio clip that will help entrain to the theta or delta levels. While the audio plays, contemplate positive affirmations; reframing statements; your vision, mission, purpose, and goals; or, some objective your working on – or simply clear your mind and meditate. Some people report experiencing a meditative "high" or even altered states of consciousness while playing them. I like meditating with binaural beats before going to bed at night. It's a very powerful reinforcing tool for positive mental states of being – and I sleep better, too. Humming, using breathing exercises, or guided imagery during binaural playback can add to the depth of the effect. If you're having some cynical thoughts about this, read the words of Napoleon Hill from his classic book, *Think and Grow Rich*, written nearly 75 years ago, "Faith is a state of mind which may be induced, or created, by affirmation or repeated instructions to the subconscious mind, through the principle of auto-suggestion." Binaural beats help you to achieve a state of auto-suggestion – self-hypnosis – in which you can repeat positive affirmations, reframing statements, etc. that you desire to manifest in your life. Do this regularly for maximum effect.

Media Fast. "Why don't you go on a media fast?" the usually very quiet nun asked me. It was almost Lent. I wasn't Catholic anymore... and she knew that. Still I was intrigued. "What's a media fast?" I asked. She then went on to explain that a media fast is a defined time period, like Lent or Ramadan, when a person consciously chooses to limit their exposure to mass media. You fast from mass media instead of from food or in addition to it.

I took up her challenge that Lent many years ago. It was one of the most enlightening and empowering experiences in my life! I have been on some type of media fast (or diet, if you will) ever since. Before that time, I didn't realize how much of a negative impact the media had on my thoughts and feelings, especially news. A media fast is a great way to help you transform negative thinking patterns while on your leadership journey. For example, you can choose to wake up to beautiful instrumental music instead of a blaring radio. That's just one way. When you go on a media fast, you can choose to fast from particular media sources and types, much like a typical fast from food. These days, I rarely listen to mass media news and carefully choose what forms of media I do.

Persistent ANTs. For those deeper, more persistent negative emotions and issues, learn everything you can about how best to understand and deal with them. Seek counsel from a trusted family member, friend, life coach, mentor, or counselor. Don't ignore or sweep them under the rug or make excuses. Act on them. Incorporate goals, objectives, and action items into your mission statement that lead you down a path of improvement.

Gratitude. This is one of my personal favorites because there are so many reasons to foster gratitude beyond dealing with ANTs. Wonderful and simple techniques to foster gratitude and the reasons why will be presented in Chapter 6, The Bridge of Gratitude. Gratitude is a powerful tool.

Our subconscious thinking patterns, beliefs, and emotions – our state of being – impacts how we consciously think, our decisions and actions, our physiology, and how we respond to our lives. There is also evidence they are influencing the subatomic field and maybe even the universe. By regularly conducting your own personal and private baggage check, you open yourself to replacing outdated, negative, self-defeating patterns with more powerful, positive ones. Recall the wise words from Dr. Dyer that opens Part I, "...you do not attract into your life what you want, you attract into your life what you are... what you *are*." That is why your state of being is so important.

We leave this chapter with an ancient, North American legend that I love to read again and again.

Two Wolves: A Cherokee Legend

> An old Cherokee is teaching his grandson about life. "A fight is going on inside me," he said to the boy.
>
> "It is a terrible fight and it is between two wolves. One is evil – he is anger, envy, sorrow, regret, greed, arrogance, self-pity, guilt, resentment, inferiority, lies, false pride, superiority, and ego."
>
> He continued, "The other is good – he is joy, peace, love, hope, serenity, humility, kindness, benevolence, empathy, generosity,

truth, compassion, and faith. The same fight is going on inside you - and inside every other person, too."

The grandson thought about it for a minute and then asked his grandfather, "Which wolf will win?"

The old Cherokee simply replied, "The one you feed."

There is a great lesson here for us. Although it is important to be aware of the "evil wolf" inside of us – of the negative baggage or ANTs we carry; it is more important to feed the good one; to pack and nurture positive, self-enhancing thoughts, beliefs, and feelings in our baggage for the leadership journey. In the chapters ahead, we will examine the most powerful and positive tools that not only outfit you for your journey, but assist you in sailing along your journey, as well.

Leadership Travel Tips Chapter 2: Baggage Check

- Since your thoughts are energy and they become things; since you can be aware of your thoughts, your energy – your state of being; and, since you can choose your thoughts; it is important to stop from time to time and conduct a baggage check.
- Together, our thoughts, beliefs, and feelings create our energy state or our state of being. It has great power – for better or worse. Be aware of your state of being.
- Negative emotions impair the effectiveness of working memory that can then lead to mistakes, misperceptions, and a downward spiral towards disaster. On the other hand, positive emotions, like enthusiasm, happiness, love, and gratitude, lead to you being energized and motivated.
- Thoughts and beliefs affect emotions and emotions affect our thoughts and beliefs.
- Your heart generates an electromagnetic field around you. Positive feeling states, such as gratitude and love, result in heart-brain coherence.
- Your heart-brain coherence can synchronize with someone else sitting just a few feet away. Your state of being can affect others around you.
- By using your emotional intelligence, you greatly improve yourself as a leader.
- Stamp out your ANTs by:
    - Being defined and aligned (see more in Chapter 3)
    - Replace ANTs using the Sedona Method and my twist on it
    - Using the Freeze-Frame Method
    - Reframing ANTs
    - Using the 100% Test
    - Using Binaural Entrainment
    - Going on a Media Fast
    - Fostering Gratitude (see more in Chapter 6)
- You do not attract into your life what you want; you attract into your life what you are. Who are you? Where are you going? What's in your baggage?

CHAPTER 3

GPS for Leaders

The research on happiness clearly shows that people who are deeply committed to whatever gives their life meaning are much happier than those who don't have this greater sense of purpose.
~ Marci Shimoff ~

I was feeling quite special as the driver pulled the black Lincoln Continental along the curb where Park Avenue meets 42nd street in New York City – right in front of Grand Central Station. It was my first time in the "Big Apple" and I was excited. It was just after lunchtime and I had a few hours before my train left to take me further on to New Haven, Connecticut. I had just finished a three-day business meeting in New Jersey and I was taking a couple of days to visit my son who was finishing his Masters in Sacred Music at Yale University. Since I only had a few hours, I planned on squeezing-in a visit to the Empire State Building before my train left. The problem was that I had this fifty-pound suitcase on wheels I didn't want to be lugging around New York, much less the Empire State building. So, I went inside Grand Central thinking there might be a locker where I could store my bag while I walked to the Empire State Building. There wasn't. But, the woman at the information counter was very friendly and helpful and gave me the address to a place somewhere on 45th Street that would babysit my bag for me. Even though it was in the opposite direction of the Empire State Building, the woman assured me it wasn't that far. A short aside: I found most New Yorkers to be very friendly and helpful. The stereotype of the New Yorker as brash and out for themselves did not ring true in my experiences at all.

So, I had to figure out how I was going to get to the baggage babysitter. "Well," I thought, "Here's my first opportunity to use that GPS navigation system on my cell phone." This was back before "apps" and you had to pay for navigation on your phone. I decided to pay the two bucks for the day and typed in the address and walked out onto 42nd Street, bag dragging behind me.

I was glad it was a cool and cloudy day as my new little lady-friend inside my cell phone's GPS program started giving me directions. I wasn't familiar with using it and I must've walked a couple of blocks before I realized that I had accidentally turned it off. I had to stop in order to restart the program and retype in the address. Not being familiar with New York and now a little flustered along with my excitement, I blindly followed the instructions to turn left down 5th Avenue, which unbeknownst to me was actually leading me away from my baggage babysitter. After walking another block, the little lady in my phone wanted me to take a right… and a block later another right up 6th Avenue. I looked up at the one-way street sign and started laughing out loud.

My little lady friend thought I was *driving a car* instead of being on foot. The GPS program was helping me to get to my baggage babysitter using the one-way streets. If you are going to use a GPS to help guide your way, you have to know how to use it. I finally did make it to my baggage babysitter and eventually to the Empire State Building.

Life Mission Statement

The Global Positioning System or GPS is fascinating technology and a great tool to get you to new destinations or through unchartered waters. I had to learn how to use the GPS on my phone. Now I can use it a lot better than I did that first time I was in New York. It has guided me on several more journeys.

What about the leadership journey? Not only is a Leadership GPS necessary in order to guide us as we make our way leading others and ourselves to new destinations, pursuing meaningful personal goals has been shown to increase happiness and initiate an upward spiral of positive outcomes and success building patterns. Without a Leadership GPS, you risk wandering in circles. The best leaders use some type of Leadership GPS to help them navigate through life. The most widely-used Leadership GPS is a Life Mission Statement. A simple Life Mission Statement consists of the following four basic elements:

The Four Basic Elements of a Life Mission Statement

- Vision, Mission, and Purpose Statement
- Guiding Principles and Values
- Goals in each of the Four Supporting Pillars
- Objectives

Discovering and regularly affirming your vision, mission, and purpose is the single most important part of your leadership journey. In one of his classic works, *Leadership 101: What Every Leader Needs to Know*, John Maxwell, internationally recognized leadership expert, speaker, and author agreed, "Vision is everything for a leader." Having a vision leads you and you lead others. Without a vision, mission, and purpose a leader is like a ship's captain without a map or GPS. Your vision, mission, and purpose are your targets, spark, and overarching

Discovering and regularly affirming your vision, mission, and purpose is the single most important part of your leadership journey.

intention to do what's meaningful to you. It is your internal compass. In our earlier analogy to getting through an airport security check, your Life Mission Statement is like your ID and boarding pass. You've got to know who you are and where you're going.

Without a vision, mission, and purpose hope is easily lost, dreams remain unfulfilled, expectations and goals are ambiguous, there is no direction, conscious intent, or control, and; life can have little meaning. In our analogy to GPS, your vision, mission, and purpose are the endpoint address, your destination. A journey without vision, mission, and purpose – without a destination – is called *wandering*. It's not a journey at all. Creating a Life Mission Statement is the first step in transforming your leadership journey. And if you already have a mission statement, now is a great time to review it and apply the following guidelines to it. Over the next few pages, you will discover how to create a powerful Life Mission Statement.

Vision, Mission, and Purpose

We start with a focus on the words *vision*, *mission*, and *purpose*. First, vision is the ability to see a much broader scope of yourself, the world, and those you serve. It is far-reaching and expansive. Your personal vision gives you a look towards a future in which the world is a much better place because of your efforts and the efforts of those you inspired, led, and served. It imagines miracles and provides hope and inspiration. Second, because of this vision, you now have a mission. Your mission is your assignment; it's the goals that further narrow your vision. Your mission is your task and your responsibility that percolates from deep within and manifests from high above – from your vision. It gives you purpose and meaning. Combined, your vision, mission, and purpose are your 'why.'

Victor Frankl survived imprisonment in four Nazi concentration camps during World War II, including Auschwitz, the largest and most-dreaded death camp. He lost his wife, his parents, and other family members to the atrocities of the Nazis. Finding meaning to life in places of such horror, slave labor, torture, and death may seem impossible. Yet this is what the famous Austrian neurologist, psychiatrist, professor, and colleague of both Sigmund Freud and Alfred Adler did – and helped others do. He explains in the now classic, *Man's Search for Meaning*, "Those who have a 'why' to live for, can bear with almost any 'how'." After World War II, he founded logotherapy, which become known as the "Third Viennese School of Psychotherapy" (coming after Freud's Psychoanalysis and Adler's Individual Psychology).

To Frankl, finding meaning is the prime motivation in life and we always have the ability to choose our attitude and find that meaning, no matter what the circumstances. When I read Frankl's book, *Man's Search for Meaning*, I could really relate. Although I know I can never fully understand what it must have been like to endure a Nazi concentration camp, I too have had times in my life that were devastating and/or terribly traumatic and difficult. I have lived through serious health issues, the loss of my high school sweetheart through a heart-wrenching divorce, and financially devastating periods, including bankruptcy. Had it not been for reconnecting to my vision, mission, and purpose during those times, I would not be where I am today; healthy and fit, happily married, and enjoying more financial abundance than I've ever had. The first step in many successful leadership development programs is finding your own personal 'why' – your very own Leadership GPS. As you discover or revisit your life's vision, mission, and purpose, keep in mind that the most powerful mission statements have four fundamental characteristics:

Expansive and Inspiring. A powerful Life Mission Statement is expansive in nature and involves a wider vision. It is not your job, career, or your profession. It is not your company's mission statement, either. It might overlap with it, but it is *yours* and it has more power for you personally.

There is a story that has several variations, which illustrates this well. It is attributed to Sir Christopher Wren, the architect of the majestic St. Paul's Cathedral in London that was built between 1675 and 1710.

> One day Sir Wren was visiting the dusty worksite for St Paul's Cathedral when he came across three strong, young men diligently working away. Sir Wren went up to the first man and asked him what he was doing. He replied very matter-of-factly, "I am laying bricks. This is what I do. I am a bricklayer." A little later, Sir Wren came across a second bricklayer and he asked him the same question. He replied, "I am making a living. I take pride in my craft and it's good to know that what I do here can feed my family and meet our needs." Finally, Sir Wren came across a third bricklayer and asked him what he was doing. With a gleam in his eye, the bricklayer replied, "Oh, I'm building the most beautiful cathedral in the world!"

Developing your own Life Mission Statement helps get you to a place where you too can have that gleam in your eye about what you do each and every day. Your mission statement drives your perspective of your life and those you serve. As we learned earlier, how we feel, think, and express our beliefs actually creates our world. Having a far-reaching, inspiring, and powerful Life Mission Statement gives us a personal and meaningful connection to what we do, just like the third bricklayer. It serves to inspire us. To the ancient Greeks, to be inspired was to have the breath of life or breath of God come within. It means literally to be 'in spirit.' Being 'in spirit' is what fills your heart with joy, whether you believe in God or not.

Having a far-reaching, inspiring, and powerful Life Mission Statement gives us a personal and meaningful connection to what we do.

Calling. Inspiration requires quieting yourself down and listening to your inner voice and heart. John Maxwell wrote, "If what you're pursuing doesn't come from a desire within – from the very depths of who you are and what you believe – you will not be able to accomplish it." Your Life Mission Statement must touch you and have personal and powerful meaning for you. For many, that means listening for God's call. I remember from a very young age, maybe as early as four or five, my mother asking me, "Alan, what's going to be your vocation?" My mother had and has great vision. She taught me from an early age that our purpose in life is rooted in God's personal call – a vocation. Jesus of Nazareth points us inward, "Nor will people say, 'Look! Here it is!' or, 'See, it is there!' For behold, the kingdom of God is within you [in your hearts] and among you [surrounding you]" (Luke 17:21). What an amazing connection! When you search your inner voice and heart or what Maxwell called 'the depths of who you are,' you are quieting yourself so you can hear the kingdom of God within you. From there your vision, mission, and purpose spring forth. After graduating from high school, I took two years to do just that – to listen very deeply. I wondered if I was being called to the priesthood and entered the seminary. After two years, I knew I was being called to service, just not as a priest. I still didn't know exactly what or how, but at least I knew to what I *wasn't* being called. I did realize that whatever job or profession I pursued; I had to be in service to others and to myself. Research shows that regardless of the job type, people who feel that they are following a calling or greater mission, experience greater satisfaction from their work and greater happiness in their lives.

Transformative. Some of the greatest ideas have come about because of a desire to change something that doesn't seem to be working. Great leaders champion a vision of change. Mahatma Gandhi had a vision of peacefully and nonviolently freeing the Indian people from British rule and oppression. Martin Luther King, Jr. had a similar peaceful, nonviolent vision of ending racial segregation and discrimination in the United States. In 1903, Henry Ford incorporated the Ford Motor Company, proclaiming, "I will build a car for the great multitude." And he did, selling over 15 million Model T cars in less than 20 years. You don't have to become famous or a millionaire for your purpose to be realized. That's not the point. You are following your calling. For example, in the late 1990's, I helped establish, along with some amazing and loving co-founders, the first non-profit critical incident stress management organization serving the greater San Antonio, Texas area. We ended up providing trainings and crisis interventions to hundreds of law enforcement, fire, and emergency medical services personnel. The powerful experiences I had through that organization and with such compassionate and altruistic people, inspired me to pursue and eventually obtain my Master of Arts in Clinical Psychology, further unfolding my own vision, mission, and purpose. That now includes inspiring and creating in myself and others a keener and deeper awareness

Great leaders champion a vision of change.

of love and loving leadership – of transforming lives and organizations. My wife influences a new set of fourth graders every year. Many come back years later to tell her what a difference she has made in their lives and they always give her big hugs. What do you want to transform, create, or accomplish? What gets you fired up?

The most powerful mission statements not only involve your inspiration and passion, but service to others.

Service-Oriented. The most powerful mission statements not only involve your inspiration and passion, but service to others. As Maxwell states in *Leadership 101* (emphasis in the original), "And if it has real value, it does more than just *include* others; it *adds value* to them. If you have a vision that doesn't serve others; it's probably too small." It serves to inspire you, to 'light your fire,' and fill your soul with passion. Service is the deepest expression of love. When we are in service to others, we are helping them meet their needs and furthering them along their journey. A mission statement not only serves our own vision, mission, and purpose, it extends a hand to help others fulfill theirs, as well. This fourth fundamental characteristic of a Life Mission Statement, service and love, is so important to great leadership that the next chapter is entirely devoted to it.

How to Make a Personal and Powerful Mission Statement

I remember the last two weeks of my first 911 paramedic job. I was about to transition from a 'field medic' to a fulltime adjunct faculty at the University of Texas Health Science Center in San Antonio teaching EMT, paramedic, Special Forces medics, nursing, and medical students.

One of the last calls I made for that service was a terrible motor vehicle accident. An elderly couple in a passenger vehicle had been broadsided by a dump truck. The amount of energy and the mass of a dump truck are no match for the side of just about any passenger vehicle. The driver's side was so utterly damaged and contorted that all of the glass had shattered like a shotgun blast into the interior and the side of the vehicle had intruded nearly halfway into the cab. The elderly man who had been driving was critically injured. He had severe head and facial trauma and was drowning in his own blood as his wife, sitting next to him, screamed in terror. I had at my disposal the latest technology and equipment. I had been blessed with some of the best training, mentors, and experience a paramedic could hope for. Our response time to the scene was unparalleled. Despite all of that, nothing I was going to do for him was going to save his life. His trauma was just too severe. One moment he and his wife were driving along a country highway, maybe talking about marigolds or what to eat for lunch, and in a flash of lightening, it was over. That man died in my arms that day.

As I offer these thoughts to you, my family and I were given the news that my father has stage 4, non-Hodgkin's lymphoma, and that it has metastasized to every part of his body. I don't know how much longer the man who taught me how to fish, who encouraged me to love with strength and character, who wrote *A Father's Prayer*, that open this book, and who time and again guided me through the lessons of manhood and fatherhood will be with us. Are you courageous enough to contemplate, for even just a few moments,

Are you courageous enough to contemplate, for even just a few moments, your last day on earth?

your last day on earth? How will you be remembered? What will you have accomplished? What will you leave behind? What is your love? Your calling? Will you leave rejoicing with the knowledge that you have heard and responded to your calling with joy and love? Or, will you leave with regret and fear?

In order to create your own mission statement, you are going to need to stop and have some 'quality time' for yourself in order to listen to your calling and contemplate some of these questions. It isn't necessary to enter the seminary, become a monk, or a hermit. All you have to do is go somewhere quiet, maybe a walk in the park, along a beach, or in the woods. Getting close to nature helps many people get in a more reflective and peaceful mood. Some people like to spend some time in a church, synagogue, mosque, or other prayerful place. You may incorporate several places over several different occasions in order to write your own personal mission statement. Wherever you choose, you will need to get away from your workplace, family, and friends for about an hour – at least for the first run at this. Some people even go on a retreat or weekend get-away in order to have some quality time to reflect, contemplate, and allow their mind to relax and open up. If you can't do it right now, schedule at least an hour for your initial Life Mission Statement development session. Make an appointment with yourself.

Here are a few suggested questions you can ask yourself to get you started with creating your own personal and powerful mission statement:

- What is the meaning of life for me?
- What do I dream about?
- What moves me, stirs my heart, and inspires me? What most often brings me joy? When do I feel like I'm 'in the flow'?
- What are the most important lessons life has taught me so far?

- What do I value most? What are my treasures?
- Look beyond yourself and to others. Look beyond your own lifetime and ask yourself, "How would I like this world to be different after I'm gone?"
- After I die, I want to be remembered for…
- What are my best talents and skills?
- What doesn't work well in my world that I wish was different?
- Simply ask, "What is the purpose of my life?"

Reflect on these questions. Just put them out there and allow them to simmer in your heart and mind. It's not necessary to have immediate answers or to allow the first answer to be the only answer. I started this process for myself in 1987 and revisit my Life Mission Statement on an annual basis, usually around the Christmas season. Others like the idea of doing it on New Year's Eve or New Year's Day. My own changes a little bit every year.

Guiding Principles and Values

Many people find writing out their guiding principles or values supportive to the Life Mission Statement process. For example, the Golden Rule is a popular guiding principle for many. I have nine guiding principles in my mission statement that I call The Nine Meditations: Love, Gratitude, Happiness, Peace, Goodness, Abundance, Holiness, Gemeinschaftsgefühl (from Alfred Adler), and Self-Realization/Holy Power. I contemplate them daily. When you stamp out the ANTs or automatic negative thoughts, you leave a vacuum. Fill that vacuum with something wonderful and positive. Contemplate them regularly to reinforce the new thought patterns you want to create. The power of contemplation is explained more fully at the end of this chapter. I prefer the early morning as I am waking up and late evening, right before I fall asleep. Choose guiding principles and values and a time for contemplation that seem right for you.

Put a 'System' in Your Leadership GPS

Simply knowing where you are headed on a journey is not enough. You must know where you are and how you are going to get there. GPS uses longitude, latitude, elevation, and time to help you navigate toward your destination – even if you get detoured, like I did in New York. It constantly measures and monitors your progress. The best Life Mission Statements employ a system of goals and objectives to help measure and monitor progress of your leadership journey, too. There is a variety of ways to support your Life Mission Statement and help you keep on track. One that I have been using since 1987 is a four-pillared approach inspired from Stephen Covey's bestseller, *The Seven Habits of Highly Effective People.* I was completely amazed when I read how Marci Shimoff explains how to build your Happiness House in her wonderful book, *Happy for No Reason.* She also advocates a four-pillared approach. She starts with a foundation of personal responsibility and ends with putting your life purpose on the top as a roof and surrounding your Happiness House with a garden of quality relationships. What amazed me the most was what she put in-between the foundation and the roof: The four pillars of her Happiness House. I have been using these same four mission-supporting pillars for over 20 years. You can see a pictorial representation of Your

The best Life Mission Statements employ a system of goals and objectives to help measure and monitor progress of your leadership journey.

Happiness House at the end of the chapter. Setting goals in each of the four pillars and working on them every day is critical to implementing and using your Life Mission Statement tool. Here is a brief and non-inclusive explanation of each of the pillars to help get you started.

The Body Pillar. The body pillar helps support your vision, mission, and purpose by optimizing your health and physical environment. Goals and objectives that people typically work on in this pillar are developing a healthier lifestyle, which may include things like a healthy diet, weight loss, detoxifying, exercise, stress management, releasing addictions, healing, and disease prevention. You can also place goals related to your home and office environments under this pillar. Some people include budgetary and financial goals in this pillar while others choose to put those under the mind pillar. We need money and things to take care of ourselves physically and to stimulate our mind. Poverty makes this difficult. The best leaders realize that wealth and success assist, but don't guarantee, a more full life. Wallace Wattles wrote in *The Science of Getting Rich* in 1910, "It is in the use of material things that a person finds full life for his body, develops his mind, and unfolds his soul."

The Heart Pillar. This pillar involves all matters of the heart and emotional well-being. Common goals include nurturing gratitude and happiness; working towards deeper love and improved relationships; learning and practicing empathic listening and conflict resolution techniques; forgiveness of self and others; and, the letting go or releasing of negative, dysfunctional feelings like fear, anxiety, anger, or jealousy. It also means being able to manage and use emotions to motivate.

> This is one pillar that many in leadership positions neglect.

This is one pillar that many in

leadership positions neglect. Some people, especially men, are taught from a very early age to suppress emotions or that they are a sign of weakness. "Big boys don't cry" is commonly heard when trying to calm an upset boy. Recall that when we were children, we were basically walking around in a hypnotic state absorbing everything around us. When it's repeated throughout childhood and culturally reinforced, it can become an ANT.

On the other hand, emotional well-being fosters effective decision-making – it helps you "think straight."

For others, as soon as you begin to talk about feelings, they roll their eyes in cynicism. They think that emotions, caring, empathy, and relationship issues aren't important to their work or that it's some kind of mushy, messy, romantic movie mumbo-jumbo where people will end up sitting around in a circle holding hands and singing Kumbaya. And yet, when we get upset, we say things like, "I just can't think straight."

Inattention to emotional distress – to getting upset – puts a leader at a severe disadvantage. When you can't think straight, you're not going to be as effective as you could be at *anything* that you do – and that goes for those you lead, too. As noted earlier, without emotion we do not make good decisions. Research has shown that negative emotions heighten people's autonomic "fight or flight" activity and narrow their attention to support only those activities that help them deal with a perceived threat, such as attacking or escaping. On the other hand, emotional well-being fosters effective decision-making – it helps you "think straight." Positive emotions actually quell the "fight or flight" response as it broadens attention; enhances thinking patterns that are flexible, creative, integrative, and efficient; and, fosters positive actions. Working on the heart pillar doesn't mean that you are weak or that it necessarily has to be all mushy. It means being aware of, managing, and using emotions so that you can be the best leader that you can.

And remember, positive emotions motivate. The word *emotion* literally means 'to set in motion or move.' Leaders have to believe in something with passion. They have to create community and teams. They have to work with their enemies. They have to persuade and motivate others. This means they have to manage emotional well-being. The research on the connections between emotional well-being and effectiveness in almost every category of human endeavors is so overwhelming that Daniel Goleman called it the "Master Aptitude" in his bestseller, *Emotional Intelligence: Why It Can Matter More Than IQ*:

> To the degree that our emotions get in the way of or enhance our ability to think and plan, to pursue training for a distant goal, to solve problems and the like, they define the limits of our capacity to use our innate mental abilities, and so determine how we do in life. And to the degree to which we are motivated by feelings of enthusiasm and pleasure in what we do – or even by an optimal degree of anxiety – they propel us to accomplishment. It is in this sense that emotional intelligence is a master aptitude, a capacity that profoundly affects all other abilities, either facilitating or interfering with them.

Your effectiveness as a leader is directly tied to your emotional effectiveness. Take this pillar, and your heart, seriously and you will discover one of the golden keys to being an effective, high-performing leader.

The Mind Pillar. The mind pillar focuses on transforming or letting go of dysfunctional attitudes and beliefs; self-esteem issues;

Great leaders have a commitment to continual learning.

developing optimal thinking patterns; daily affirmations; and, intellectual growth. The former Dean of Academics at the Army Management Staff College, Ursula G. Lohmann, PhD, advises military leaders (emphasis in the original), "Successful leadership and adaptation feed on the opportunity to learn. Good leaders never slack off learning, they make it conscious, and they take every opportunity to apply it... Leader is or ought to be synonymous with *learner.*"

Great leaders have a commitment to continual learning. There seems to be a never-ending list of available self-improvement books, courses, websites, blogs, online research articles, and ezines – and so many of them are free! Traditional or formal education continues to offer financial advantages. According to a 2005 L. William Seidman Research Institute report, if you have a bachelor's degree, your average annual income will be seventy-five percent higher than someone who simply completes high school. That means that with that bachelor's degree, you will earn over $1 million more than the high school graduate will over the course of your respective careers. Higher education is also associated with lower crime rates, greater civic participation, enhanced worker productivity, and a higher quality of life. Peter Drucker goes a step further, "The basic economic resource is no longer capital, nor natural resources, nor labor. It is and will be knowledge... value is now created by 'productivity' and 'innovation' both applications of knowledge at work."

I remember the Thanksgiving of 1990 very clearly. My brother-in-law and I were sitting outside after dinner chatting about life. I was a young paramedic and started lamenting about how I had never finished college after my seminary years and that if I went back, it would probably take me 10 years to complete a degree and graduate. I remember him saying, "Alan, look at it this way. Ten years from now, you can be just as you are now: a paramedic without a degree. Or, you can be a paramedic *with* a degree. It's your choice. It's up to you." Ten years later, I was walking across the stage in cap and gown. Five years after that, I earned my Master of Arts degree in Clinical Psychology. This book represents at least two years of goals and objectives that support my Life Mission and Guiding Principles and Values. Believe me, if I can do it; you can, too. Broadening your perspective, deepening your knowledge, and increasing your self-awareness, no matter how you choose to pursue it, will benefit you and those you lead and serve.

The Spirit Pillar. A deeper spiritual life or a connection to spirit is not necessarily a religious one, nor is it a requirement that you believe in God or a higher or Supreme Being. That doesn't mean it can't or shouldn't involve religion or theism, because for many it does. It's just not a requirement. What the spirit pillar more broadly involves is a deepening and/or expanding awareness of interconnections (between living things or within the universe), relationships, virtues, hope, possibilities, a sense of contact with divine power, and/or whatever it is for you that gives you 'spark' or vitality.

Expansive goals in this pillar involve things like creating quiet time for contemplation, meditation, or prayer; developing trust and peace; nurturing virtues and goodness; charitable acts and gifts; and, religious or volunteer work. This means heightening your awareness of and increasing your participation in connecting to others, nature, your higher or inner self, God, the Universe, Life Source – whatever fits best with your belief system. For example, one of my goals under this pillar is, "I take time each day (morning and evening) to contemplate and meditate."

Goals and Objectives. Each of the four pillars supports your Life Mission Statement. Where your vision, mission, and purpose statement is expansive and far-reaching, each of the four pillars narrows the focus a bit. Here you set goals that will help you achieve your Life Mission. The goals and objectives you set inside each pillar allow you to put your Life Mission Statement into practice. These goals are not things you already do or do well. They are the future milestones of your journey – where you are headed. They are just 'stops' along the way, that when reached, help you to know that you have made it just a little bit further towards your destination.

You can see how different pillars share a lot of overlap. For example, those who exercise regularly report greater happiness and self esteem (heart pillar), think more clearly resulting in improved problem-solving (mind pillar), and some even report spiritual experiences while exercising. It's okay if a goal overlaps with other pillars. The idea is to get it written down and begin working on it. Goals in each of the pillars are to be written using Contemplation Rule #1 (below): Write them in the present tense, positively, and with the energy and feelings of *having*. For example, a goal for the body pillar might be, "I am vibrant, energetic, healthy, and physically fit." Then, daily contemplate your goal in the spirit of having and gratitude.

They are just 'stops' along the way, that when reached, help you to know that you have made it just a little bit further towards your destination.

Goals are further broken down into objectives that are more tangible and measurable behaviors. An objective that supports the above goal may be, "I enjoy

30-minutes of aerobic exercise four times a week." Objectives are specific and measurable. Write them down in a day planner, on a 'To-Do List.' Or, do like I do and schedule them in your Outlook calendar. That way, they are more easily managed when conflicting objectives arise – which they often seem to do.

Once ingrained into a healthy habit, many objectives become so much part of your life that you will find it unnecessary to schedule them on a 'To-Do List' or calendar. Perform the activity of setting at least one goal in each of the four pillars (Body, Heart, Mind, and Spirit) and writing out the objectives necessary to reach that goal. Of course, you can have as many goals as seems necessary to fulfill your Life Mission. If these four pillars don't seem to work for you, feel free to create ones that do.

I encourage you to research your goals and discover how others have achieved success as part of writing your objectives. Consult books, research articles, experts, and supportive mentors. Take courses, if necessary. Learn all you can about your goals to increase your odds of success. One mistake some people make is going to current coworkers, friends, or family members who may not be supportive, who may have failed at similar goals, or may either be jealous or misunderstand that you are creating a new you that is destined for greater happiness and success. Avoid naysayers. They will only generate negative emotions and doubt as they vibrate from a place of lack, want, or negativity rather than a place of having and gratitude.

Many goals, like graduating from college or raising children, may take many years to complete and remain on your Life Mission Statement year after year. Only the step-by-step objectives change as the project moves along. Other goals are continuous and life-long and only adapt in their expression and meaning.

Be open and adaptive with the process. As you learn and grow and as new life experiences come your way, the steps and objectives that you thought would bring you to your goals may turn out to be something you never thought of. The universe has a strange way of surprising us from time to time. Be open to that and be okay with changing them – even the big picture – if you need to (emphasis on the word *need*).

Figure 2. Your Happiness House

Based on: Shimoff, Marci. (2008). *Happy for No Reason.* New York: Simon & Schuster, Inc.

Objectives are the specific and measurable behaviors or steps that help get you to a goal. Goals are the milestones that support your vision, mission, and purpose. When completed and used as a daily action tool, your Life Mission Statement gives you powerful and meaningful connection to what you do, inspires you, and gives meaning and focus to your life. It provides measurable progress towards goals and as you complete goals, gives you a great sense of satisfaction and accomplishment.

Contemplation

My great uncle Joe and I were talking in his modest Austin home about a year or so before he died. He was born in 1901 and was 93 at the time. I sat in utter amazement as he described Texas life in the early 1900s. There were no cars. Many people traveled simply by walking from place to place. I remember him talking about how lucky the new immigrant Mikolaj family was to have a mule-pulled wagon on the farm. When it rained, travel ceased. No one went anywhere because the dirt roads turned into thick mud. There were no paved and landscaped boulevards. There was no intricate highway system. There was no running water, no electricity, no radio, or television (much less cable or satellite). There were no telephones or airplanes. Space travel, cell phones, and personal computers weren't even imaginable. Yet in his lifetime, all of these things *were* imagined, contemplated, and realized. None of these amazing advances could have happened without someone mulling over some difficulty, challenge, or new possibility. Someone contemplated them. As Wayne Dyer noted in one of my favorite books, *Excuses Be Gone*, "Contemplation is the mental activity behind all inventions – indeed, behind all of creation."

Spending some time each day contemplating your vision, mission, and purpose and your guiding principles and values provides you with the inspiration for the bigger picture. This *is* important work – but it's only half of the equation. The other half is contemplating or visualizing the steps or objectives. The

Spending some time each day contemplating your vision, mission, and purpose and your guiding principles and values provides you with the inspiration for the bigger picture.

process of reaching your vision is where your time is spent; so – and this is important – make time in your contemplation for visualizing and energizing with emotion the steps you will do *today*. See yourself in the process of carrying out each step along with how it feels to be making that progress – even if it seems like they are baby steps.

One of the most powerful tools you can take with you on your leadership journey is the regular and consistent practice of contemplation.

One of the most powerful tools you can take with you on your leadership journey is the regular and consistent practice of contemplation. Consistent, focused, and positive contemplation of your vision, mission, purpose, guiding principles, and goals results in their manifestation. The problem may be that you were not taught how to contemplate productively. You may be contemplating the wrong thing or going about it in the wrong way. Those nasty subconscious beliefs and old thought patterns– and the feelings that come with them – just keep resurfacing.

Contemplation Rule #1

Have you ever found yourself wishing for something or daydreaming about how your life could be different? Maybe you want to find that 'special someone' or you want your 'special someone' already in your life to be more romantic or listen better or any number of issues. Maybe you want more money. Maybe you wish you could be less anxious in certain circumstances. Then we snap – and reality calls. Moments later, we are lamenting about how terrible our love life is or we are back to worrying about what bills may come in the mail today – and we continue complaining over and over to whomever will listen while we generate negative energy. These negative thoughts and energy-vibrations will only attract what you *don't* want. Remember, like attracts like. Wayne Dyer, PhD explains it so well (emphasis in the original):

> The more you ponder the impossibility of having your desires show up, complain about life's unfairness, and get upset about what continues to manifest, the more those very things define your reality. That's because whatever you focus on invariably shows up in your life – be it what you want or what you *don't* want. So if you're always thinking or talking about what's wrong with your life, then you're attracting exactly what you don't desire.

One of the problems that most people have when trying to use the Law of Attraction and contemplation is that they think about what they *want.* On the surface it seems like that's the whole point, right? However, thinking about *what you want* is expressing and vibrating with the feeling and energy of the lack of something. We are basically saying, "I don't have [fill in the blank] and I want it." Even our prayers often reflect this kind of thinking. A similar but even more powerful word we often use is *need.* "I *need* love." "I *need* more money." There is a hole, emptiness, or craving associated with the expression of wanting or needing. We are thinking and vibrating with lack. Hale Dwoskin also explains this eloquently in *The Sedona Method:*

> Wanting equates to lack. It does not equal having. Our lives are limited by our tendency to focus on the struggle that leads up to having, rather than having itself. When we let go of wanting, we therefore feel more like we can have. We also notice a corresponding increase in what we actually have.

Having, on the other hand, expresses and vibrates with a completely different type of energy and feeling. There is a sense of wholeness, joy, peace, and even gratitude. In mathematics, a negative takes away from something else and a positive adds to it. It's the same with thoughts, feelings, and beliefs. It is imperative that you cut away and release negative feelings, thoughts, and beliefs and replace them with the positive thoughts and feelings associated with having and gratitude. Move away from *wanting* and towards *having*. It's why we hear, "The rich get richer and the poor get poorer." It's all about where your focus and energy are. Charles Haanel, put it this way in 1912:

> A plant will remain visible for some time after its roots have been cut, but it will gradually fade away and eventually disappear, so the withdrawal of your thought from the contemplation of unsatisfactory conditions will gradually, but surely, terminate these conditions.

Contemplation Rule #1: Word your affirmations and goals in the present tense, positively, and with the energy and feelings of *having*. Think, imagine, feel, and speak as if it is true. As Haanel said, "Hold in mind the condition desired; affirm it as an already existing fact. This indicates the value of a powerful affirmation or goal. By constant repetition it becomes a part of ourselves. We are actually changing ourselves; are making ourselves what we want to be." Change saying, "I want or need [fill in the blank]" to "I have or am [fill in the blank]." If you are looking to change your world, you must begin to do something different: think differently. As Albert Einstein is so often quoted, "Insanity: doing the same thing over and over again and expecting different results." In order to do something new you must think something new – and contemplation will make it a positive habit. You've got to get outside of your comfort zone.

Contemplation Rule #2

Since the 1950s, positive affirmations have been a part of cognitive psychology. It is called cognitive restructuring. Right in line with the New Thought Movement, the basic idea of cognitive restructuring is that people's emotions and behavior are greatly affected by what they think. If you consciously change the habits of what you say to yourself and what mental images you present, you can make your life happier and more productive – you can accomplish positive change. The key? Consistency. Predating cognitive psychology by almost 50 years, Haanel wrote (emphasis added):

> The subconscious mind cannot argue controversially. Hence, if it has accepted wrong suggestions, the sure method of overcoming them is by the use of a strong counter suggestion, ***frequently repeated***, which the mind must accept, thus eventually forming new and healthy habits of thought and life, for the subconscious mind is the seat of Habit. That which we do ***over and over*** becomes mechanical; it is no longer an act of judgment, but has worn its deep grooves in the subconscious mind.

How intense is your desire to manifest positive change, happiness, and success? Your commitment, diligence, and persistent discipline are going to make all the difference. Haanel notes that, "Character is not a thing of chance, but it is the result of continued effort." You must develop new habits – and contemplation is a regular habit of thought, reflection, study, and feeling all rolled together. In the beginning, developing a new habit takes effort. After a while, it becomes second

How intense is your desire to manifest positive change, happiness, and success?

nature. Think about the time when you were first learning to drive. It took great concentration to coordinate all of the tasks that comprise driving. Today, you can cruise effortlessly through town and by the time you get to where you're going, you don't even remember most of the trip. It was all so automatic. In order to transform your new thoughts into automatic ones, it will require daily contemplation.

So first, pick a quiet time that you can contemplate every day. When I first started daily contemplation, I knew I was trying to reach deeper parts of myself and my subconscious mind. So, I chose a time when my mind is more closely resonating with subconscious frequencies: when I first wake up in the morning. Many monastic traditions awake and meditate early in the morning. Jack Canfield, known as America's success coach and founder and co-creator of the billion-dollar book brand *Chicken Soup for the Soul* also recommends a morning intention, visualization and releasing practice. For me, a morning contemplation practice quickly became a part of my routine and now it seems to take little effort to start. I don't even think about it much. It has become a habit that I find very powerful and rewarding in and of itself. But you can contemplate anytime. Pick a time that seems right for you. You may find, as I did, a desire to contemplate more frequently. I've since added a nightly contemplation before I fall asleep each night and often find myself taking a few minutes during the day to simply sit back and focus on my vision, mission, purpose, guiding principles, or goals. It re-energizes me and fills me with enthusiasm.

You can also read about a topic or listen to lectures, presentations, or interviews related to your vision, mission, purpose, guiding principles, and goals during the day. This definitely enhances contemplation. You can also purchase or download free binaural audio clips that help entrain

The busier and more stressful your life is, the more you need to take time out and contemplate.

your brainwaves to the theta or delta levels to use during contemplations. Whatever time you choose in your day, start with a contemplation practice of at least once a day for about 10-15 minutes for 3 weeks. That will ingrain the habit. As that becomes a part of your daily routine, add other times of contemplation, especially when you are busy and stressed. Make sure that you are choosing a time that you will be undisturbed so you can really focus. The busier and more stressful your life is, the more you need to take time out and contemplate.

Contemplation Rule #2: Incorporate the contemplation of your vision, mission, purpose, guiding principles, and goals on a regular and consistent basis – at a minimum for 10-15 minutes a day to start. As self-help author and motivational speaker, Anthony "Tony" Robbins said, "For changes to be of any true value, they've got to be lasting and consistent."

Contemplation Rule #3

Contemplation Rule #3 states that your vision, mission, purpose, guiding principles, goals, and affirmations must be energized with positive emotions. It is closely tied to Contemplation Rule #1. When you form a clear picture of what you want and enter that experience fully, as if it already exists, the feelings of what that state of being is like begin to manifest. Wallace Wattles advises in a classic work, *The Science of Being Great*, "Form your mental vision of yourself with care. Make the thought-form of yourself as you wish to be, and hold this with the faith that it is being realized, and with the purpose to realize it completely." As you contemplate in this fashion, allow the positive emotions to flow as if what you're contemplating is true.

There is no coincidence that the greatest inventors, scientists, spiritualists, and leaders are called visionaries. Some of the greatest scientists used visualization. Albert Einstein is most famous for this on more than one occasion to solve complex problems in physics. He called his visualizations *thought experiments*. For example, he imagined what it might be like to ride on or along with a beam of light. When doing this, he was able to "see" light as if it were still. From this visualization, the theory of relativity was born. Haanel further instructs, "From this it is evident that in order to express power, abundance or any other constructive purpose, the emotions must be called upon to give feeling to the thought so that it will take form."

Contemplation Rule #3: Your vision, mission, purpose, guiding principles, goals, and affirmations must be energized with positive emotions.

Contemplation Rule #4

I have used the analogy of a journey in this book, but many agrarian cultures have used the analogy of seeds and plant growth to the same end. I can really relate. My mom grew up on a sharecropper cotton farm in central Texas and she passed on a love of plants to me. I have a variety of plants growing around and in my patio. I water them regularly, pull out the weeds, and turn them from time to time so that the whole plant gets equal sunlight. It is pleasing to watch them grow and radiate with life.

Despite what I do to nurture them, however, I am not the one who gives the plant life. The same is true of the vision, mission, purpose, guiding principles, and goals that you contemplate. In this analogy, contemplation is the watering, weed-pulling, and other things we do to help a plant grow. Once our vision, mission, purpose, guiding principles, and goals are planted, our contemplation of them – the nurturing of the planted seed – follows a natural principle of growth. Thomas Troward wrote over 100 years ago:

> The principle of growth is that of inherent vitality in the seed itself, and the operations of the gardener have their exact analogue in Mental Science. We do not put the self-expansive vitality into the seed, but we must sow it, and we may also, so to speak, water it by quiet concentrated contemplation of our desire as an actually accomplished fact. But we must carefully remove from such contemplation any idea of a strenuous effort on our part to make the seed grow. Its efficacy is in helping to keep out those negative thoughts of doubt which would plant tares among our wheat, and therefore, instead of anything of effort, such contemplation should be accompanied by a feeling of pleasure and restfulness in foreseeing the certain accomplishment of our desires. This is that making our requests known to God with thanksgiving which St. Paul recommends, and it has its reason in that perfect wholeness of the Law of Being which only needs our recognition of it to be used by us to any extent we wish.

Contemplation Rule #4: Allow and be patient with your contemplation in a spirit of gratitude. When we try to force or become impatient with the principles of natural growth with our leadership and ourselves we violate Contemplation Rule #1.

Not a Done-Deal

Once you've created your own personal Life Mission Statement, you must understand that it is not a done-deal. Keep in mind that it is *not* written in stone. Because your Life Mission Statement gives you vision, mission, and purpose, you must refer to it often and be ready to adapt it as you discover and learn. I encourage you to continue to revise it until you are completely comfortable with it. Bounce it off a mentor, life coach, friend, or special person in your life. Some people, like my wife Leah, seem to know their purpose with clarity right off the bat. Others, like me, need time. I have gone from downright floundering through life to a more complete and mature mission statement that seems to develop and clarify a little more every year. As each New Year approaches, I encourage you to re-read this chapter and go through the process again. I also encourage you to read what other authors have to say about their perspectives of the process. Some great sources are *The Seven Habits of Highly Effective People*, by Steven Covey, *Success Intelligence*, by Robert Holden, PhD., and *Happy For No Reason*, by Marci Shimoff. See if your mission statement changes and becomes clearer each year, too.

Keep it with you or posted where you can see it every day. Read and re-read it. Contemplate it. Use the Four Rules of Contemplation and allow it to soak into your being. After awhile, it will become burned into your memory. After you first create it, review it several times a day for at least three weeks (21 days) and contemplate on it and your guiding principles and values using the Four Rules of Contemplation at least once a day. Thereafter, review and contemplate it as often as seems necessary to keep you and your life on track. The times that we need to reflect on it most are during the busiest and most stressful times. Taking time out to re-center and re-focus is a crucial part of effective leadership. As I mentioned before, I contemplate my guiding principles and values every morning and every night on a continual and routine basis. If I get stressed or busy, I take time-outs to reconnect to purpose, mission, and vision and guiding principles and values.

The times that we need to reflect on it most are during the busiest and most stressful times.

Only then am I ready to focus on the goals and objectives that manifest them into reality.

It is in the moment to moment that major goals are achieved. It is imperative to stay in the now. If all I did was sit around and belly button stare, I'd never get anything done. Like the Zen proverb teaches, "Before enlightenment; chop wood, carry water. After enlightenment; chop wood, carry water." The morning contemplation gives me my 'spark' for the day. I love that 'belly button staring' time; but then, I get to work on my objectives – my To-Do List. Focusing on what's important *now* – being in the present moment – is how goals are achieved (more on this in Chapter 9). Immerse yourself in your work – the steps and objectives. Get into flow. However, don't underestimate the power of daily contemplation. It is sometimes in those morning moments of silent reflection (and evening, too) that insights and key steps that I couldn't see before come to me. I connect to inspiration. Spending a few moments each day reflecting on the *why* will often lead to an insightful *how*. Having your very own Leadership GPS is what makes your vision real. As Charles Haanel instructs, "The world within is the practical world in which the men and women of power generate courage, hope, enthusiasm, confidence, trust and faith, by which they are given the fine intelligence to see the vision and the practical skill to make the vision real."

It is here that some brief words about time management and priority setting must be said. We all have objectives, assignments, and problems that arrive in our world that seem like *I* didn't put on my plate or ask for. My boss schedules another meeting, my direct report calls out sick, 'corporate' wants another report, both phones are ringing, and I have 150 unanswered emails in my inbox – and that's just at work! This section is not intended to ignore these real parts of everyday life. Demands are placed on our time and every leader is given exactly the same twenty-four hours in every day. However, it is beyond the scope of this text to delve into the specialty niche of time management training. If that issue is a concern for you, I highly recommend *The One Minute Manager* by Kenneth Blanchard, *How to Live on 24 Hours a Day* by Arnold Bennet (in the free press and available online), and *First Things First* by Stephen Covey.

Now it's time for you to write your own personal Life Mission Statement. As you do, recall the words of Walt Disney, "If you can dream it, you can do it."

BONUS MATERIAL: See the next page for a template that is a great tool to get you started. There is also a handy link to download your own customizable Life Mission Statement as featured on the next page. Here's what you do:

- Go to: www.alanmikolaj.com
- Click on the "Order the Book" tab.
- Click on the red Bonus Material box at the bottom of the page.
- Enter the password "bonus1"
- Click the DOCX icon labeled "Life Mission Statement"

____
(Name)

Life Mission Statement - ______
(Year)

MY VISION, MISSION, AND PURPOSE IS:

GUIDING PRINCIPLES OR VALUES:

Body Goal:	*Heart* Goal:	*Mind* Goal:	*Spirit* Goal:
Objective #1:	Objective #1:	Objective #1:	Objective #1:
Objective #2:	Objective #2:	Objective #2:	Objective #2:
Objective #3:	Objective #3:	Objective #3:	Objective #3:
Objective #4:	Objective #4:	Objective #4:	Objective #4:

Leadership Travel Tips Chapter 3: Turn On and Contemplate Your Leadership GPS – A Life Mission Statement

- Create a powerful Life Mission Statement by using the four fundamental characteristics of Vision, Mission, and Purpose:
    - Expansive and personally inspiring (vision and purpose);
    - Come from deep within or have a sense of calling from God (mission and purpose);
    - Transformative (purpose); and,
    - Service-oriented (mission and purpose).
- Write out your own personal Guiding Principles or Values
- Write out at least one goal under each of the four Mission-Supporting Pillars:
    - Body
    - Heart
    - Mind
    - Spirit or Higher-Self
- List your supporting objectives in a day planner or 'To-Do List' or schedule them in your Outlook calendar.
- Use the Four Rules of Contemplation. Contemplate key aspects of your Life Mission Statement on a daily basis.

Part II

The Journey

That's why we say, "I knew in my heart it was right (or wrong)."

Because we did.

Have you ever set out on a new venture, which scared you, but which you knew on a deep level was the right thing to do?

Have you ever held back from a scary new venture, while you felt that there was something inside you urging you on?

That's your heart guidance system in operation. Follow it.

You'll be glad you did!

~ Wes Hopper ~

CHAPTER 4

The Highway of Happiness

We do not become happy because we are successful; we become successful because we are happy.
~ Robert Holden, PhD ~

Dr. Holden sums up very nicely one of the most powerful findings from the newest school in psychology, positive psychology. Let's take a brief look at what the research has discovered through a couple of fictitious characters; one named Happy Worker, who we'll call Hap for short, and Sappy Worker, who – you guessed it –we'll call Sap.

Because Hap is positive and happy, she is more likely than Sap to hook a second job interview when looking for work. Once she lands the job, Hap will earn more money than Sap. Hap's supervisor rates her more positively and she demonstrates superior performance and productivity. In every way, Hap is noticeably a much better employee. Hap is hardly ever absent from work, whereas Sap just isn't as dependable. Hap is punctual, cooperative, and always seems willing to help her team mates.

Customers just seem to flock to Hap, too – and not only do they love her, they ask for her by name and keep coming back. She performs better than Sap on interpersonal, managerial, and decision-making tasks and it's highly likely that she'll be promoted into a managerial job much sooner than Sap – and she'll handle being that leader much better than Sap, too. It comes as no surprise that Hap's work group is one of the most successful and profitable in the company. She's the kind of employee who tends to stick with the company and she likes her job. Sap, on the other hand, is just one of those employees that edge up the turnover rate in the company, adding to the costs and headaches of finding replacements. Over the years, Hap continues to be happy and satisfied with her work, and her work group has the highest productivity, customer satisfaction ratings, and profit margins, and the lowest turnover and accident rates in the company.

Hap's close friends notice a spillover effect between her personal and professional life. Hap, and people like her, are more likely to get married than Sap and her type are. Once married, Hap's marriage is more fulfilling and satisfying than poor Sap's marriage is. Hap has a strong social network of family and friends, too. People just seem to like Hap more and want to be her friend. Part of the reason for her interpersonal success is her great conflict-resolution skills – she just seems to have a knack for collaborating with others.

Hap exercises more, has fewer accidents and injuries throughout her lifetime, has a higher pain threshold, a stronger immune system, and is generally healthier than Sap. If Hap does get sick or requires surgery, she'll recover faster than Sap. In the end, she'll live longer than Sap, too – even if they both have a heart attack or get cancer.

Some say her happiness and success are because she attends church regularly or others that she has a fulfilling life-philosophy or personal faith that gives her meaning and purpose in her life. But they all admit that she enjoys volunteer work helping others, both on and off the job.

One of the most important things about Hap is that she sets goals that are meaningful to her and her success in life and she progressively works towards them. Hap's positive and happy outlook on life has given her the skills and resources to be successful!

From World War II until the new millennium neared, the science of psychology had chiefly been concerned with mental illness and how to treat it – it was a science of pathology and healing. The vast majority of psychology focused on what was wrong with or what distressed people, institutions, and society. That all changed in 1998 when Martin E. P. Seligman, the father of positive psychology and one of the world's leading psychologists, became president of the American Psychological Association (APA) and made positive psychology the theme of his term. Positive psychology research has blossomed since then and the revelations are profound, eye-opening, and empowering for leaders and business.

Positive psychology is the study of positive emotions, positive character, and positive institutions. Studying human strengths, what makes us better, and what makes us lastingly happier dominate the subject matter. One of the main goals of positive psychology is to understand and support workplaces that foster satisfaction and high productivity. A forerunner of positive psychology, American physician, psychologist, philosopher, and Harvard professor, William James, famously said over one hundred years ago, "If we were to ask the question: *What is human life's chief concern?* one of the answers we should receive would be: *It is happiness.*"

The connections in the research between happiness and effectiveness in almost every category of human endeavors are overwhelming.

Characteristics of Happy People

- More likely to secure job interviews
- Earn more money
- Are rated more positively by supervisors
- Demonstrate superior performance and productivity
- Better handle managerial positions
- More punctual
- Less likely to show counterproductive workplace behaviors such as, absenteeism, turnover, job burnout, and retaliatory behaviors
- Are more cooperative and willing to help workmates
- Instill customer loyalty and have higher customer satisfaction ratings
- Have lower work accident rates
- Have happier relationships, including marriages
- Have strong social network of family and friends
- Demonstrate better conflict-resolution skills
- Attends church regularly or has a fulfilling life-philosophy that gives them meaning and purpose in life
- Engage in volunteer work, both on and off the job
- Sets goals that are meaningful to their success in life and progressively works towards them
- Are healthier; having fewer accidents and injuries, a lower pain threshold, and a stronger immune system
- Live longer
- Enjoy more financial prosperity

Why Nurture Happiness?

Ed Diener and Martin Seligman answer the question, 'Why is nurturing optimism, happiness and subjective well-being or SWB[1] an important

[1] Serious researchers usually call happiness, *subjective well-being,* or SWB, in the literature and other constructs describing aspects of happiness, such as *optimism*, *positive affect*, *global well-being*, *hedonic well-being*, *life satisfaction*, and *eudaimonic well-being*, while differentiated in the research, will just simply be referred to as happiness or SWB in this text.

goal?' First, existing evidence indicates that across the board, people high in SWB function more effectively than people lower in SWB. They are likely to have more successful relationships, to be more productive at work, to have higher incomes, and to have better physical and mental health. In almost every way, happy people are more successful. One of the indispensable qualities of great leaders is that they are inwardly happy and nurture that happiness for themselves and others.

Some people might try to avoid responsibility for their happiness by blaming their genetics and saying something like, "Happy Worker just got lucky and has better genes than Sappy Worker." As it turns out, the answer is a more complex than that. Most of us actually have a disposition towards a more positive subjective well-being or what Diener and Scollon call a "positive offset." In other words, most people are happy.

Ed Diener, PhD is one of the most prominent SWB researchers in the world today. He and his colleague, Richard Lucas, report in a review article that the very highest and most conservative estimates of the variance of genetics on happiness in the research is about fifty percent for current real-time happiness levels and about eighty percent for long term happiness. Using those numbers still leaves a considerable 20-50% of the variance from our environments – events and things that we can control. The most widely accepted heritability for the genetically determined set point for happiness is fifty percent. In their three-factor model of happiness, renowned happiness researchers Kennon Sheldon, PhD from the University of Missouri Columbia and Sonja Lyubomirsky, PhD from the University of California Riverside, produce evidence that the "set point is not really a set *point,* but rather, a set *range.* That is, people may have considerable latitude to be located *above* the central point" (emphasis in the original). Their model identifies three primary factors that influence happiness: The happiness set point, life circumstances, and intentional activity.

Figure 3. Three-Factor Model of Happiness

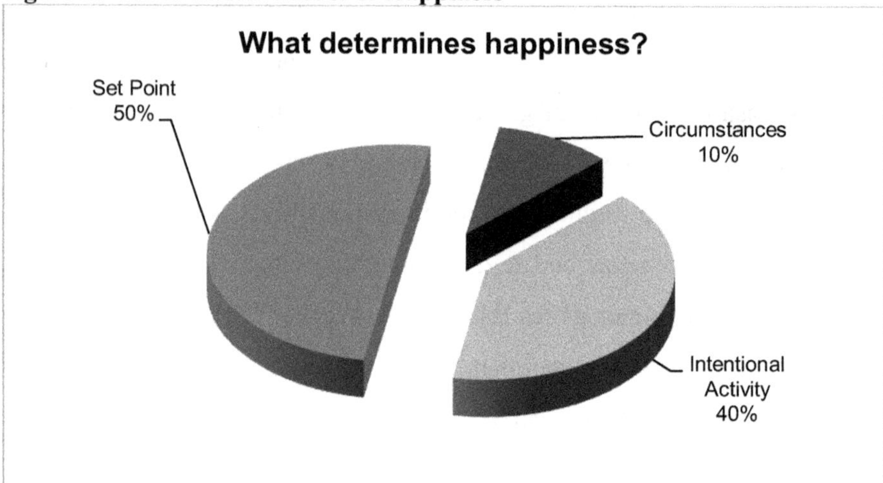

Sheldon, K., & Lyubomirsky, S. (2004). Achieving Sustainable New Happiness: Prospects, Practices, and Prescriptions. In P. A. Linley, & S. Joseph (Eds.), *Positive Psychology in Practice* (pp. 127-145). Hoboken, NJ: John Wiley & Sons. Used with permission of the publisher.

Although genetics (the set point) does play a major role in our happiness, we have, as illustrated in the above graph, a serious bit under our own personal control (intentional activity). That should catch the interest of leaders at every level of business. Don't miss this powerful finding: We can influence our happiness.

Happiness Leads to Success

Psychologist Robert Holden, PhD is another pioneer in positive psychology and an expert on happiness. Most famously known for his work as the director of The Happiness Project, Dr. Holden has spent years researching happiness and coaching people and organizations on how to be more authentically happy and successful. In his book *Success Intelligence*, he wrote, "I witnessed so many apparently intelligent people chasing after success in the most foolhardy and bird-brained manners. They seemed willing to pay for their cockeyed success with peptic ulcers, broken marriages, and crazy lifestyles. They were manic, hyper, and busy – to the point of distraction. They might have gotten A's for effort, but not for intelligence." I see it all the time – people so busy and caught up in MBOs, deadlines, emails, meetings, reports, and such, that they forget to pay attention to their state of being, purpose, and authentic happiness. Dr. Holden has found that real success *requires* happiness.

Real success *requires* happiness.

We are enculturated to believe that money and success will bring us happiness. When we land the great job, get the corner office, drive that sexy car, have the latest and greatest 'toys,' find 'Mister or Miss Right,' and have lots of money, suddenly and magically we will be happy. The 'carrots' of our culture are held out in front of us our whole lives and we are taught from a very early age that they will bring us happiness and fulfillment. And yet, despite great affluence and abundance in the United States and other countries, many people feel empty. Something is missing and they are still searching for meaning and happiness. This is what David G. Myers, PhD from Hope College in Michigan, calls "The American Paradox." Even though personal income and GNP have consistently risen in the United States, happiness levels and social well-being have decreased. The US isn't alone. He wrote, "The same conclusion – that economic growth has *not* produced increased personal or social well-being – is true of European countries and Japan." He represents this paradox in the graph below. As Americans' personal income doubled from 1970s into the new millennium, the percentage of people reporting that they are very happy actually fell.

Figure 4. The American Paradox

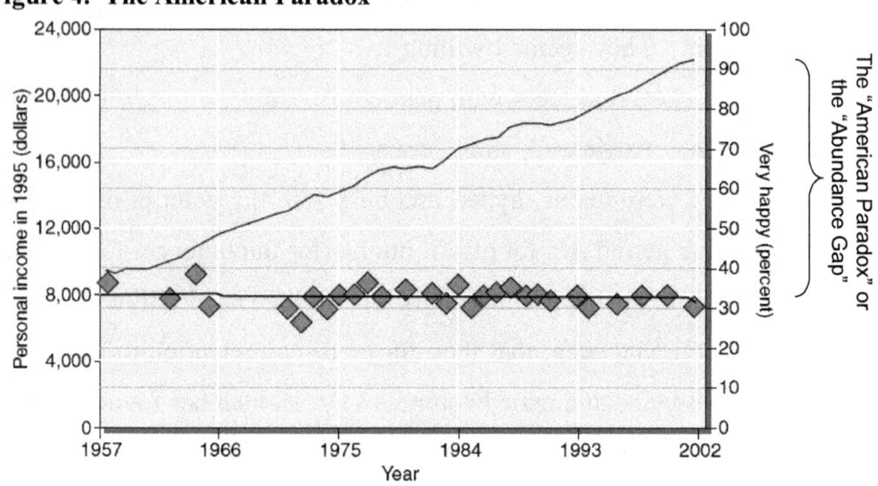

Myers, David G. (2004). Human Connections and the Good Life: Balancing Individuality and Community in Public Policy. In P. A. Linley, & S. Joseph (Eds.), *Positive Psychology in Practice* (pp. 641-678). Hoboken, NJ: John Wiley and Sons. Used with permission of the publisher.

Famous Princeton University happiness researchers, Daniel Kahneman and Alan B. Krueger report similar findings on wealth and happiness in the *Journal of Economic Perspectives*. Between 1994 and 2005, the average real income in China rose by two hundred and fifty percent! Over 15,000 Chinese were polled during this period. Similar to findings from the US, the percentage reporting that they were satisfied with their lives fell and the percentage of those reporting that they were dissatisfied rose. Karen Newquist calls this phenomenon the Abundance Gap – as abundance flourishes, life satisfaction and happiness levels decrease. Kahneman and Krueger attribute this paradox to adaptation or habituation. We quickly adapt to the beneficial gains and happiness from everything from monetary rewards to marriage and return to a baseline or set point or even worse, find ourselves even more dissatisfied and unfulfilled. The research has well-established that once income brings individuals out of extreme poverty, it has little long-lasting effects on happiness or life satisfaction.

Consider the findings of arguably the most well-known and respected positive psychology and happiness researchers, Ed Diener of the University of Illinois and the Gallup Organization and Martin E. P. Seligman of the University of Pennsylvania and the father of positive psychology. They compared data on life satisfaction from many groups. Individuals were asked to indicate on a 1 (completely disagree) to 7 (completely agree) scale, their answer to the following statement "You are satisfied with your life." Four is the neutral or midpoint. Interestingly, groups who did not have the 'luxuries of life,' were just as satisfied as are some of the wealthiest people in the world. Even, slum dwellers in Calcutta were above the midpoint, indicating that they are satisfied with their life. They highlight the fact that the African Maasai of East Africa are a herding people who have neither electricity or running water and live in huts made from dung. And yet, they reported being almost as equally satisfied with life as were the richest Americans.

Table 2. Life Satisfaction from Various Groups

Group	Rating
Forbes magazine's "richest Americans"	5.8
Pennsylvania Amish	5.8
Inughuit (Inuit people in northern Greenland)	5.8
African Maasai	5.7
Swedish probability sample	5.6
International college student sample (47 nations in 2000)	4.9
Illinois Amish	4.9
Calcutta slum dwellers	4.6
Fresno, California, homeless	2.9
Calcutta pavement dwellers (homeless)	2.9

Diener, E., & Seligman, M. E. (2004). Beyond Money. *Psychological Science in the Public Interest, 5* (1), p. 10. Washington, DC: Sage Publications. Used with permission of the publisher.

This and other research from positive psychology on wealth, happiness, life satisfaction, and success has generated a maxim that has also been preceded by motivational speakers and authors on success and prosperity for quite some time: *Success does not lead to happiness; rather,*

Success does not lead to happiness; rather, happiness leads to success.

happiness leads to success! As Dr. Holden said in our opening quote to this chapter (emphasis in the original), "The conclusion of all my work with Success Intelligence is that *we do not become happy because we are successful; we become successful because we are happy.*"

One of my favorite authors on personal development, Wayne Dyer, PhD, foreshadowed these ideas on success, intelligence, and happiness in the mid-1970s in his first book, *Your Erroneous Zones*. He said, "A truer barometer of intelligence is an effective, happy life lived each day and each present moment of every day. If you are happy, if you live each moment for everything it's worth, then you are an intelligent person."

Predating the positive psychology movement by almost 2000 years, Epictetus, the great and venerable Stoic philosopher, said, "All human beings seek the happy life, but many confuse the means – for example, wealth and status – with that life itself." The bottom line is that when you nurture happiness for yourself and others, you are nurturing success.

Happiness is Learned

Dr. Seligman's early research also demonstrated that optimism and happiness are learned. An abundance of further research has clearly correlated optimism, SWB, and happiness with success, both personal success and professional success. The causal relationship in experiments has also shown happiness and success to be reciprocal or bidirectional – that means that personal and professional success cause happiness *and* happiness causes personal and professional success. It works both ways.

And while that might seem contradictory to the earlier statement,

Boehm and Lyubomirsky recently reviewed the research in an article in the *Journal of Career Assessment.* While recognizing this bidirectional causality, they walked away convinced that "positive affect can bring about successful outcomes in the workplace." Happiness is primary.

You may have heard about the downward spiral of abuse, depression, or addiction. It seems that happiness can cause a reverse, upward spiral. According to Julia Boehm and Sonja Lyubomirsky, "That is, happiness can foster particular job characteristics, which, in turn, enhance one's happiness and activate an upward spiral over time." You can activate this upward spiral for yourself and those you serve when you add nurturing happiness to your repertoire of skills as a leader. This book contains a wealth of strategies on that spiral staircase to happiness and success.

Employee Engagement

Leaders in every avenue of business – from CEOs to frontline employees – are talking about employee engagement. Employee engagement is a companion of happiness. It could even be called its twin sister. While employee engagement might mean different things to different people, it is clear that employee engagement is not simply employee satisfaction.

Engaged employees are not only happy and successful employees, they also contribute to the success of their organization.

BlessingWhite, an expert global consulting firm on employee engagement, states in a 2008 report that if we equate employee engagement with only employee satisfaction, it "is only as good as the organization's last round of perks or bonuses." Most definitions include both some aspects of employee satisfaction and business outcomes or employee contributions resulting from that satisfaction. In other words, how is employee satisfaction affecting the bottom line? If you are not using this type of measure, you may be missing some important information about your team, department, or organization. An engaged employee is someone who is fully involved in their work, enthusiastic about it, and thus acts in a way that furthers their organization's interests. Engaged employees are not only happy and successful employees, they also contribute to the success of their team and thus, the organization. It is a sound confirmation of the 'happy-worker' hypothesis. A happy worker is a productive worker who helps the success of the organization.

The BlessingWhite report also discloses some dismal numbers on employee engagement in North America. Over seventy percent of American workers reported being less than fully engaged – with nearly twenty percent reporting being fully disengaged! Gallup further estimates that those disengaged employees cost US companies between $292-$350 billion annually. On the bright side, organizations that rank in the top twenty-five percent on employee engagement have been shown to grow earnings per share (EPS) over two and a half times that of organizations with below average employee engagement! The bottom line is that it pays to have engaged employees.

On the bright side, organizations that rank in the top twenty-five percent on employee engagement have been shown to grow earnings per share (EPS) over two and a half times that of organizations with below average employee engagement.

The major meta-analysis conducted by the Gallup Organization mentioned above gives us some of the most powerful insights into employee engagement and successful business outcomes to date. The report was no small feat. It included nearly 8,000 business units, almost 200,000 respondents, and culminated over 30 years of research. The authors averaged together 12 survey items that defined employee engagement from an employee well-being survey. They then correlated levels of employee engagement with levels of business unit success over time. Four composite key outcomes defined successful business units: low employee turnover, customer satisfaction, productivity, and profit. These are the hallmarks of high-performing work groups.

High Employee Engagement Equals Leadership Success

The meta-analysis reveals, "work units with high levels of employee engagement have a much greater chance of business unit success, as measured by our composite criterion." As you can see in Table 3 below from the study, each of the 12 items are positively correlated with at least two or more of the four key outcomes necessary for successful business unit performance. Some of them, such as recognition and caring, correlated with all four success outcomes. This is strong evidence that increasing employees' positive emotions and employee engagement leads to successful business outcomes. The authors concluded that "behaviors that increase the frequency of positive emotions lead to increasing clarity of expectations, the understanding and use of resources that is congruent with company goals, individual fulfillment in work, a bonding of individuals through a sense of caring, ownership for the altruistic and tangible impact of the company, and learning that it is in line with this shared mission. In the long run, this is what is good for the employee and the company."

Table 3.

How Employee Engagement Relates to Business Unit Performance

Item	Turnover	Customer	Productivity	Profit
Know what is expected	x	x	x	
Materials and equipment	x	x		
Opportunities to do what I do best	x	x	x	x
Recognition/praise	o	o	o	x
Cares about me	x	x	x	o
Encourages development	o	x	o	x
Opinions count	o	x	x	x
Mission/purpose	o	o	x	x
Committed—quality	x	o	x	x
Best friend		x	o	x
Talked about progress		o	o	
Opportunities to learn and grow	x	x	x	x

Notes. o = Positive, generalizable relationship.
x = Strongest generalizable relationships.

Harter, J. K.; Schmidt, F. L.; Keyes, C. L. (2002). Well-Being in the Workplace and its Relationship to Business Outcomes: A Review of the Gallup Studies. In C. Keyes, & J. Haidt (Eds.), *Flourishing: Positive Psychology and the Life Well-Lived* (pp. 205-224). Washington, D.C.: American Psychological Association.

When employees know what is expected and have the basic tools to do their work, feel recognized, cared for, respected, fulfilled, and have opportunities for growth, then they are more likely to enjoy what they do and stick around. Engaged employees and their work teams apply themselves more effectively, increasing productivity. They serve customers better, increasing customer satisfaction and loyalty. When both employees and customers are happy and loyal, employee turnover goes down, and productivity goes up. Profits increase.

Unfortunately, they report, "managers fall short in encouraging and rewarding their employees' use of talents." The MBA core curriculum offered at most business schools includes courses in accounting, business strategy, economics, IT courses of one sort or the other, finance, operations management, statistics, and the like. When a graduate lands that first job as a supervisor, manager, or director, the training and orientation typically involves company policies, performance management programs, internal computer programs necessary to perform the job, MBOs of the position, productivity reports and their deadlines, and so on. Rarely do you see courses or training in fostering positive emotions in employees.

High-performance success doesn't happen automatically, by magic, or because of luck. It happens because supervisors, managers, directors, vice presidents, and CEOs – leaders – expand their skill-set to incorporate fostering employee engagement as part of who they are as a leader. In other words, they help meet the basic needs of their employees with genuine care and concern, develop and nurture relationships, and provide opportunities for growth and development – in a nutshell, they are concerned with their employees' happiness. Taking the highway of happiness and inviting your team along is the way to success. Applying the strategies in this book will help you do just that!

Leadership Travel Tips Chapter 4: The Highway of Happiness

- In almost every way, happy people are more successful.
- Once income brings individuals out of extreme poverty, it has little long-lasting effects on happiness or life satisfaction. Money doesn't buy happiness.
- Success does not lead to happiness; rather, happiness leads to success.
- We not only have a great deal of personal control over our happiness; happiness is and can be learned.
- High performing teams have high employee engagement.
- High-performance success happens because leaders expand their skill-set to incorporate fostering employee engagement as part of who they are as a leader.
- High employee engagement leads to reduced turnover, higher customer satisfaction, higher productivity, and higher profits.
- High employee engagement equals leadership success.
- Taking the highway of happiness and inviting your team along is the way to success.

CHAPTER 5

A Path of Love

What's love got to do with it?
~ Tina Turner ~

After my divorce, I was single for many years. I was intensely studying psychology and I devoured any course, research article, or book on love, relationships, marriage, and divorce that I could find. I also found myself in a new technological 'dating scene.' eHarmony, Yahoo Personals, Match.com – I tried them all. I was as intellectually and professionally interested, as I was personally interested, in this thing called *love*.

I had quite a few first dates and I must admit that I must have been a bit of a shock to many an unsuspecting woman. When the initial first date jitters settled and the conversation turned beyond simple pleasantries, I would often ask my date, "What's love to you?" More often than not, the answers I heard centered on emotions and romance. When my date then turned the question on me, I would tell her that through my studies and life experiences I had come to the conclusion that love was not an emotion – that I believed it definitely has emotional elements to it – it's just that there seems to be much more to love than simply emotions or feelings. I would say something like, "If love is just an emotion and I suddenly feel anger or something else towards you, then I wouldn't 'love' you anymore – at least for those moments. Would I? But I know I can feel angry about something someone has done and still love them." As you might suspect, I had far fewer second dates than first. Huey Lewis and the News put it quite powerfully in song, "More than a feeling… that's the power of love!"

This brings up a major problem with the word *love*. I say the word *love* and scenes of Hollywood, romantic movies, passionate love, or some variation, often come to mind. Sex and sex appeal, romance, who's with whom, and infidelities dominate the media culture's discussion of love. When we stop and think about it, we know that there are many variations and depths to love. The problem is that the word *love* can mean so many things. M. Scott Peck, MD said in his timeless classic, *The Road Less Traveled*, "…our use of the word 'love' is so generalized and unspecific as to severely interfere with our understanding of love." I couldn't agree more.

I can love pizza, a movie, or a hot cup of coffee. I can love my home. I can love my pet. I can love Christmastime. I can love my job. I can love my children, parents, best friend, lover, or spouse – and each of these 'loves' are different. There is a range of ways to experience and define love – romantic love being only one of them. Our culture tends to overemphasize and focus on romantic or passionate love – to the point that it has become idealized and idolized into a cultural myth.[2] When it comes to personal and professional development, life mission, career, work, and of being a leader, it seems that love is often put to the side – and it may be partly due to the ambiguity when the word *love* is mentioned. We don't

---

[2] For one of the most discriminating, valuable, and readable discussions on the topic of love (and much more) that is still just as pertinent today as the day it was written, I refer you to and highly recommend Dr. Peck's, *The Road Less Traveled*.

want to take the risk of being misunderstood; that we are not talking about a weak and sentimental feeling, but something more powerful that requires great courage, discipline, and awareness. And yet, if there is one principal quality of great leaders that our inquiry should focus on, it is love.

What's Love Got to Do With Leadership?

Tina Turner asks a poignant question, "What's love got to do with it?" Does the idea of discussing love in the context of career or leadership cause you to stop and balk? Even just a little? Then you're in good company! Tamara Woodbury, executive director of one of the largest Girl Scout councils in the country, points out in the *Oxford Leadership Journal*:

> It is common belief that 'real' leaders are shrewd, decisive, action-oriented, results-driven, competitive, and accountable only to the bottom-line. Our society reveres measurable results, financial success, analytical competence, and often, cutthroat competition. We tend to be skeptical of things that cannot be seen and measured, even our own feelings. We like to win, and we like winners... Reflective, intuitive, collaborative, compassionate, and loving qualities are not often considered to be characteristics of 'winners' and are rarely valued as leadership skills, especially when embodied by men."

I am writing this section of the book while on Christmas holiday break. Among other classic holiday movies, my wife and I ritually watch *Scrooged* every year. In this classic remake of Charles Dickens' *A Christmas Carol*, Bill Murray plays Frank Cross, a cutthroat, competitive TV executive. Frank's shrewd and impersonal nature jumps out early in the movie. During the following exchange with his secretary, Grace Cooley, played by Alfre Woodard, the film captures the stereotypical cold, competitive, and uncaring leader right after he just fired one of his staff members on Christmas Eve and learns that his boss has hired a consultant to help him with his current project and he's feeling threatened:

Frank: Grace! I need a full report on a guy named Brice Cummings. He's an LA slime ball.

Grace: OK, um… you're due at Helmsley Palace at seven o'clock and I'm gonna leave. I've got to take my son to the…

Frank: No you're not. You're staying here with me. We're working late.

Grace: But I have to take my son to the doctor.

Frank: GRACE! When I work late, YOU work late!

Grace: But I made the appointment two months ago!

Frank: [sarcastically] I DON'T CARE!

Frank: [grabbing Grace] We're indivisible. If I'm workin' late, you GOTTA work late! If you can't work late, I can't work late! If I can't work late, I CAN'T WORK LATE!

These and many real-world examples typify what some might call an old paradigm of leadership. This old paradigm depicts a leader whose only concern is his or her own advancement, image, and the legendary 'bottom line' – one who believes that people are to be used and underlings should simply do what the boss says. When questioned with "Why?" answers, "Because I'm the boss!" And yet, some of the most influential leaders in human history were models and messengers of love: Buddha, Confucius, Mahatma Gandhi, Jesus of Nazareth, Martin Luther King, Jr., Nelson Mandela, Mother Teresa of Calcutta, John Woolman (American Quaker and abolitionist), and Lao Tzu, to name only a few.

The most powerful relationships we have in our lives are with those people who lead us and with those whom we lead – in which leadership is a central element of the relationship. Parent-child, friend-friend, girlfriend-boyfriend, spouse-spouse, teacher-student, coach-player, boss-employee, – it is relationships like these that have the most influence in our lives and where the lessons of love and life are cultivated.

The most powerful relationships we have in our lives are with those people who lead us and with those whom we lead.

It is well accepted that the desire for interpersonal attachments, the need to belong, is a fundamental, innate human motivation – love is a basic human need. It is in and through attachments, relationships, and personal bonds that love is born, developed, and experienced. If we want to be masterful leaders, we must recognize the clear road sign on our journey that love is fundamental to everyone (that includes you and those you lead) and that continually learning more about love and actualizing what you learn are high priorities. Walk with me for just a while down the path of love and you may come to the same conclusion that I did – love's got *everything* to do with it!

What is Love?

Like Dr. Peck, I too must concede that I realize that by attempting to examine love, we are attempting to "examine the unexaminable and to know the unknowable." Love can seem mysterious and enigmatic. It's not easy to measure and put on an MBO, spreadsheet, or report. Even so, there is still great value for the leader to walk down and examine the path of love. As Robert Holden, PhD so famously instructs the seeker of success and happiness who is setting goals and developing a life mission, "If your definition of success has little or no measure of love in it, get another definition." Love is difficult to define and may be more difficult to give – and yet it is absolutely necessary for the successful and masterful leader of our times.

Is Love an Emotion? My first date discussions about whether love is an emotion or something else stand in good company. Throughout the literature on love, there are some theorists who describe love as an emotion and others who maintain it is as something else – an attitude, a cultural construct, or a goal-oriented motivational state, for example. Despite the discussion in the literature, you will be hard-pressed to find love on a list of basic human emotions, because most emotional theorists do not consider love as one of the basic human emotions. Yet, researchers from the University of California-Davis and Illinois State University report that [emphasis in the original] "the research clearly establishes that [lay] people *believe* that love is an emotion and there are emotional components to love." Whether love is an emotion or not may be moot and best left to the social scientists to hammer out. What *is* clear from the research and our experience, however, is that love has emotional elements associated with it, one way or the other – and emotions move or motivate human behavior. That's something powerful for the leader to keep in mind.

Types of Love. Love is often described by the style of love or by the type of relationship. Unlike English, the ancient Greek language has four different words for love: *storgē*, *philía*, *éros*, and *agápe*. *Storgē* is a simple and natural affection, such as parents have for their children. *Philía* is the love associated with friendship and is a virtuous love that also includes a sense of loyalty to family, friends, and community. It is part of the root of the name of the famous city, Philadelphia, the "City of Brotherly Love." *Éros* is an intimate and passionate type of love usually, but not necessarily, associated with sexual desire and longing. This is where we get the modern word

Agápe love is primarily motivated by the interest and welfare of others and that it is volitional.

erotica. Finally, *agápe* is a deep brotherly or familial, self-sacrificing, unconditional, and volitional type of love that was not associated with romance, passion, or affection. It stands apart from the other forms of love in that it is primarily motivated by the interest and welfare of others and that it is volitional or is made by choice. *Agápe* love is the type of love most often mentioned in the Bible.

Robert Sternberg of Yale University presented an interesting and now famous triangular theory of love. It posits that there are three components to love that can be expressed in the form of a triangle: intimacy, passion, and decision/commitment. Any relationship can be described by the depth or intensity of each of the components or three vertices of the triangle. For example, *nonlove* or casual day-to-day encounters are low in all three components. There isn't much intimacy, passion, or commitment with the sales clerk ringing up the groceries or the barrister at Starbucks.

Friendships, or what the ancient Greeks called *philía*, are characterized by high intimacy and low or no passion and commitment. When we have a good friend, we share our ups and downs and intimate secrets and fantasies. But, friends come and go throughout our life without any long-term, formal commitment – and good friends are not usually characterized with sexual or romantic passion. When that happens, romantic love or *éros* is born.

Characterized in the model by high intimacy and passion, *romantic love* doesn't involve much in-depth decision-making or commitment. It's what's known as 'friends with benefits' – the benefits being the passionate sensualities. The vertex of decision/commitment has two aspects: a short-term decision that you love someone and a long-term commitment to maintain that love. It is often commitment that carries the deeper relationship through difficult times. Contrary to that, we often hear about the break-up of someone in a romantic, passionate relationship because of the slightest, little thing – because there is no commitment.

Figure 5. Sternberg's Triangular Theory of Love

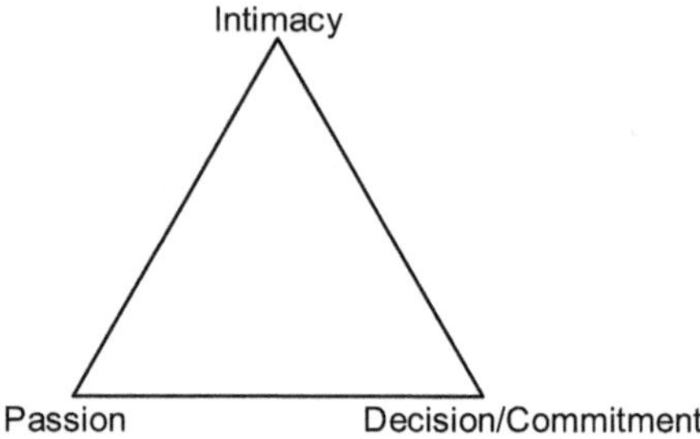

Based on Sternberg, R. J. (1986). A triangular theory of love. *Psychological Review*, *93* (2), 119-135.

The pinnacle of the model is *consummate love* or complete love – a love that balances and encompasses all three components (pictured above).

Table 4.

The Triangular Theory of Love: Types of Relationships

Type of Love	Intimacy	Passion	Decision/Commitment
Nonlove or casual interactions	Low	Low	Low
Liking or Friendship	High	Low	Low
Infatuated Love or "love at first sight"	Low	High	Low
Romantic Love or "friends with benefits"	High	High	Low
Empty Love or the "stagnant relationship"	Low	Low	High
Companionate Love (e. g., the long-term married who's passion has died down)	High	Low	High
Fatuous Love	Low	High	High
Consummate Love	High	High	High

Based on Sternberg, R.J. (1986). A Triangular Theory of Love. *Psychological Review*. 93:2, 119-135.

It is important to note that sex and romance are not the only sources of passion in Sternberg's model. Self-esteem, nurturing, affiliation, and self-actualization are among the needs that make-up passion in the model. Passion in this sense is anything that motivates us into action. Therefore, passion is not necessarily sexual. In romantic relationships, passion can transform over time into the intense desire of helping someone rise and grow into their highest potential – and that facet of passion has great importance for the leader, no matter what type of relationship it is. One objective of great leaders is to help those you lead become successful. If they are successful, you consequently are too.

Differently shaped triangles emerge depending on the intensity of each of the three components (i.e., type of relationship). For example, romantic love or 'friends with benefits' would look something like the triangle below. They are high in intimacy and passion, but have little or no decision/commitment.

Figure 6. Romantic Love or 'Friends with Benefits' Triangle

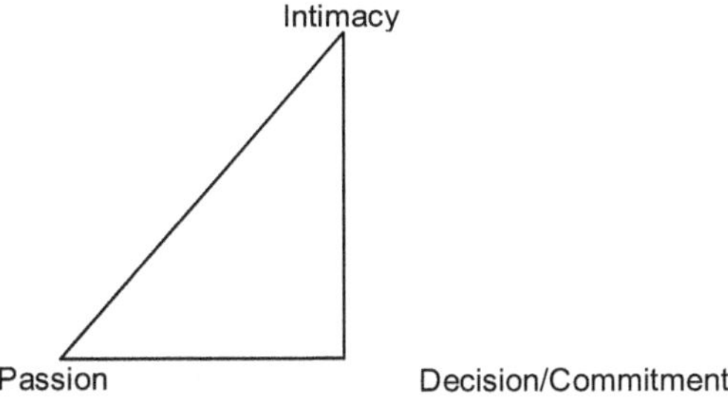

Based on Sternberg, R. J. (1986). A triangular theory of love. *Psychological Review*, *93* (2), 119-135.

Loving One's Job

"Choose a job you love, and you will never have to work a day in your life." We have all heard the famous quote by Confucius. But what if there's more to it than that – simply choosing a job you love? Could the triangular theory of love be applied to our jobs?

Although Sternberg's triangular theory and many other theories and research about love did much to advance our understanding of love, most of the research and application of those theories centered on romantic, intimate relationships. In 2010, the prolific Canadian researcher, professor, and Canada Research Chair in Occupational Health Psychology at Saint Mary's University, E. Kevin Kelloway, PhD and colleagues, offered some ground-breaking connections between Sternberg's triangular theory of love, the love of one's job, and happiness.

In their rubric of loving one's job, the "valued object" of love does not necessarily have to be another person. It can also be other living things ("I love my pet"), a possession (I love my car"), or an activity ("I love my job").

Our jobs are a central aspect of our lives and directly affect our happiness and well-being. When we are passionate about our work, experience a sense of intimacy with the people at work, and are committed to our organization or work group, we love our job. This is Sternberg's consummate love applied to our job: high passion, high intimacy, and high decision/commitment.

When those you lead love their jobs and are happy, it not only helps you with turnover (and other positive outcomes), they will, on average, simply do better in *all* areas of their lives. When you help people love their jobs, you help them become happier – and when you help them become happier, you help them become more successful in life.

Passion for Work. High passion for work is thought of as the excitement, enthusiasm, and personal rewards and fulfillment from the actual job performed. It goes beyond job satisfaction – simply being content or satisfied with one's job. When passionate about our work, we find our work important. There is meaning to it and we're excited and enthusiastic about it. Therefore, there is an element of longing or desire to do it. Performing our job feels good.

I remember the first job I ever had. I was about twelve years old and a neighbor who raised prize-winning beagles needed some help taking care of them. My job was to clean out their kennels and give them fresh food and water every day – for one dollar a day! Shoveling out those kennels and hosing them out was not very fun. Even though I came to really care for those beagles, my passion for that job was not very high. I contrast that with other jobs I have had that I *did* have high passion and enthusiasm for – EMS Paramedic, Director of Youth Ministry, Instructor of Psychology, Training and Field Operations Specialist, mentor/coach, and author. Those jobs are or were a sheer joy. Not surprisingly, high passion for one's work is associated with higher levels of productivity and well-being. When we are passionate about our work, we do it better and are happier and so are those you lead.

Healthy Work Relationships. The second vertex of loving one's job, intimacy, is defined by healthy, high-quality relationships at work. Healthy relationships at work are associated with all kinds of positive outcomes including group cohesion, productivity, job performance, and well-being. A powerful aspect of intimacy is that it promotes a desire to enhance someone else's welfare and well-being. When that is mutually shared, positive feelings of trust, partnership, and teamwork grow and are reinforced. As the leader, you set the tone and quality of relationships. You are looked to for the 'group rules' – what will be tolerated and what won't. We will examine relationships in more depth in Chapter 7.

Affective Commitment. Finally, Kelloway and his colleagues borrow a definition of commitment to work first identified by Dr. John Meyer, professor and chair of the Graduate Program in Industrial and Organizational Psychology at the University of Western Ontario and colleagues – *affective commitment*.

Affective commitment is an emotional attachment to, identification with, and involvement in the organization. You *want* to be there as

This places the responsibility of cultivating affective organizational commitment squarely on the leader.

opposed to *having* to be there. Some people feel like they have to be at work because of some necessity or that they *should* be there because of some obligation or outside pressure. That might be a form of commitment, but it is not affective commitment. Affectively committed employees have a sense of belonging to the organization – they feel like they are part of the team and make a difference. Because of this, they are willing to apply themselves toward organizational goals making them valued employees. Finally, because of this identification and commitment, they want to stay with the organization, reducing turnover. Other positive outcomes associated with this vertex are better attendance, job performance, and positive workplace behaviors.

Interestingly, Meyer and colleagues report supporting evidence that demographic variables such as age, education, organizational tenure, marital status, and work experiences, play a minor role in developing affective commitment. This means that leaders trying to recruit and hire certain 'types' of people predisposed to organizational commitment is "less effective than will [be] carefully managing their experiences following entry." This places the responsibility of cultivating affective organizational commitment squarely on the leader. The ability to create an environment in which people want to work – one where you can trust the leaders, effort is recognized and rewarded, talents are encouraged, community is built, the larger purpose is clear and linked to the job, honest communication is fostered, and high performance is pursued – is critical to the master leader who wants to increase employee engagement and love of one's job. This is congruent with the 2011 BlessingWhite report that releases the discovery that managers and executives are *the* key to employee engagement in all of these areas.

Beyond Employee Engagement. Based on empirical research, this tripartite model of loving one's job goes beyond the simple two-pronged definition of employee engagement – employee's personal job satisfaction plus their contribution to the company's success. It takes into account what an employee thinks and how an employee feels about the work they do, their work relationships, and the company itself. The measure of job satisfaction by itself may not be enough, since job satisfaction and affective commitment measurements overlap. Dr. John Meyer and colleagues concluded "...that job satisfaction and affective organizational commitment should both be considered in efforts to understand and manage employee behavior" because of the strong correlation between the two.

Triangular explanations of employees' love of their jobs can be used to help you achieve this. For example, one employee can love what they do and who they do it with, but if the job conditions and leadership (the organization) are terrible, the love of their job will suffer. Another worker may be fully committed to the organization because it's such a great company, have great relationships at work, but not really care for the actual job they do. Finally, a worker could be passionate about their work, be fully committed to a great organization, but can't stand the people they work with. All three vertices must be positive in order for someone to love their job. Whether you are a leader in a company or any other organization or group, you can now look at each members' love of their job or role through this triangular model and adapt your approach towards each of them accordingly.

According to the Bureau of Labor Statistics, the average American works 1,768 hours each year. That's a lot of time to be doing anything other than what you love. The advice of Confucius rings clear, "Choose a job you love, and you will never have to work a day in your life."

A Leader's Definition of Love

As we have seen, there are many types of love. Let's differentiate other types of love from a leader's love – whether in a company, school, family, or other organization. A leader's definition of love can be described as a complex combination of feelings, creative energy, volitional decision, and actions/service that stem from an innate need to connect, relate, support, and mutually nurture and serve that which leads to the discovery and growth towards both of your greater or higher selves – what Abraham Maslow called self-actualization.

Emotional. First, love is emotional or possesses emotional elements. As we discovered in Chapter 2, the treasures of the heart have tremendous power. Emotions are powerful motivators of present and future behaviors. I recall the words of Dr. Darren Weissman, "Emotions transform energy; energy creates movement; movement is change; and change is the essence of life." Life is constantly moving and changing and at what seems an ever-increasing rate. One hallmark of leadership is how we manage change. Almost everything we move towards or away from (change) is motivated in some way by the emotions we feel. When we deny our feelings or numb ourselves to them, we cannot make good decisions and are therefore less effective as a leader. However, when properly harnessed, emotions have the power to positively influence almost every aspect of our lives.

Take a moment here and now to think of someone you love and who loves you. Visualize your love as vividly as possible. Now, begin to become aware of the feelings that come with the awareness of your love. How or what do you feel? Warmth? Joy? Concern? Care? Secure? Desire? Empowered? Delight? Glowing? Gratitude? Serenity? You can call forth love's energy.

Positive emotions, such as love and gratitude, have power for you and those you lead.

Positive emotions, such as love and gratitude, have power for you and those you lead. By purposefully focusing on and harnessing love's emotive and motivational power, we spark in ourselves and in others a movement – a movement towards something new and better. If you're ever feeling negative or self-defeating emotions, remember some of the techniques from Chapter 2 that help eliminate ANTs. Charles Haanel masterfully instructs, "There is no getting away from the law of love. It is feeling that imparts vitality to thought. Feeling is desire, and desire is love. Thought impregnated with love becomes invincible." That leads us to the second quality of love.

Creative Energy. In addition to being emotional, love is a source of energy used to motivate, create, and connect. Buddhist monk, psychologist, and bestselling author, Jack Kornfield, PhD, wrote in his classic book, *A Path With Heart,* "Whatever we choose, the creations of our life must be grounded in our hearts. Our love is the source of all energy to create and connect." Einstein devoted much of his life to investigating energy. He taught that all of reality is energy. This is well-accepted science. As we learned earlier, there is an underlying energy field to all of space and time called the Zero Point Field or ZPF.

Astrophysicist, Bernard Haisch, explains in his book, *The God Theory*, how for the first 300,000 years after the Big Bang, the universe was dominated by non-visible forms of electromagnetic radiation (light energy). He believes that the creation process itself – of matter, the sun, stars, and ultimately each of us – may be intimately linked to the electromagnetic ZPF. He connects "Let there be light" from the religious and esoteric traditions with quantum physics and then develops a rational theory about God. Since God is recognized as the source of creation and is connected to love for so many of us, it may be beneficial to explore that.

God has been depicted as some sort of bearded 'father' that exists in a heavenly palace guarded with pearly gates – and many people believe this place and this bearded image to be physically real in some way. Is it possible that God is much more than that? Humanizing God forces the question, "How can God be physically real in an actual space-time place called heaven and still be infinite and the creator of all things?" Dr. Haisch eloquently explains (emphasis in the original):

> The argument for a material God creating a material universe can only take you in circles. After all, if God is made of matter – even some kind of "super-matter" – then who made *that*? Logically, you have to postulate an even higher-order of creator for your country-club heaven…
>
> God as the creator of masculine and feminine archetypes and beings cannot possibly be identified with one or the other gender; if the essence of both come from God they must in some fashion be attributes of God the Creator, the manifest God.

Whatever God is, God is probably not a physical being seated on a physical throne in a physical palace in some undisclosed, undiscovered kingdom floating in the clouds or the heavens. The logic that God is immaterial is only pointed out so that we might entertain that God may be something else.

There is a passage from the Christian tradition which might help us see God beyond a physical, bearded deity. It has long been an inspiration and an enigma to me and one that I ponder often. It is simple and yet quite profound. It's in the First Letter of John and it states, "God is love" (1 John 4:8) – and it tells us this twice. This simple and yet powerful phrase about the nature of God is saying that the very essence or being of God is love – and the word used for *love* in the original ancient Greek is *agápe.* God and love are equal. The Source of the universe, including each one of us, is love. I like to sit outside beholding the abundance of life – the plants, trees, birds, bugs, clouds, stars – and contemplate the miracle of it all. What John is saying is that all of that and the rest of the universe, including you and me, comes from and owe our existence to Love. Love is *the* Creative Source of everything and everything is energy.

I am not the first to be inspired by love and leadership and make connections to the passage from the New Testament. One year to the day before his assassination, Martin Luther King, Jr., in his famous speech at Riverside Church in New York City in 1967 proclaimed:

> This oft misunderstood, this oft-misinterpreted concept [love], so readily dismissed by the Nietzsches of the world as a weak and cowardly force, has now become an absolute necessity for the survival of man. When I speak of love, I am not speaking of some sentimental and weak response. I am not speaking of that force which is just emotional bosh. I am speaking of that force which all of the great religions have seen as the supreme unifying principle of life. Love is somehow the key that unlocks the door which leads to ultimate reality. This Hindu-Muslim-Christian-Jewish-Buddhist belief about ultimate – ultimate reality is beautifully summed up in the first epistle of Saint John: "Let us love one another, for love is God…"

The creative energy of love is not weak and sentimental. On the contrary, as Reverend King tells us, it is a force – a unifying force that is the supreme principle of life. Leaders who use the creative energy force of love have made a giant step towards a more profound and sublime power on their journey.

So, underlying all of reality is energy. That energy is an unseen bubbling sea of electromagnetic energy. Strangely, our hearts produce an electromagnetic field that can be measured and harnessed. Recall the Institute of HeartMath's profound discoveries concerning the electromagnetic field emanating from your heart? That field is powerful – more powerful than the brain's field – and when you focus on love and appreciation, that field brings your entire being into greater coherence and fosters well-being on every level. When your state of being is coherent with love, gratitude, and happiness, you make better decisions and are more effective – and you inspire others to do the same. Love, and possibly other positive emotions and thoughts, are a creative energy source. Love's energy has the power to transform; it is creative.

The most miraculous example of this for me is the process of pregnancy and childbirth. I remember sitting in anatomy class many years ago learning about fertilization and how absolutely amazed I was at the miracle of life. That didn't even compare to the actual experiences of my children's pregnancies and births. Relationships are also creative. When we connect, relate, and support each other, something mysterious happens. Relationships become causative in our life, even difficult or painful relationships. Have you ever said or heard someone in the final stages of recovering from a severe break-up say something like, "I wouldn't be the same person today if I hadn't lived through it"? The passion of the artist, entrepreneur, inventor, author, leader, teams, organizations, and societies striving to create something new are also examples of how love is a creative source. As bestselling author Michael E. Gerber wrote, "The passion of the entrepreneur is not to run a successful business – not to run a business someone else invented – but to invent a unique business that becomes successful." Leaders are charged with creating things and events with, for, and through those they lead. Love's creative energy is there to help you do that.

Volitional Decision. Erich Fromm, the illustrious social psychologist, psychoanalyst, and humanistic philosopher, saw responsibility as one of four mutually interdependent fundamental elements of love (the other three being care, respect, and knowledge). In his classic book, *The Art of Loving*, he wrote, "But responsibility, in its true sense, is an entirely voluntary act; it is my response to the needs, expressed or unexpressed, of another human being." When we exercise our responsibility, we are exercising our ability to choose – our 'response-ability,' our freedom – between a myriad of alternative responses.

Viktor Frankl said, "Between stimulus and response there is a space. In that space is our power to choose our response. In our response lies our growth and our freedom." Stephen Covey calls this the freedom to choose. That choice is a "gap" between a stimulus and our response. Becoming aware of the gap is a fundamental step in loving.

When things happen – especially in stressful times – we tend to react from our gut or automatically. If that gut reaction was built from negativity (like fear, unworthiness, anxiety, jealousy, etc.), then that's when the ANTs come creeping out. For example, my wife is Filipina. Although she speaks fluent English, her original,

Becoming aware of the gap is a fundamental step in loving.

native language is Tagalog. Generally, this isn't a problem for us. But sometimes, there can be a bit of a communication gap. I remember one day we were working on our budget and a program got 'stuck' on the computer and it wouldn't close. I was trying everything – two or three times. As I tried each maneuver, I would tell her what I was trying. We were both getting frustrated. To my surprise, she kept asking me over and over to try something I had already tried several times – and I told her I had *already* told her I had told her! In retrospect, it seems almost comical. But at the time, both of us were frustrated. I reacted from my gut, lost my temper, and huffed out of the room to cool down. I didn't catch the gap.

However, when we *are* able to catch the gap – between the outside stimulus and our inner response – we realize that we get to *choose* our response. We are in better touch with our values and how we want to *be* as a leader and as a person. As Dr. Frankl said, it's in that gap where growth and freedom are. The catch? We must be aware of it!

For love to be volitional and responsible, the leader must amplify the ability to respond – the 'response-ability' – by increasing awareness. We have to know about the "gap." One of the greatest skills to expand awareness is listening – to both our inner self and others. Active or empathic listening bridges across to the action/service aspect of love. It takes extreme effort to do well. Very few of us are taught how to listen, and yet, as leaders, listening consumes a large portion of our time. It is a fundamental skill of the best leaders, so we will examine listening in more detail in Chapter 8, The Communication Expedition. Generally,

For love to be volitional and responsible, the leader must amplify the ability to respond – the 'response-ability' – by increasing awareness.

though, when speaking of leadership and awareness, more often than not, what is meant is *self*-awareness.

Dr. Dyer agrees, “Taking charge of yourself begins with awareness” and taking charge of yourself is one of the first steps towards leading others. When we couple our knowledge and skill with greater self-awareness and more cognizance of our environment and others, we become more effective. To be aware is to have knowledge; and knowledge, wisdom, and awareness are continually evolving – just as life is, and we along with it. Awareness, or what some call mindfulness, then, is something we must work at all of our lives.

Become aware of your state of being. Have a quiet time. It’ll help you find your gaps as you go through the day. It will increase your ‘response-ability’.

There are many techniques and practices for increasing awareness: study and readings, journaling, yoga, prayer, meditation, voluntary service to others, ceremonial practices, fasting, and a variety of wonderful psychotherapies. Chapter 3 gives some basic instructions in contemplation, yet another powerful way to increase awareness.

So, take some time today – and everyday – to become more self-aware. Become aware of your state of being. Have a quiet time. It’ll help you find your gaps as you go through the day. It will increase your ‘response-ability’. It will make you a more effective leader. It will help you to love more authentically.

You may choose one or many ways to expand your awareness but be cautious. There is no ‘absolute right’ way to practice increasing awareness. As Jack Kornfield cautioned, “Remember, the practices themselves are only vehicles for you to develop awareness, loving-kindness, and compassion on the path toward freedom. That is all." Don't let the means to an end become the end itself. The end here – the goal – is to increase awareness so that you can make the most effective choices; responsible choices that lead to the greatest good for yourself and others, towards both of your greater or higher selves. In the words of Wayne Dyer, "Awareness allows me to perceive possibilities rather than difficulties, to feel connected to my Source of being and see the outcome as working rather than failing."

So in addition to having emotional and motivational elements and being a creative energy source, love is also a choice rooted in responsibility and awareness. When we accept responsibility for ourselves and our choices, we are no longer a victim and escape the blame game. When we shirk our responsibility of awareness and love by blaming someone else or external circumstances, we allow others to define who we are, our perception of circumstances, and give them power over us. Viktor Frankl recognized the volitional character of love and the acceptance of the responsibility to choose your attitude in the worst of circumstances in his famous bestseller, *Man's Search for Meaning*:

> We who lived in the concentration camps can remember the men who walked through the huts comforting others, giving away their last piece of bread. They may have been few in number, but they offer sufficient proof that everything can be taken from a man but one thing: the last of the human freedoms – to choose one's attitude in any given set of circumstances, to choose one's own way.

When I read Dr. Frankl's work, I'm inspired. If he and others could find purpose, meaning, and love in the Nazi concentration camps during World War II, then there is hope for all of us. We may need to remind ourselves of it daily, but we can choose awareness and responsibility – as leaders, we can choose love. When we feel like we *have* to, then we are probably experiencing something more consonant with obligation, coercion, or neurotic infatuation or dependency. On the other hand, whenever we endeavor to discover and nurture growth towards a greater or higher self, we do not *have* to, we have chosen to love. Love is a decision, a decision to act.

That is why those who seriously examine love and leadership, eventually talk about will. The apex of James Hunter's leadership model is the will. He said, "Love is always built on the will." When speaking on love and the work of attention, Dr. Peck wrote, "Attention is an act of will, of work against the inertia of our own minds." Our will is our attitude, our personal choice, our intention, and our discipline. We manifest our will when our intention and our volitional decision are put into action.

Action/Service. We can be in touch with the emotional elements of love, the creative energy and power of love, and even be aware of our volitional decision-making power or will, and yet, if we don't *do* something, we do not love. Dr. Peck recognized the connection between the volitional and behavioral aspects of love. He said, "Love is an act of will – namely, both an intention and an action." Our intention is our will or voluntary decision to love, to act. Action is how we carry that intention or decision out. He elaborates on this action aspect further, "Love, then, is a form of work or a form of courage." Sometimes, maybe often at first, it can indeed be frightening to 'put ourselves out there' for someone. This is when our will is required.

Love is a decision, a decision to act.

It takes awareness of two things: What a person needs and what you have to offer to help meet those needs in order to serve the person's greatest good or higher self. Feelings of care and concern (emotional elements) fuel the creative energy that gets the mind deliberating about and recognizing what a person needs and how to accomplish that best (volitional/decision elements). What you do – your action – is your gift. In the words of Dr. Fromm (emphasis in the original), "Love is an activity, not a passive affect; it is a 'standing in,' not a 'falling for.' In the most general way, the active character of love can be described by stating that love is primarily *giving*, not receiving."

Action and giving are work. Work requires effort. One could argue that this action-aspect of love is the quintessence of what great leaders do and are. When we decide to focus our attention and awareness on the object of love (whether that's a project, goal, or person) and make a decision to love, we shift our thinking away from whatever preoccupies us at the moment and attend to that 'special something' or that 'special someone.' We are aligning our feelings of care and concern with action. That is congruence or authenticity. It is also service. *Service* is defined as "an act of helpful activity." When we choose to love no matter what the circumstances, we are answering the questions, "What is the best helpful action I can offer? How can I best serve?" Sometimes the best answer to that question is "Nothing." An act of restraint is still a gift. More often than not, we find that there *is* something that we can do or give.

One of the best books that I've read on this aspect of love is *The Servant: A Simple Story About the True Essence of Leadership* by James Hunter. Written in fable format, the main character, John Daily, is a businessman whose life is falling apart. He is failing miserably in each of his leadership roles as

This action-aspect of love is the quintessence of what great leaders do and are.

a boss, husband, father, and little league coach. At the behest of his pastor and wife, he reluctantly attends a weeklong leadership retreat at a remote Benedictine monastery, along with a pastor, a drill sergeant, a school principal, a women's basketball coach at a university, and a head nurse at a birthing hospital.

Love is a gift, especially a gift of self.

The monk who facilitates the leadership retreats turns out to be a former business executive and Wall Street legend. Brother Simeon guides John and the group to a realization that is both simple and profound: The true essence of leadership is not power, but authority and influence, which is nurtured through love, relationships, service, and sacrifice. Brother Simeon teaches the group about *agápe* love and challenges them with a new leadership paradigm, "Remember, the role of leadership is to serve, that is, to identify and meet legitimate needs. In the process of meeting needs, we will often be called upon to make sacrifices for those we serve." He defines love as a verb and as behavior-based, "…the act or acts of extending yourself for others by identifying and meeting their legitimate needs." Love, then, is an action.

Legitimate needs is important to point out. Have you ever walked through a Walmart with a toddler? Every few feet it's, "I want that! I need that!" But do we buy the toddler everything she thinks she wants or needs? Of course, not. What about an alcoholic or drug addict? They may sincerely believe that they need another drink or fix. But when we love with awareness, we recognize that these do not serve their greatest good, higher self, or self-actualization. Not to compare those we lead to toddlers or drug addicts, but it's important for leaders to be aware of the concept of legitimate needs. We don't give those we lead or love everything that they think that they want or need either. We use our listening skills, collaborative efforts, awareness, knowledge, and experience to help determine what the legitimate needs really are. Leaders must also learn to balance their own needs, the needs of customers/clients, direct reports, and the needs of the organization. Then, we use decision-making skills to arrive at how we will best serve them. The action/service is our gift.

The idea that love is an action-item gift, especially a gift of self, reverberates among the best minds. Dr. Peck calls this aspect of love *attention*, *work*, and *courage*, Dr. Fromm *giving*, and James Hunter *service* and *sacrifice*. Dr. Stephen Covey wrote, "Proactive people make *love* a verb. Love is something you do: the sacrifices you make, the giving of self, like a mother bringing a newborn into the world. If you want to study love, study those who sacrifice for others, even for people who offend or do not love in return."

Love, then, for the leader is this complex combination of the elements of emotions, creative energy, volitional decision, and service or giving. It is not sentimental, soft, or weak. It takes great courage, strength, and discipline to integrate the interdependency between these elements and to demonstrate love. Being aware of the power of each element and putting them into practice helps us to be a masterful leader and nurtures greater love, happiness, and success for ourselves, our teams, and our organizations.

The New Millennial Leader

When the causes of the Great Recession of 2007 were being investigated, reporters, the Security and Exchange Commission, and Congress repeated allegations of fraud, the abandonment of integrity, and putting profits before employees, investors, and clients by the leadership of major institutions that resulted in a worldwide financial meltdown. Jeff Clark,

Senior Editor, Casey's Gold and Resource Report, thinks this may only be the tip of the iceberg. He describes the response of government leaders as "the biggest financial deception of the decade." Deception, fraud, cutthroat competitiveness, greed, selfishness, and exploitation are diametrically opposed to the fundamental qualities of true leadership. It could be argued that the single most important factor leading to the financial crisis of our times was that there was a paucity and failure of leadership; those at the root cause were only *filling* leadership positions. They were not truly leading; nor were they leaders in any sense of the modern understandings of leadership.

The tough, 'old-school,' cutthroat, competitive, impersonal, manipulating, power-wielding leader of the past who is accountable only to the bottom-line has proven to be a failed archetype for the new millennium. When taken to extremes, it results in the types of abuses and catastrophic failures exemplified in organizations like Enron, WorldCom, Bear Stearns, Lehman Brothers, Fannie Mae, Freddie Mac, and AIG. For some, this may seem like a radical paradigm shift and for others, it not only makes intuitive sense; they have already realized the new demands on the new millennial leader and are actively pursuing them. J. Martin Hays, PhD and Choule Youn Kim, PhD Candidate of the Australian National University agree:

> Conventional leaders and leadership of the past are insufficient to meet the demands of the 21st Century. As we enter the new millennium, our world is characterized by unprecedented complexity, paradox, and unpredictability. Change is rapid and relentless. Today's leaders face demands unlike any ever before faced. Standard leadership approaches that have served us well throughout much of history are quickly becoming liabilities. Conventional wisdom regarding leadership and many of its habits

> must be unlearned. The strong, decisive, charismatic, and independent leader and leadership we have idealised, strived to be, depended upon, and longed for may prove counter-productive in the new millennium and undermine a sustainable future. The challenges and opportunities of the 21st Century call for a new type of leader and leadership, indeed an entirely new and different way of thinking about leadership and of developing future leaders.

The call has been made for a new type of leader – a New Millennial Leader (NML) – to meet the demands of our times and the foreseeable future. What is the NML like?

A Loving Leader. The strongest attribute of the new millennial leader is that of a loving leader – and I qualify that with our definition above. Recall that according to the BlessingWhite report, only twenty-nine percent of employees reported being fully engaged, while seventy-one percent reported being less than fully engaged and nineteen percent reported being fully disengaged. What does employee engagement have to do with love and leadership?

Recall what employee engagement is: An engaged employee is someone who is fully involved in their work, enthusiastic about it, and thus acts in a way that furthers their organization's interests. BlessingWhite also reported that many leaders are not taking the steps to foster employee engagement – meeting the basic needs of their employees with genuine care and concern, developing and nurturing relationships, and providing opportunities for growth and development. These elements of fostering employee engagement read like a textbook definition of love. Remember, it was organizations with high employee engagement that were the most successful and profitable.

An ideal to strive towards is that of the loving, servant leader, such as Mahatma Gandhi, Jesus of Nazareth, or Martin Luther King, Jr. There is a passage from the Christian tradition's gospel of Luke during his account of the last supper that captures this beautifully. It is often overlooked and yet very instructive, no matter what your religion. Jesus is quoted to have said (emphasis added), "The kings of the Gentiles are deified by them and exercise lordship [ruling as emperor-gods] over them; and those in authority over them are called benefactors and well-doers. But this is not to be so with you; on the contrary, let him who is the greatest among you become like the youngest, and him who is the chief and leader like one who serves" (Luke 22:25-26). Although new voices call for a New Millennial Leader (NML), the idea of a loving, servant leader is not new and the rewards for both the leader and those she leads are many.

Knowledge Leaders. There are leadership models related to the loving leader: knowledge management, transformational leadership, and servant leadership. The connections between the servant leadership model are obvious. But what about the other two?

Knowledge management derives from Peter Drucker's "knowledge worker" and the "Information/Knowledge Worker Age." He and others point out that we have become a knowledge-based society and that a knowledge-based revolution is taking place.

Almost half of this knowledge is what is called *tacit knowledge*. Tacit knowledge is an individual's personal knowledge in their mind that includes experience, expertise, judgment, intuition, and even their savoir-faire. It's not easy to capture, articulate, or write down. How leaders encourage the sharing and collaboration of this knowledge for the benefit of teams and organizations, comprise knowledge management. Drucker asserts "that knowledge has become *the* resource, rather than *a* resource" and introduced the idea of the knowledge worker of the new millennium.

He said, "The most valuable asset of the 21st-century institution, whether business or non-business, will be its knowledge workers and their productivity." *Explicit knowledge*, knowledge that can be more easily captured, articulated, written down or codified, and stored, may also be included as part of knowledge management. The challenge for the NML is to encourage the sharing of the more elusive tacit knowledge.

NMLs integrate their personal leadership skills and use technology in order to capture and share tacit knowledge. At first glance, knowledge management would not seem to particularly fit into a discussion about a loving leader – until research made a connection between effective knowledge management and transformational leadership styles. But first, what is transformational leadership?

Transformational Leader. According to one of the leading experts in transformational leadership, Bernard Bass, PhD, superior leadership performance occurs when leaders "elevate the interest of their employees, when they generate awareness and acceptance of the purposes and mission of the group, and when they stir their employees to look beyond their own self-interest for the good of the group." It is person-centered; the leader cultivates the needs of the follower – a reverberating trend in current leadership models. Transformational leaders possess four qualities:

1. **Charisma/Challenge to Grow.** Transformational leaders provide vision, mission, and convince employees to break through barriers – they tap the need of followers to champion a cause. They foster self-efficacy and positive feelings about what can be accomplished, even inspiring greatness, rather than fostering fears of what cannot be done. They instill pride, respect, and trust.

2. **Idealized Influence/Integrity/Inspiration.** Transformational leaders set high expectations and do the right thing themselves rather than what may be easy, thus leading by example and earning the admiration of those they lead. They have a high moral commitment to themselves and to those they lead. They are credible.
3. **Intellectual Stimulation.** These leaders encourage careful problem-solving, challenge employees to think for themselves, and value intelligence and rationality. They are not the type of leader who 'has all the answers.'
4. **Individualized Consideration or Love.** Transformational leaders give each employee personal attention. They individually coach and advise their employees. They use empathy and compassion and are genuinely concerned for the well-being of those they lead, thus building strong relationships with them.

Again, when we compare our definition of love with the description of the transformational leader, we find many similarities. What's amazing about transformational leadership is its effectiveness. The effectiveness of transformational leadership has strong support in the literature within various types of organizations. It has been shown to enhance employee safety and well-being as well as organizational performance at every level. Since transformational leadership has proven so effective and beneficial in all types of organizations and knowledge has become *the* resource of our times, could there be a relationship between them?

Chris Crawford, PhD, Assistant Provost for Quality Management and a professor at Fort Hays State University in the Department of

What's love got to do with it?

Leadership Studies, wanted to know the answer. He tested over 800 students in a graduate degree program on their behavioral aspects of knowledge management and compared that to their leadership style. The powerful results led him to conclude, "Among the most specific findings in this research study is the strong relationship between transformational leadership and knowledge management behaviors." Those that did not espouse a follower-centered approach (i.e., transactional or laissez-faire leadership styles) did not correlate with knowledge management at all. Being a technically savvy, knowledge-oriented leader and a loving or transformational leader are key qualities of the NML.

At the beginning of this chapter, Tina Turner asks, "What's love got to do with it?" When it comes to leadership, loves got everything to do with it! We are confronted with the most challenging demands ever facing leaders – leaders of relationships, leaders of groups and teams, leaders of industry and organizations, leaders of governments. When we harness the power of positive emotions, we inspire love of ourselves and for those we lead. When we actualize love's creative energy – we create and innovate. When we exercise our 'response-ability' with awareness – we choose to enact our will with love. When we are in service by focusing on the needs of those we lead – their well-being and growth, higher self, or self-actualization – we love them. When we love with this vision, we transform; we transform towards innovation, personal well-being and happiness, effectiveness and self-efficacy, productivity and profits, success, and a better world. This is the New Millennial Leader. The words of Solomon are inspiring, "Hatred stirs up disputes, but love covers all offenses" (Proverbs 10:12).

The Three Questions

One of my favorite short stories is *The Three Questions* by Russian author, Leo Tolstoy. Many consider him to have been one of the world's greatest novelists. This story, originally written in 1885, masterfully captures three great lessons for leaders who want to better walk down a path of love. The leader in Tolstoy's lovely parable is a king in search of the answers to the three most important questions in life:

- How can I learn to do the right thing at the right time?
- Who are the people I most need, and to whom should I, therefore, pay more attention than to the rest?
- What affairs are the most important and need my attention first?

BONUS MATERIAL: You can find your own copy of this lovely story and the answers to the three questions on the Free Bonus Material link on my website. You will also find some amazing quotations on love for your reflection. Here's what you do:

- Go to: www.alanmikolaj.com
- Click on the "Order the Book" tab.
- Click on the red Bonus Material box at the bottom of the page.
- Enter the password "bonus1"
- Click the PDF icon labeled "The Three Questions"
- Click the PDF icon labeled "Reflections on Love"

Leadership Travel Tips Chapter 5: Walk a Path of Love

- The most powerful relationships we have in our lives are with those people who lead us and with those whom we lead – in which leadership is a central element of the relationship.
- If we want to be masterful leaders, we must recognize the clear road sign on our journey that love is fundamental to everyone (that includes you and those you lead) and that continually learning more about love and actualizing what you learn are high priorities.
- A person can love their job. Research shows that when we are passionate about our work, experience a sense of intimacy with the people at work, and are committed to our organization or work group, we love our job.
- You can now look at each members' love of their job or role through this triangular model and adapt your approach towards each of them accordingly.
- A leader's definition of love can be described as a complex combination of feelings, creative energy, volitional decision, and actions/service that stem from an innate need to connect, relate, support, and mutually nurture and serve that which leads to the discovery and growth towards both of your greater or higher selves or self-actualization.
- The challenges and opportunities of the 21st century call for a new type of leader and leadership: the New Millennial Leader.

CHAPTER 6
The Bridge of Gratitude

Being in a state of gratitude actually creates magnetism, and of course, a magnet draws things to itself. By giving authentic thanks for all the good you now have, as well as the challenges, through this magnetism you'll start the flow of more good into your life. Every successful person I know is grateful for everything they have.

~Wayne Dyer ~

Popular culture gives us a clear idea of how to achieve happiness – earn more money and buy more stuff. That message isn't just in the media. Political, educational, and business institutions also send us messages about the belief that having the best things in life and personal wealth will bring happiness – and Americans are buying it.

Researchers from the University of British Columbia and the Harvard Business School asked people to predict how happy or unhappy they would be if they were earning incomes different from their own and then compared their predictions to the actual happiness levels of people at those incomes. When it came to higher income levels, people were pretty good at predicting how happy people are. However, when it came to lower income levels (below the median), people really missed the mark.

People tended to think that earning less money meant being

significantly less happy than people actually are – the lower the income, the worse the prediction (see Figure 7). People who earned higher incomes believed that less money equals less happiness the strongest of all. In other words, rich people think poor people are unhappy because of their economic plight. People at lower incomes thought that earning twice as much money would also double their happiness, even though the actual change in income would only result in a seven percent increase in happiness. In other words, poor people think more money will make them happier. Most Americans *do* believe that money can buy you happiness.

Figure 7. Happiness and Income: What Americans Believe

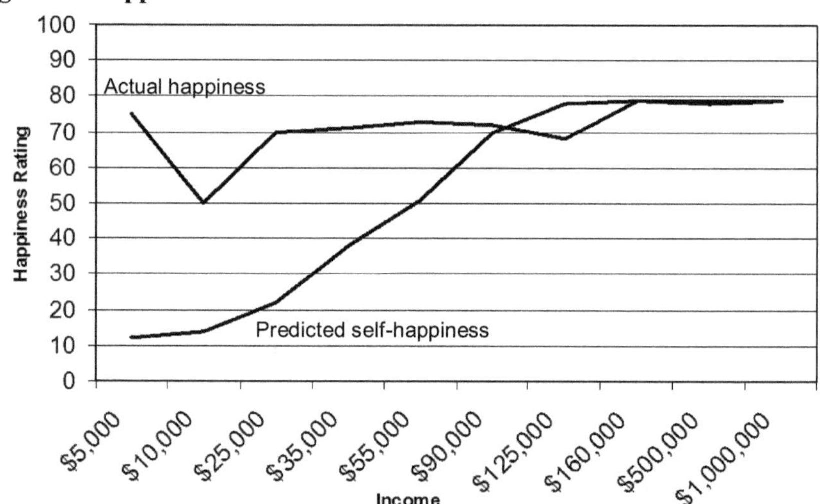

From: Aknin, L. B., Norton, M. I., & Dunn, E. W. (2009). From wealth to well-being? Money matters, but less than people think. *The Journal of Positive Psychology*, *4* (6), 523-527. Reprinted by permission of the publisher (Taylor & Francis Ltd, http://www.tandf.co.uk/journals).

Here are a few surprising facts from the research about wealth and happiness:

- Beyond poverty, increases in personal wealth do not typically result in increased happiness.
- The wealthiest people aren't that much happier than other people are.

- The relationship between wealth and happiness is surprisingly weak or very modest at best.
- Happiness levels in the US have remained stable or slightly declined despite a doubling of income and GDP in the past 50 years.
- People who strongly desire wealth and money are less happy or even unhappy compared to those who do not.
- Cross-sectional, longitudinal, and experimental evidence supports the idea that happiness leads to successful outcomes in the workplace and personal life.

As we learned in Chapter 4, success does not lead to happiness rather; it is happiness that leads to success – in every major life domain. Since it is happiness that leads to success and it isn't necessarily money that leads to happiness, the question then becomes, "What *does* lead to happiness?"

The Bridge of Gratitude

The Bridge of Gratitude changed my life. On the back cover of this book is a picture of Stone Mountain Covered Bridge, located in Stone Mountain State Park in Georgia. It crosses Stone Mountain Lake connecting the traveler to Indian Island inside the park. It is a powerful reminder to me of how the Bridge of Gratitude transformed my life – as it has for countless others. It is also a symbol of journeys and transformations. When I took the picture, I had recently finished the first Go Gratitude Experiment in 2005 (www.gogratitude.com) in which I had been on a 42-day journey of focusing on gratitude. Engendered by Stacey Robyn, I spent a few minutes reading an inspirational email on gratitude and taking account of the things I was grateful for in my life. So, while visiting my sister near Atlanta, I decided to make a pilgrimage to Stone Mountain. I was just beginning to realize that the Bridge of Gratitude had given me a fresh start – a new beginning – and that bridge has become a symbol in my life of how gratitude can lead to happiness. You see, I had crossed into a new way of being. I felt joyous, peaceful, and happy – not an ecstatic mania type of happiness – but a resilient, deep, sublime, and subtle joy. Crossing the Bridge of Gratitude allowed me to see my current circumstances from a different view. It carried me across from where I was to a place of sanctuary, appreciation, and joy.

Of all the travel tips in this book, I have to say, that for me, learning to cross the Bridge of Gratitude was personally the most powerfully transforming event in my personal and professional development. Gratitude is the bridge to happiness. But why and how? What is it about feeling grateful or what Benedictine Brother David Steindl-Rast calls 'Great Fullness' that is so transforming?

What is Gratitude?

There are plenty of self-help groups, motivational speakers, authors, and religious, spiritual, and cultural traditions that espouse the regular practice of grateful thinking to enhance spiritual, psychological, and social functioning and well-being – happiness. Promoting the positive power of gratitude is ubiquitous across history, cultures, and religions. Gratitude is a universal human phenomenon.

I define gratitude as a cognitive-affective state characterized by the recognition of having received some good or benefit from a benefactor, whether distinct or more ethereal. It is the awareness of having received something good or desired accompanied by a warm, joyous, admiring, and appreciative feeling. Gratitude also fosters a desire to 'pay it forward.' There is a sense of indebtedness that is felt toward a benefactor, God, or other ethereal mental images (personages, society, one's nation, nature, the universe, etc.) that motivates further giving. This then creates a spiral of giving, receiving, and repaying. It is no wonder that the symbol and logo of GoGratitude is a spiral shaped 'g' and circle.

Figure 8. Go Gratitude Symbol/Logo

It is in this vein that Robert Emmons and Charles Shelton define gratitude as a *moral affect*. It is an emotion that results from and promotes moral behavior. The benefactor is motivated by empathy and concern for another person and offers a gift, which then fosters gratitude in the beneficiary. The beneficiary then 'pays it forward' propagating the cycle. This interaction promotes future prosocial behaviors in both the giver and receiver.

Gratitude Research

On the back cover of M. J. Ryan's beautiful book, *Giving Thanks: The Gifts of Gratitude*, is a single quote, "Gratitude creates happiness." The idea that gratitude is a bridge to happiness, and therefore to success in life, is not new. Over 2,500 years ago, Buddha said, "Wise men try to express their appreciation and gratitude by some return of kindness, not only to their benefactor, but to everyone else." Every major religious tradition across the centuries advocates gratitude as a means of worship, prayer, or attainment to higher levels of being. More recently, there has been an explosion of discourse on gratitude. A recent search on Google revealed nearly 600,000 scholarly 'hits' and over 30,000,000 website results. A

People who daily focus on gratitude are more attentive, determined, energetic, enthusiastic, excited, interested, joyful, and strong than those who do not.

similar search for gratitude in the books department on Amazon.com produced nearly 1,600 results. Gratitude is a popular topic.

While there are many inspiring works and words on the benefits of gratitude, the best way to determine whether nurturing or practicing gratitude actually *does* lead to happiness and enhanced functioning is to put gratitude to the test scientifically.

Renowned gratitude researchers Robert Emmons and Michael McCullough did just that. In one study, they had participants write down up to five things they were grateful for at the end of each week for 10 weeks. They also included a "hassles" condition in which participants had a similar weekly report but instead, wrote down up to five hassles or irritants. Included was a control condition in which participants were simply prompted to report five events that had an impact on them. Those in the gratitude condition reported fewer physical illness symptoms, spent more time exercising (nearly 1.5 more hours per week), were more optimistic about the upcoming week, and rated their life as a whole more positively compared to those in the other conditions.

They continued this line of investigation in a second study. This time, they varied the conditions slightly. Instead of weekly reports, they now asked participants to fill out daily reports at the end of each day over a two-week period. The gratitude and hassles conditions remained essentially the same as in the first experiment. They changed the control condition to a 'downward social comparison' condition. Downward social comparison is when we compare ourselves to someone less fortunate. As you would suspect, writing down five things you are grateful for on a daily basis greatly enhanced the power of evoking gratitude. In addition, those people who daily focused on gratitude reported being more attentive, determined, energetic, enthusiastic, excited, interested, joyful, and strong than the other participants. This constellation of emotions is what positive psychologists call *positive affect.* It's one of positive psychology's lingo for being happy. Here is where we begin to connect the dots. A daily focus on gratitude for just two weeks evoked increased happiness – and we know that happiness leads to success. Those in the gratitude condition were also more likely to report that they helped someone with a personal problem or offered emotional support that day. In addition to increasing happiness, gratitude also evokes prosocial behavior.

Because the second study did not replicate the health and exercise benefits noted in the first study, they decided to conduct one more study with the increased power of focusing on gratitude on a daily basis – but over a longer period this time. They also wanted to use a different sample – a sample of people with a chronic illness. So, for 21 days, the participants in the gratitude condition wrote down up to five things they were grateful for at the end of each day. As before, gratitude evoked increased positive affect (or happiness) and more satisfaction with life as a whole. Those focusing on gratitude were also more optimistic about the future. Interestingly, they got more sleep, too! However, there were not the same effects on health/illness reports. An additional twist was added to this last study: Immediately after the 21 days were over, they asked the spouses and

Gratitude leads to happiness and happiness leads to success.

significant others of the participants what they thought of them. The loved-ones of someone who daily focused on gratitude saw their significant other as happier (increased positive affect) and more satisfied with their lives. The effects weren't simply something happening subjectively to the person who focused on gratitude, but someone close to them in their lives could see the effects, too. Studying the effects of daily gratitude over 21 days was compelling.

In a landmark collection on the practical applications of positive psychology, gratitude and happiness researchers concluded that "gratitude is a key element for sparking positive changes in individuals, families, and organizations." MJ Ryan and Wayne Dyer are right. Gratitude creates happiness and acts as a magnet to increase the flow of good things into your life.

When Do People Feel Gratitude?

The perception that another person (the benefactor) has intended to promote your well-being is cited as the most frequent cause of gratitude. The benefactor can also be something nonhuman, such as God, fate, or some other intentional or ethereal force (e.g., Mother Nature, Life Force, the Universe). More gratitude is created when the act meets three criteria: It is perceived as intentionally provided, at some cost to the benefactor, and valuable to the recipient/beneficiary.

Gratitude creates happiness and acts as a magnet to increase the flow of good things into your life.

When someone goes out of their way or has to interrupt their normal routine to give me a gift, no matter how small, it just means more. I remember my last birthday with joy and deep gratitude. My wife secretly collaborated with my boss and coworkers to decorate my cubicle and classroom with streamers, balloons, and candy the night before my birthday. You can imagine my surprise when I walked into work on my birthday morning! This act met the three criteria for increasing the intensity of gratitude. First, it was intentional. My wife had to plan and collaborate with my work team in order to pull-off the surprise. Second, there was the personal cost of time, energy, buying the supplies, decorating, etc. Finally, I love simple surprises over extravagant gifts and my wife and work team took the time to know that about me and used that awareness to give me something that was of value to me. Without buying expensive name brand gifts, my wife and coworkers gave me one of the best birthdays in recent memory. They also have my enduring gratitude. The research also shows that unexpected benefits or gifts, like my birthday surprise, appear to generate the most gratitude. Some of the best benefits and gifts we receive on our life journey are the ones we didn't see coming and are least expected. Since gratitude leads to happiness, it should be no surprise that the benefits are very similar between the two. Go to the bonus material on the website to see some of the benefits of gratitude cited in the research.

Gratitude is also a strong reinforcer of positive, prosocial behavior.

Gratitude as Reinforcer

Gratitude is also a strong reinforcer of positive, prosocial behavior. Expressions of gratitude have been shown to reinforce kidney donation, volunteering behavior, and to increase productivity in workers. A simple thank-you note was shown to increase tips from patrons and produce higher response rates on mail surveys. As a leader, it pays to know your

You can use gratitude as a way to enhance happiness and success for yourself and those you lead.

people. Those who are high in need for approval are more strongly reinforced by beneficiaries' expressions of gratitude. Money and reward programs are wonderful tools, but sincere praise and a 'thank you' are simple, easy, may be more powerful – and it's free!

Most of us know from taking an introductory psychology course that the most effective reinforcement is done as soon after the behavior as possible. Gratitude as a reinforcer can be done verbally, written, via email, or with an eCard. The more quickly the expression of gratitude follows the behavior, the more that particular and similar behavior is reinforced. You can use gratitude as a way to enhance happiness and success for yourself and those you lead.

How to Nurture Gratitude

In a 2007 report, thirty-seven percent of workers said that their supervisor failed to give them credit when credit was due. Nothing feels better than being recognized for doing a good job. Here are some simple and cheap (some are even free) techniques that you can use to foster gratitude for yourself and those you serve and lead.

Reward and Award. The best leaders know to reward as quickly as possible and to make it something special – an award of some kind. Be creative! Have fun with it! I know one director who gives out a monthly "Wonder Woman Award" with a funny picture of Wonder Woman on it. Weekly "Woo Hoo's!" surprising a staff member, a monthly gift card (they don't have to be expensive), or simple certificates can all can show your appreciation. Make sure you state *specifically* why the person is receiving it. While notes, cards, and emails can be useful as reinforcement, a general rule of thumb is: Reward in public, correct in private. People usually love being recognized in front of their peers. When you vary the reason or metric for why a reward/award is given, your staff won't know which one you will happen to pick. For example, one month you might reward customer satisfaction and the next, revenue and a few months later, reduced overtime or expenses. It's a good idea to balance your fun and creativity with your profession and organizational culture. Using rewards and awards are powerful gratitude tools that are inexpensive or free.

The Power of a Leader's Gratitude. It's important for leaders to recognize that when the benefactor is someone higher in relative social status or power, a gift is seen as more deliberate and meaningful, compared to say a family member or coworker. This leads the recipient to feel and express more gratitude. This is in part because benefits from equals may be considered obligatory or habitual in nature and so, not as powerful. As a leader, when you praise, thank, and provide your direct reports benefits of any type, your authentic words and actions have power. In their bestseller, *How Full is Your Bucket?*, Tom Rath and Donald Clifton, PhD, wisely noted, "Great recognition and praise can immediately transform a workplace."

I remember going to my boss and telling her that I was interested in a Project Manager position that our company had opened up. In addition to her general moral support, I needed her approval on an internal form in order to apply. Not only did she provide me both; she went out of her way to find books, programs, and examples of my work to support my application. Then, despite her busy schedule, she made the time to personally coach me in preparation for my interview.

Great recognition and praise can immediately transform a workplace.

Suddenly, whether I got the position or not didn't matter as much. I felt deeply grateful because of her support and the knowledge that she believed in me and wanted me to do better – and she didn't have to do what she did. No reward program can engender the loyalty and gratitude that her actions did.

The Tell *Your* Boss Technique. Another strategy that puts this research finding to great use is the Tell *Your* Boss technique. Here's how it works. You and your boss collaborate beforehand on this gratitude/reward technique. First, you write a note or send an email to *your* boss about one of your direct reports or team members – or anyone - you genuinely believe has done something well. Be specific. Then, your boss responds to that individual, either in writing or in person, thanking them for doing such a great job. As a direct report, knowing that my boss told her boss that I did a great job increases the feelings of gratitude and reinforcement. Not only did my boss think I did a great job, she told her boss about it, and then the head honcho herself came and told me, "Thank you." Wow!

Change every 'I have to' into 'I get to.' I first heard of this strategy of nurturing gratitude during a one-on-one with my boss. She heard it in a sermon at her church and shared it with me. Jeff Herring also wrote about this online. Here's the gist. Do you ever wake up in the morning and grudgingly say, "I *have* to go to work!"? There's something that happens inside our heads when we say, "I have to" to ourselves. There is instant rebellion against whatever it is we 'have' to do. "I have to" seems to automatically lead to negative emotions and self-talk. We are raised to believe that being 'made' or forced to do anything is no fun and restricts our freedom. This sense of obligation leads down a spiral of negative emotions and self-talk. "I *have* to go to work" turns into "I *have* to face the traffic and that always sucks" and we can easily spiral downward from there.

However, when we change every "I have to" into "I get to," it can lead to positive self-talk and gratitude. Here's how. When you change "I *have* to go to work" into "I *get* to go to work," you begin to think of all of the advantages and blessings of having a job. You might think, "My work allows me to pay my bills and provide for my family" or "I enjoy contributing and doing something I love" and those thoughts can lead to a feeling of gratitude. This simple change in language helps us see the positive side of things and to count our blessings.

Barry Schwartz and Andrew Ward of Swarthmore College study choices that people make and how different factors surrounding our decisions affect our happiness. They said, "We can vastly improve our subjective experience by consciously striving to be grateful more often for what is good about a choice or an experience, and to be disappointed less by what is bad about it." Next time you catch yourself saying, "I have to…" about anything, change it around and find the positive about that activity and say, "I get to!"

Next time you catch yourself saying, "I have to..." about anything, change it around and find the positive about that activity and say, "I get to!"

Gratitude Rock. Here's a simple technique to nurture gratitude that was featured in the movie *The Secret* by Lee Brower. He tells the inspiring story of how this idea developed and how it transformed his life on his website. After admitting his twelve year old daughter, nicknamed 'Mariposa' or 'butterfly' in Spanish, into a substance abuse treatment

Carry a small stone in your pocket and each time you notice it, think of something you are grateful for in that moment.

facility, he went away for a few days to do some introspection and work. While strolling along the beach, his gaze was drawn to a dark colored stone. He couldn't resist from picking it up. On the back was the image of a butterfly in flight. He sent it FedEx to her and told her that every time she touched it, to think of something she was grateful for. He found his own rock and did the same. He said, "Sincere gratitude is the lubricant that allows the law of attraction to work for us."

Here's how it works. Find a small stone and carry it around in your pocket. I've been doing this for a couple of years, now. I conduct a brief blessing ceremony for my gratitude rock and for myself before sticking it in my pocket (I'm on number three – I've lost the first two). I trust wherever those first two gratitude rocks are, they are emanating gratitude around them. Every morning when I pick it up off the nightstand to put it in my pocket, I say at least one thing I'm grateful for – sometimes more. Every night when I'm putting my things away, I do it again. Then, throughout the day, whenever I notice it in my pocket, I think of something I'm grateful for. This helps increase being grateful and happy about my day in a spontaneous way.

I really notice the transforming power of gratitude induced by my gratitude rock when I notice it in my pocket during an especially difficult or challenging moment in my day. It's at these moments that I clearly can catch what would have been a negative downward spiral and, at the very least, stop it and oftentimes; reverse the situation into something positive.

It's impossible to feel authentic gratitude and negative emotions at the same time.

The Gratitude Letter and Visit. Originated by Chris Peterson at the University of Michigan, this strategy has scientific proof that it works. Here's what you do: Spend some time reflecting on a person in your life who has been especially kind to you but whom you've never properly thanked. Then, sit down and write a detailed gratitude letter to that person. In the letter, explain in concrete and specific terms why you're grateful. After you've completed the letter and you're satisfied with it, schedule a visit with that person. During your visit, read the letter aloud to them. Research by Martin Seligman, PhD and colleagues revealed that this technique produces large positive changes in happiness for up to one month, not to mention the positive changes it can do for your relationship with that person.

The Gratitude Journal. Of all the techniques, this one is by far my favorite because of its power and long-term effects. Here's what you do: As late in the day as possible, but before you're too sleepy, sit down and write down 3-5 things that you are grateful for that day. After each entry, also write down why you think each event happened or why you're grateful for it. Do this for a minimum of 21 days. The technique only takes about 5-10 minutes. I've found that couples or friends who do this together and share it, report more profound effects.

Martin Seligman, PhD, the father of positive psychology, and colleagues reported in 2005 on answers they found to the question, "What really works when trying to increase happiness?" One of the

The Gratitude Letter and Visit technique has been shown to increase happiness for up to a month.

most powerful interventions that really worked at increasing happiness was practicing a form of a daily gratitude journal that they called the 'Three Good Things in Life' intervention. Participants were simply instructed to write down three things that went well each day and the reason why for one week. Some participants liked this practice so much that they continued to practice the gratitude journal well beyond the instructed timeframe. The results supported Emmons and McCullough's earlier research on gratitude.

Whether someone wrote down three good things for one week or continued beyond the study's instructions, happiness levels continued to increase as each month went by. Those who continued beyond the one-week instruction saw even greater increases in happiness compared to those who did it for just one week. Happiness levels were assessed at one week, one month, three months, and six months. It took about a month for the increases in happiness to become statistically significant, whether done for a week or more than one week. So, a little patience in the beginning is necessary. The happiness levels continued to rise after that – even out to the six-month happiness measurement. It absolutely amazes me that something so simple *and free* can have such a powerful and long-lasting effect on happiness.

Keeping a Gratitude Journal for as little as 21 days will increase your happiness for up to six months!

You can go out and buy a fancy journal, a simple spiral binder, or use something as handy as scratch pieces of paper held together with a paper clip or stapled. After doing this technique for 21 days, you can vary it to help keep it fresh. Instead of writing it down, create a daily mental gratitude journal during meditation.

My wife and I often conduct a verbal gratitude journal during or after dinner. It doesn't matter; the effects are the same – increased happiness!

Other techniques shown to enhance gratitude are meditation, progressive muscle relaxation, and imagining being forgiven by someone you've harmed in some way.

Crossing the bridge of gratitude leads you to the land of increased happiness. Increased happiness brings you increased success – in every major life domain. As Wayne Dyer's last step in his ten-step program for creating a stress-free, tranquil life states in *The Power of Intention*, "Stay in a state of gratitude and awe. Go on a rampage of appreciation for all that you have, all that you are, and all that you observe." I close this chapter on the bridge of gratitude with a quote from the international best-selling book, *Optimal Thinking*, by Rosalene Glickman, PhD:

> If you don't appreciate what you have, you may as well not have it. When you count your blessings, you can generate your most positive feelings. It is truly in your best interest to develop and maintain an Optimal attitude of gratitude.

BONUS MATERIAL: You can download and view a handout on the Benefits of Gratitude on the Free Bonus Material link on my website. Here's what you do:

- Go to: www.alanmikolaj.com
- Click on the "Order the Book" tab.
- Click on the red Bonus Material box at the bottom of the page.
- Enter the password "bonus1"
- Click the PDF icon labeled "The Benefits of Gratitude."

Leadership Travel Tips Chapter 6: Cross the Bridge of Gratitude

- Remember that gratitude is a bridge to happiness and happiness precedes and leads to success in life.
- Nurture gratitude. Here are some suggestions:
    - Use Award and Reward on a regular basis
    - Use the Power of a Leader's Gratitude
    - Use the Tell *Your* Boss Technique
    - Change every 'I have to' into 'I get to'
    - Carry and use a Gratitude Rock
    - Write a Gratitude Letter and Conduct a Gratitude Visit
    - Start a Gratitude Journal and write in it daily for at least 21 days

CHAPTER 7

Relationship Road

Personal relationships are the fertile soil from which all advancement, all success, all achievement in real life grows.
~ Ben Stein ~

In the evenings throughout the pregnancy of my first son, Benjamin, I routinely took out the stethoscope and listened for the baby's heartbeat. He would kick up on his mother's belly and I would push back. I would talk to him and marvel at the miracle. Inevitably, I would end our nightly escapade by singing to him the alphabet song. You know the one? It has the tune of "Twinkle, Twinkle, Little Star" but the lyrics go through the alphabet.

When the day of delivery finally arrived, he came out wailing. A nurse wiped him up, gave him a quick looking over, swaddled him up, and handed him to me; still crying. My wife had some minor complications that needed her attention. The doctor and other staff were busy. Like a lot of new fathers, I stood in a state of shock holding and looking at this helpless infant crying away. I was concerned about my wife and found myself torn about what to do next. The crying was obviously not helping the situation any. All I could think to do was sing that silly alphabet song.

So, I drew him in tight and looked down at him and started softly singing, hoping not to disturb the important work right in front of me.

As soon as I started singing, my new son instantly stopped crying, opened his eyes, and looked at me. Our eyes actually locked. I slowly rocked him and continued singing as we both stared at each other. I began feeling the most powerful feelings of amazement, wonder, tenderness, bonding, and belonging with this tiny, young creature. As I neared the end of my silly song, I became aware of the fact that the room had become abruptly and absolutely quiet. I looked up, and to my surprise, everyone in the room was staring at me and my new son in utter amazement. It was a miraculous moment.

Bonding, or what is also called attachment, is a powerful experience! According to the research, it happens quite effortlessly and in every culture. After that first experience with my child's birth, I was compelled to repeat similar experiences with my second son's and my daughter's pregnancies and childbirth.

The Need to Belong

The need to belong – the need to form and maintain strong, stable relationships – is both innate and universal. We are born to connect and belong. In an extensive literature review and formation of a comprehensive theory of attachment as a fundamental human need, Roy Baumeister of Case Western University, and Mark Leary of Wake Forest University said, "We suggest that belongingness can be almost as compelling a need as food and that human culture is significantly conditioned by the pressure to

The need to belong is both innate and universal. We are born to connect and belong.

provide belongingness." Belongingness is now well-accepted as a universal human need.

The most powerful relationships we have in our lives are those in which leadership is a central element of the relationship.

Our first relationships are with our parents or primary caregivers. Those relationships serve as a model or foundation for future relationships – a prototype, if you will. There is convincing, cumulative evidence from so many researchers over the past 60 years that early caregiver/parental bonding and attachment later becomes an integral part of all of our most important relationships, work, and well-being "from cradle to grave" – as psychologist, psychiatrist, and attachment theorist pioneer, John Bowlby once wrote. The most powerful relationships we have in our lives are those in which leadership is a central element of the relationship. At work, healthy relationships are associated with all kinds of positive outcomes including group cohesion, productivity, job performance, and well-being. An employee's relationship with the leader, their boss, can be the single most important relationship at work.

In their New York Times bestseller, *First Break All the Rules: What the World's Greatest Managers Do Differently*, the Gallup Organization's Marcus Buckingham and Curt Coffman offer some powerful insights and guidance for those who want to be great managers. They report, "The talented employee may join a company because of its charismatic leaders, its generous benefits, and its world-class training programs, but how long that employee stays and how productive he is while he is there is determined by his relationship with his immediate supervisor." By now, most of us have read or heard about that one very

People don't quit jobs, they quit bad bosses.

popular conclusion from their book and the Gallup Organization's research in one form or another: *People don't quit jobs, they quit bad bosses.*

The main components and recommendations of the rest of their work are positive, however. They offer research-driven, practical steps that managers and other leaders can employ to help make them great, too. You see, up to a certain point, the needs that employees have are less about money, and more to do with how they're being treated, how valued they feel, whether they are appreciated, and their talents developed. For the employee, it's as much or more about the need to belong, fulfillment, and relationships. When we 1) Feel needed, 2) Do fulfilling and meaningful work, and 3) Have a great relationship with our boss, we love our work – and our relationship with our boss has much to do with the first two. Our relationship with *our* boss makes all the difference in the world for us at work – and the same is true for those we lead. So, much of this depends directly on you, the leader.

That means getting down to the hard work of relationship-building. It means listening and identifying strengths and needs. It means providing the tools that employees need to do their work. It means taking the time to notice and recognize good work. It means showing that you care and walk down a path of love, as described in Chapter 5. It means taking the time and effort to know that different people require different things from you.

Buckingham and Coffman tell us about a distinction between the conventional wisdom that we treat all employees the same and an attribute of the great managers they studied, "Their path is much more exacting. It demands discipline, focus, trust, and, perhaps, most important, a willingness to individualize." When we focus one-on-one with each direct report in special and meaningful ways, we are on the roads of leadership and success. Remember, the word *lead* means to "cause to go with one" or "to travel" and *success* means "to go." Great leaders recognize the need to belong while traveling down Relationship Road. While on that road, how we communicate helps to determine whether our journey is abundant in joy and ends in success or is woeful and a dead-end. And if you think you have to be smart to go down Relationship Road, consider what Daniel Goleman wrote in his bestseller, *Emotional Intelligence*:

> These [people skills] are the social competences that make for effectiveness in dealing with others; deficits here lead to ineptness in the social world or repeated interpersonal disasters. Indeed, it is precisely the lack of these skills that can cause even the intellectually brightest to flounder in their relationships, coming off as arrogant, obnoxious, or insensitive. These social abilities allow one to shape an encounter, to mobilize and inspire others, to thrive in intimate relationships, to persuade and influence, to put others at ease.

There is a difference between traditional measures of intelligence and traveling confidently down Relationship Road.

One of the most robust findings in the literature about happy people is that they have more friends and better relationships. They have better social support networks. As it turns out, satisfaction with your marriage and family life is the strongest correlate of happiness. Successfully traveling Relationship Road brings you joy and happiness and that happiness is contagious.

In a unique analysis of nearly 5,000 people, researchers from the University of California, San Diego and Harvard University mapped the participant's happiness and the connections between them. What they found was amazing. Not only do happy people tend to cluster together, they spread their happiness out around them, up to three degrees of separation; for example, "to the friends of one's friends' friends." They concluded, "Happiness, in other words, is not merely a function of individual experience or individual choice but is also a property of groups of people. Indeed, changes in individual happiness can ripple through social networks and generate large scale structure in the network, giving rise to clusters of happy and unhappy individuals." As happy, socially competent leaders, we spread happiness – and as we learned, happiness leads to success.

The Communication Expedition

Our ability to communicate is one of the most important tools of leadership. It's how we send and receive important information, motivate, and show that we care. The first step of effective communication is attention. Attending to someone's growth – loving someone as defined in Chapter 5 – does indeed take work and effort. As Dr. Peck said, "The principal form that the work of love takes is attention… By far the most common and important way in which we can exercise our attention is by listening." Listening is one of the most important skills, if not *the* most important skill, while on the Communication Expedition. I call it an expedition because every time we communicate with another while on the leadership journey, it can be a unique and exciting adventure – an opportunity to both learn and grow. Have you ever been on an expedition? There's a sense of excitement and anticipation as you set out. When we view our communications as an expedition, we are setting out to discover something new – although it may not always be pleasant or what we expect. We put aside our preconceived notions and look to see what will be revealed to us. We are open and ready for anything.

Listen

Most of us are not taught how to listen and communicate well. Like me, you've probably taken a communications class of some sort while in college. I remember learning how to write a business letter, email etiquette, resume composition, persuasive speech presentations, and the like. However, leaders are rarely taught empathic listening or what is also called active listening. According to a 2007 report in *Leadership Quarterly*, almost a third of employees surveyed disclosed that their supervisor gave them the "silent treatment" in the past year. That's disappointing since so much of what a leader does involves listening and communication.

Marion Spendlove, research fellow at Aston University, maintains that people skills, which include the competency of listening, are paramount to leadership. Many companies and organizations list communication skills and listening as core leadership competencies. The book stores are full of works on improving communication in your relationships, too, whether at work or in your most intimate relationships. In his classic bestseller, *How to Win Friends and Influence People*, Dale Carnegie wrote, "Dealing with people is probably the biggest problem you face, especially if you are in business. Yes, and that is also true if you're are a housewife, architect or engineer." In their New York Times best seller, *Crucial Conversations: Tools for Talking When Stakes Are High*, the authors unveil an important lesson from their research (emphasis in the original), "Twenty-five years of research with twenty thousand

Listening is one of the most important skills, if not *the* most important skill, while on the Communication Expedition.

people and hundreds of organizations has taught us that individuals who are the most influential – who can get things done, *and at the same time* build on relationships – are those who master their crucial conversations." And in his New York Times best seller, *The 21 Indispensable Qualities of a Leader,* John Maxwell includes listening as one of those twenty-one indispensable qualities saying, "The ear of the leader must ring with the voices of the people." Making the Communication Expedition part of your leadership journey and successfully negotiating Relationship Road are crucial to happiness and success.

Multitasking

I remember a picture I ran in our newsletter of one of our supervisors after she had returned from a vacation. She was busy going through the hundreds of emails in her inbox and at the same time, she was holding a cell phone in one hand up to one ear and her landline up to the other – trying to talk to two different people at the same time. On the one hand, it was an amusing photo capturing someone multitasking and we could all relate to her predicament. Who hasn't tried to go through email while on mute on a conference call? On the other hand, it can also remind us how easy it is in our fast-paced world not to truly listen. As Dr. Peck said, "For true listening, no matter how brief, requires tremendous effort. First of all, it requires total concentration. You cannot truly listen to anyone and do anything else at the same time."

While we may *think* we are listening and doing something else, the truth is that our brains are not wired to

While we may *think* we are listening and doing something else, the truth is that our brains are not wired to multitask.

multitask. We are most likely only *selectively* listening or even worse, simply pretending to listen. What most of us call multitasking is actually just rapid shifts of attention between tasks (reading and responding to emails) and sensory input (auditory in the case of the conference call). That quick shifting of attention back and forth, does not allow the type of focus required for empathic listening. The type of effort required to truly listen to someone else demands that we stop what we're doing and focus.

Now that doesn't mean that we could or even should use empathic or active listening all of the time. First, it would be too exhausting and sometimes office chatter is just simply that, chatter. Rather, the most effective times to use empathic listening are:

- When the other is emotional (e.g., anxious, joyous),
- The subject matter seems to have great value or meaning for the other, or;
- The person is speaking from their heart.

We choose empathic listening to create connectedness, respect and value, to foster appreciation and trust, to allow self-discovery, and to encourage growth and learning – we are fostering a deeper kind of relationship.

Interest and Respect

However, research shows that when we do choose to actively, empathically listen, we give concrete evidence that we respect and value someone and that encourages the other to return that respect and value in the future – either back to us or to someone else. John Baldoni, leadership consultant, coach, speaker, and author, wrote, "The roots of effective leadership lie in simple things, one of which is listening. Listening to someone demonstrates respect; it shows that you value their ideas and are willing to hear them."

Great leaders are great listeners.

Interestingly, the Latin root of "respect" – *respicere* – means "to look back" or "to look again." If we want to show respect, we must take a second look at another; we must look past the first impression, the prejudices, and automatic thoughts and try to connect to their story, their history, and their personal journey. We just might learn something in the process, too.

Finally, when we listen, we use one of the most powerful tools available to encourage change and learning – and that's what great leaders always seem to do best. Carl Rogers, arguably the most influential psychologist in American history and founder of humanistic psychology, asserted, "Over the years, however, the research evidence keeps piling up, and it points strongly to the conclusion that a high degree of empathy in a relationship is possibly the most potent and certainly one of the most potent factors in bringing about change and learning." How do we foster meaningful connections with those we lead? Listen. How do we gain their respect? Listen. How do we foster change and learning? Listen. Great leaders are great listeners.

Silent

The first lesson in active or empathic listening is the lesson of silence. Notice that the word *silent* is the anagram of the word *listen*. Both words have the same letters. There is something wonderful in that for me. In order to listen, one must be silent. Now of course, a physical silencing of the mouth and vocal cords are required – but that's not the crucial lesson here about listening and silence (although for some, even this can be a challenge). The more difficult and basic work of listening is silencing our inner thoughts, judgments, and distractions about what's being said and about who is saying them.

One phenomenon that interferes with an internal quieting is what I call *The Bigger Fish Story Syndrome.* We've all have it. It's what classically happens when one fisherman is telling another about his latest catch. As the first fisherman is telling his story about the big fish that he recently caught, fisherman #2 is already remembering, planning, and thinking about his own bigger, more exciting fish story. He can't wait to tell fisherman #1 his own story and he might even interrupt him to do so. Whether it's an actual fish story, a new car story, or a story about what's bugging them, instead of truly listening to the other, our tendency is to think about our own response and story while the other is still talking. We have our experiences and thoughts. We have our agenda. Things have to be done. So does the other; and back and forth it goes. Carolyn Schwartz, ScD, from the University of Massachusetts Medical School, said that we live in what she calls the "dyadic monologue culture." We all just keep telling our bigger fish stories – carrying on our monologue – but no one is really listening. It takes great discipline to put that, and more, aside and actually open up to and focus on the other person. Dr. Peck affirmed, "An essential part of true listening is the discipline of bracketing, the temporary giving up or setting aside of one's own prejudices, frames of reference and desires so as to experience as far as possible the speaker's world from the inside, inside his or her shoes."

When we silence our minds and focus on what it must be like for the other – what Dr. Peck calls *bracketing* – we create an open space. New knowledge, respect, appreciation, connections, and growth will always fill that space. We must quiet ourselves in order to fully listen. In his brilliant book, *Why Good Things Happen to Good*

Notice that the word *silent* is the anagram of the word *listen.*

People, Stephen Post, PhD, quotes the famous psychologist, Dan Gottlieb, PhD describing this silence as he struggled with becoming a quadriplegic:

> There was a new silence inside me, and in the silence I was able to hear people's hearts. We can only hear with our heart when the noises of the ego are quiet. That's when we're open. And when we're open, we attain the kind of security everybody longs for – the security that people build fences to find, buy guns to find, marry each other to find. It can be found when we listen with our hearts.

In order to listen, we must remember the anagram of *listen* and be *silent* so we can listen with our hearts.

The frontal lobes of the brain are the newest part of our brain. It is responsible for what is known as *executive functions*. In addition to the higher abilities of conceptual thinking, recognizing and learning patterns, decision-making, planning, and organization, one of the most important executive functions of the frontal lobe is *inhibition*. It is because of our frontal lobes that we can inhibit and delay thoughts and actions in order to delay higher-order gratification and outcomes. That is why empathic listening is such work. We have to make the choice to inhibit our thoughts, emotions, and actions – one of the highest functions of our intellect – and that will take practice.

It is not by accident that these functions are called *executive*. They are indeed higher, leadership functions of the brain – and you. You must use your frontal lobes and dual-focus in order to actively listen. First, you must monitor your feelings, thoughts, prejudices, and reactions and actively quiet them. Second, you must attend to the other and to what is being said from "inside their moccasins."

A general rule of thumb when empathically listening is that when the speaker pauses, wait *at least* three seconds. The other may be organizing their thoughts, processing, and deciding where to go next. Become comfortable with silence during this crucial type of communication. Don't rush to say something or ask another question. Let silence be a space that the speaker is encouraged to fill.

A general rule of thumb when empathically listening is that when the speaker pauses, wait *at least* three seconds.

If I think a period of silence has distracted the speaker and allowed them to wander so far away inside their head, I may paraphrase the last thing they said or say something like, "I wonder what you're thinking right now." Or, like I used to tell my children after an unusually long pause, "I can't hear your inside voice." Use listening to show you are attentive – to show you care.

Enhance Your Silence Skills

If you want to increase your empathic listening skills, you can practice and enhance your executive function of inhibition by regularly practicing mindful meditation, contemplation (as was described in Chapter 3), yoga, or other meditation practices. There's a simple technique you can try.

Basic Meditation

- Sit quietly in a comfortable position (sometimes I like to lay down), close your eyes, and turn your focus on your breathing.
- Next, feel the air as it comes in through your nose breathing first deep down into your belly, and then letting your middle chest, and then finally, your upper chest fill.
- At full inspiration, hold the breath in for a few seconds and then slowly, but naturally, let the air flow back out through your nose.

- To help get me started, for the first few breaths, I may say in my mind to myself as I breathe in, "Breathe in the gift." And as I breathe out, "Breathe out gratitude."
- After doing this for several breaths (whatever feels comfortable to you – I vary between 3-9 breath cycles), let your breathing simply be relaxed and automatic. Many find that it naturally slows and becomes shallower. Just let your breath be. Simply be aware of it.
- As your breathing relaxes and you focus on your breath, the objective is to not think. Clear your mind of thoughts and just be aware of your breath, body, and the sounds and sensations in and around you. If a thought enters your awareness, which it will, simply acknowledge it, let it go, and return to your breath, body, and sensations. Let your body, heart, and mind be still.

Try doing this for just ten minutes every day. Mornings and evenings are really ideal times, but I find that even five minutes during lunch can be so refreshing. You may find that as you become more comfortable with the practice that you want to increase the time and have more extended meditations. Choose times and places that work best for you. Although there are so many benefits to meditation and contemplation, the benefit of enhancing our inhibition/silence skills prepares us to become a better listener. The next time someone is speaking and we choose to actively, truly listen, we can simply take in one of those deep slow breaths, hold it for a few seconds, and let it out. Our mind and our heart will be better prepared to open and create an empty space that the other is invited to fill as we truly listen.

Get the Story

Once we create an empty, quiet space between ourselves and the other, we can now allow the person to fill that space with their story. We are now simply present. I liken this part of empathic listening to becoming an investigative journalist who wants to 'get the story' from their prized source or a wise old hermit who has all the time in the world and whose only interest is learning the landscape from another's vista. The key difference in this type of listening is that we are trying to understand the inner world of another, regardless of our own views and current state. We want to understand what something means *to the other.* We create that silence and space, put aside our thoughts and judgments, and truly try to 'get inside' the other person's experience. We ask ourselves, "What's this like for her?" Contrast that with trying to discover what the inner world of the other means *to me.* When we try to understand what someone is saying through our own lenses, we color and influence, we judge, and we risk missing a golden opportunity to really connect.

Empathic listening is not an evaluation or analysis, but rather, an attempt to connect and participate with the other. There is no plan, no agenda – it is a flow of being. We do that by creating a space, being present to the other, and asking open-ended questions. "What?" "When?" "How?" and "Where?" questions are typically used to get things going. Then we simply allow. We pause. We wait. We listen. Open-ended questions encourage self-examination and self-disclosure by the other. The person is given an opportunity to frame and reframe their experience through the process of our

Empathic listening is not an evaluation or analysis, but rather, an attempt to connect and participate with the other.

questioning and listening and their thinking and sharing. As they do that, we, the empathic listener, enter their private world and accompany them on their journey for a while. We become sensitive to the changing flow within the person, sensing meanings, communicating and checking those with the individual, and helping the person to experience the meanings more fully. All the while, as an empathic listener, we do this without losing our own sense of self, knowing we can return to our own world at any moment we choose.

Checking in on content, experiences, and meanings are an important part of empathic listening. We reflect, translate, and interpret what is said into valued meaning for the speaker. It is not simply parroting back what the other says. Actually, research shows that parroting is actually counterproductive and can be irritating to the speaker. By checking in from time to time, we aren't trying to solve the issue. We are simply trying to understand and 'be' with the person in their world.

We also aren't analyzing. Because of that, we avoid asking, "Why?" You may ask, "Why don't ask *why*?" Think about why-questions. What one word must begin the answer to a why-question? *Because.* When someone must answer a question with *because*, she or he instantly becomes defensive, whether they wanted to or not. By avoiding why-questions, we allow and we respect. When we parrot, ask why, analyze, offer advice or solutions, and interject our own experiences, we are subtly communicating that *my* thoughts and experiences are more important and what you're experiencing is not. Rather, through the trial and error of non-judgmental questioning, silence,

Checking in on content, experiences, and meanings are an important part of empathic listening.

listening, creating space, encouraging, reflecting, translating, interpreting meaning, and checking in, we dissolve aloneness, create connectedness, create respect and value, foster appreciation, allow self-discovery, and encourage change and learning. As Carl Rogers wrote in 1975, "a finely tuned understanding by another individual gives the recipient his personhood, his identity." We give the person permission to accept and love themselves.

Emotions guide us to meaning and are the motivator of behavior.

Genuineness

As we listen empathically, we stay particularly aware of emotions – both our own and those of the other. Emotions guide us to meaning and are the motivator of behavior. We must be self-aware during the encounter so that we can remain genuine. When outlining the most important elements in "growthful" relationships, Carl Rogers asserted, "In the ordinary interactions of life – between marital and sex partners, between teacher and student, employer and employee, or between colleagues, it is probable that congruence is the most important element. Such genuineness involves letting the other person know 'where you are' emotionally."

What Carl Rogers called *congruence*, we might simply call being real or genuine – not fake, or putting on a façade or front. If the other perceives fakeness on our part, trust will be destroyed. So, as we listen and interact we must be our true self. Rosalene Glickman, PhD, advised, "Your purpose in relationships is simply to be your best self, regardless of the circumstances." It doesn't mean that we say anything or everything that pops into our heads or always share what we're feeling. Rather, our genuineness is based on the belief and understanding of the reason *why* we have chosen empathic listening in that particular moment – to create connectedness, respect and value, to foster appreciation and trust, to allow self-discovery, and to encourage growth and learning – we are fostering a deeper kind of relationship. We share what we hope will add to those ends – even if it may sometimes be unpleasant. It is sometimes appropriate to share anger, sadness, disappointment, etc.

So, there are occasions when it is appropriate to interrupt or interject. Sometimes, we may not understand what the other said or is saying. If something is not clear, then it's okay to question. At other times, even though we try to keep our internal silence, we get lost in our own thoughts while someone is speaking. That's okay. Honestly admit that, and ask the person to repeat what they just said. They'll appreciate that more than if we pretend we understood and try to fake it. It's also okay to interrupt someone to give them feedback about a decision that may be self-defeating. Sometimes, as we monitor ourselves as the other speaks, what is said will trigger negative emotions, thoughts, and reactions. If we are upset, we will not be the most effective empathic listener. It's okay to take a 'time-out' to refocus and continue later.

Remember, the empathic listener does not give advice. If we say things like, "You should…" or "Why don't you try…" we do not give the person the chance to come up with their own answers – one's they are more likely stick to. Contrast empathic listening with instructions, coaching, or corrective feedback – very different types of communication. When empathically listening, we also don't necessarily give comfort or encourage. That might sound strange, but phrases such as, "Hang in there. Everything's going to be okay" placate rather than encourage processing and further sharing. They tend to either shut the conversation down or cause the speaker to get the impression that, deep down, you really don't care.

Validation

One of the most powerful empathic listening tools is *validation*, or what humanistic psychology calls, *a reflective statement*. Hearing a validation statement from someone can be extremely powerful. I remember a time my boss used a validation statement after I shared my thoughts and feelings about my wife and I thinking about having a child. She has never had children and I've already 'been there, done that.' My boss' statement was quite simple, actually. She said, "You must be a little frightened by the thought of having another child now that you're a little older and already have grown kids." My heart warmed and I felt freed and at the same time, appreciation for her understanding and caring.

When you express a validation statement, the other person hears their problem or situation *as they are experiencing it* from someone else. Someone outside understands – and this often seems like the first time to the speaker. It can be eye opening and the feeling of truly being listened to and understood fosters appreciation, admiration, and greater self-awareness. Here's the basic formula for a validation/reflective statement:

"You feel ______ (insert what the person is most likely feeling) because ______ (insert the reason or situation causing the feeling)."

For example, "You feel disappointed because the report was lacking the detail you needed." You don't have to be talking about a big deal or a life crisis in order to use a validation statement. It can be used whether the situation and emotions are positive or negative. Validation can be used in empathic listening for several reasons:

- As a 'check-in' to see if we are fully understanding the other
- To help the other become more aware of their experience
- To communicate empathic understanding

We can vary the formula depending on our style or state.

Variations of the Validation Statement

"It makes sense that you feel ______ (insert what the person is most likely feeling) because ______ (insert the reason or situation causing the feeling)"

"I think just about anyone would feel ______ (insert what the person is most likely feeling) because ______ (insert the reason or situation causing the feeling)."

"If I had experienced ______ (insert the reason or situation causing the feeling) I think I would feel ______ (insert what the person is most likely feeling), too."

This form of listening requires conscious, purposeful effort on our part. It is not intended to be used all the time. There are times when we actively discourage speaking and ask people to be quiet and hold their thoughts, input, and questions – such as when we are explaining a new process or there is a speaker in front of a group. Other times, we may simply be too busy and just let people chatter as we go about important or critical functions. Many times, we selectively listen, picking up only on those things that are particularly relevant or directed to us.

However, we know that as effective leaders, we must frequently foster motivation, employee's self-esteem, employee engagement, belonging, personal and professional growth, and our relationships with those we lead. We're trying to bring out the best in them. Therefore, choose regular and frequent times to interact and empathically listen to those you lead. Schedule regular one-on-ones that don't necessarily focus on your agenda, metrics, or your issues. These times are meant to hear about the other's needs and issues. Dr. Peck wrote, "True listening, total concentration on the other, is always a manifestation of love." That gift of yourself – your attention, listening, and love – manifests rewards on both a personal and professional level – and they can last a lifetime. As the 'One-Minute Manger' said, "How on earth can I get results if it's not through people? I care about people *and* results. They go hand in hand."

The Solution

Sometimes the other who is speaking is struggling with an issue and really does want or need a solution to a problem, and yet, the empathic listener does not offer advice or easy solutions to the other. As we empathically listen, reflect, and help clarify meaning, the other reframes their problem more clearly. Solutions they hadn't seen before may become readily apparent – and because they weren't given advice, talked down to, judged, or given an easy solution to try, they now have strong ownership of the solution. However, even with the best of empathic listening, some people still struggle to see the best alternatives and solutions, for whatever reasons.

There are several techniques that can help coax someone closer to discovering their own solution. In her enlightening book, *Optimal Thinking*, Rosalene Glickman, PhD, recommends that we ask some variation of the following question, "What's the best thing you can do under the circumstances?" If it's a more complex problem, she recommends asking, "What are your best options for resolving this?" or, "What are the most constructive, productive actions you can take?"

One way of helping someone to see possible solutions I really like and use, is called 'the Overnight Miracle.' After empathically listening and arriving at an effective validation, I ask, "If a miracle were to happen tonight and when you woke up in the morning your problem was completely solved, what would have to have changed?" Then, continue to use empathic listening to help someone arrive at their own miracle solution. Having the question posed this way often reveals to the person that they haven't quite thought things through as thoroughly as they thought.

Recent research has revealed that we are actually hard-wired towards empathy.

Recent research has revealed that we are actually hard-wired towards empathy. A neural basis of empathy, known as *mirror neurons*, activate in our own brains, cortical areas where the body is represented and emotional centers as we observe and listen to others. Giacomo Rizzolatti and Laila Craighero concluded, "The observation of emotionally laden actions activates those structures that give a first-person experience of the same actions. By means of this activation, a bridge is created between others and us." In a 2006 edition of *Scientific American*, David Dobbs called the discovery of mirror neurons the biggest neuroscientific discovery of the past decade. They aid us in learning movement, language, cultural transmission, our ability to feel, understand intention and meaning, and empathy. In addition to empathy, mirror neurons provide the biological basis for the well-known contagiousness of yawns, laughter, and good or bad moods.

Benefits of Empathy

Research on empathy demonstrates clear benefits for both the speaker *and* the listener. As a leader who chooses to listen with empathy or love, we get to share the joys of others and feel good about giving someone an opportunity to talk about something important. Another perk is that we are prized by those we listen to. They come to see us as someone who cares about them and understands them. We are someone they can go to and rely on in times of need. An icebreaker I often use to open some of my classes is a short version of the gratitude journal. Each participant names one thing they are grateful for and why. One of the responses I often hear is, "I am thankful for my (insert 'boss,' 'spouse,' 'family,' etc.) because I can always turn to them and rely on them in times of need." They honor them, almost venerate them, because they care, listen, and love. An interesting health benefit of empathic listening is that it lowers blood pressure and resting heart rate. As we learned earlier, true listening takes that silencing of the mind that is akin to meditation – and that calms *us*. When we reduce stress and calm the heart, mind, and body, we gain a whole host of health benefits. Finally, when we empathically listen, we model a higher-order skill set. Others begin to learn the deep rewards of empathically listening, pass that on, and become better listeners to others and to you! You foster positivity.

The benefits for the other who is being listened to, experience a profound feeling of being heard and understood. This has a calming effect that facilitates further opening up, intimacy, and appreciation. This fosters relationships – not just with us, but with others, as well. They feel less alone and less isolated and more connected. They feel happier and happier people are healthier, too. Finally, empathic listening helps makes sense of a puzzling situation or experience. They can more easily see solutions or steps towards solutions that they may have never seen before. They get more work done.

In 2010, a collaborative and eloquent study published by researchers from Michigan State University, University of Florida, Singapore Management University, and the University of Notre Dame investigated the role of manager empathy on employee well-being (which is linked to team and organizational success). They found that

The benefits for the other who is being listened to, experience a profound feeling of being heard and understood.

empathic managers tended to have employees who reported less physical/illness (somatic) complaints, were more positive and happy, and who felt like they made more progress on their daily work goals than employees of non-empathic managers did. Empathic managers "foster a climate of understanding and support that is associated with greater happiness following daily accomplishments at work." Their report concludes, "Combined, our results suggest that empathic managers may have a beneficial impact on their employees that is both direct (by influencing average levels of somatic complaints) and indirect (by influencing average strength with which progress or failure at work goals is associated with daily well-being).

The Magic Ratio

Daniel Gottman, PhD began researching marriage in 1972. Today he is the author or co-author of 190 published academic articles and author or co-author of 40 books. Along with his wife, Dr. Julie Schwartz Gottman, Dr. Gottman was the co-founder of the Gottman Institute and is an emeritus professor of psychology at the University of Washington. He is executive director of the nonprofit Relationship Research Institute, which was originally the Family Research Laboratory, affectionately known as "The Love Lab." He wanted to know why marriages either succeeded or failed – and he found answers. His contributions to the understanding of marriage and relationships have won him awards and the admiration and gratitude of countless people. Before Gottman, the best marital therapy of the day had only a thirty-five percent success rate and after one year, that number dropped by half. Compare that to an eighty percent success rate for Gottman's groups. One of his major contributions was what he dubbed 'the magic ratio.'

> The magic 5:1 ratio can be used to predict—with remarkable accuracy—everything from workplace performance to divorce.

Using innovative study designs, Dr. Gottman studied over 650 couples for over fourteen years. From microsecond to microsecond, his teams coded video interactions of how couples talk to each other, their facial expressions, how much they fidgeted, and how they gestured. In addition, they measured heart rates, how much they sweat, breathing, and other measures of stress. In one study of seventy-nine couples, Gottman achieved a ninety-three percent accuracy rate of predicting divorce or marital stability. Throughout all his research, he can boast a whopping ninety-one percent average accuracy rate for predicting divorce – and he can do it in about five minutes. He said, "Amazingly, we have found that it all comes down to a simple mathematical formula; no matter what style your marriage follows, you must have at least five times as many positive as negative moments together if your marriage is to be stable." Negative experiences are just that much more powerful than positive ones. It takes about five positive experiences to outweigh just one negative experience. Since Gottman's original research, it is now known that the magic 5:1 ratio can be used to predict—with remarkable accuracy—everything from workplace performance to divorce.

According to professor emeritus of psychology and public affairs at Princeton University and Noble laureate, Daniel Kahneman, PhD, people have twenty thousand (20,000) moments every day. Research has documented how all of us automatically classify those moments (incoming stimuli) as either positive or negative (good or bad) – and that we are hard-

This hard-wired hyper-alertness to threats, potential threats, and negativity explains the appetite for negative, fear-based news media and the magic ratio.

wired to pay attention to the negative or bad moments and that negatively-valenced events have greater impact on us than positively-valenced events of the same type. Why? Evolutionary psychologists contend that it was key to our survival as a species.

Imagine it's the prehistoric period. Two couples are standing hand in hand looking at a beautiful waterfall. One couple is primarily focused on the beautiful waterfall and the positive feelings for each other. The other couple is attentive to the positive, but is also on high alert for anything negative. They're slightly more attuned to possible negativity – especially anything detrimental to their survival. They happen to notice that a ravenous tiger is stealthily approaching and run away. The other couple? Well, let's just say the tiger ate well that day. Humans attuned to negative environmental stimuli tended to survive. This hard-wired hyper-alertness to threats, potential threats, and negativity explains the appetite for negative, fear-based news media and the magic ratio. The problem is that it doesn't serve us well in most modern day-to-day encounters and situations.

Dr. Gottman has a great analogy. Imagine a stereo system that is divided into a left speaker and a right speaker. The left speaker emits positive messages and the right speaker emits negative, threatening, or fear-based messages – both at the same time. If the volume of the two speakers is about equal, our natural propensity is to tune into the negative, right speaker. It takes turning up the power to the positive, left channel five times until we can achieve a level that accentuates our attention to the positive. It is vital that we cultivate our awareness and expression of the positive.

The effects of the magic ratio are not limited to marriage relationships. Mapping complex interdependencies, researchers from Meta Learning and the University of Michigan Business School used an innovative and complex nonlinear model to arrive at a positivity/negativity ratio (P/N) displayed by high and low performance strategic business unit management teams. They confirmed that what Gottman found true for successful marriages was also true for high performance business teams. The accuracy of their model (positivity/negativity ratio or P/N of 5.614 for high performance teams) mirrors Gottman's ratio. Also mirrored were the medium performance teams with a positivity/negativity ratio (P/N) of 1.855 and low performance teams with a P/N of 0.363. Gottman found that the closer a couple got to a 1:1 positive to negative interaction ratio, the more likely they were to divorce; the closer a couple got to 5:1, the more likely they were to stay together. High performance business teams also share a positive 5:1 ratio and poor performing business teams are closer to a 1:1 ratio or less.

The higher positivity/negativity ratio that high performance teams displayed to one another broadened the choices available to the teams. It created "emotional spaces" that opened possibilities for action that the medium and low performing teams just didn't have. Their higher negativity restricted

The higher positivity/negativity ratio that high performance teams displayed to one another broadened the choices available to the teams.

emotional spaces that closed possibilities for action. In the words of the researchers, Marcial Losada and Emily Heaphy, "Emotional spaces are created by the P/N ratios: high ratios create expansive emotional spaces and low ratios create restrictive emotional spaces." Think about the last time you felt anxious, jealous, impatient, frustrated, or even angry. Those types of negative feelings restrict our thinking and options. When I'm pissed-off, there's not much more I can think about besides getting even. Contrast that with a time you felt joyous, free, 'in the flow,' appreciated or appreciative, or loving. When we feel good, our creative energy provides us with more expansive and productive options than when we feel bad. Remember the research on happy people? It has been repeatedly demonstrated that happy people aren't just feeling better – they are performing better in almost every major aspect of life. This is also true of happy marriages and high-performing business teams.

Gottman lists nine ways to show more positivity in our relationships that will help us increase those emotional spaces and choices. What's interesting is that showing interest, showing that you care, gratitude, and empathic listening are among them.

Nine Ways to Demonstrate Positivity in Your Relationships

- Show interest
- Be affectionate
- Show that you care
- Show gratitude/Be appreciative
- Show your concern
- Be empathic
- Be accepting
- Joke around
- Share your joy

Conflict Management

There is oftentimes an unspoken taboo about conflict, especially at work. That's because most of our experiences with attempts at conflict resolution turned out to be anything but resolution. Conflict so often turns into ego-driven, sarcastic, contempt, attacks, and defensiveness. Who wouldn't want to avoid that? In his bestseller, *The Five Dysfunctions of a Team*, Patrick Lencioni lists *fear of conflict* as the number two dysfunction of teams. But truly, all great relationships and teams, whether at work, in marriage, as parents, coaches, between friends – must all face conflict.

There are two types of conflict: productive conflict and unproductive conflict. Lencioni wrote, "It is important to distinguish productive ideological conflict from destructive fighting and interpersonal politics." He further points out that *both* types of conflict produce passion, emotions, and frustrations. Conflict can be messy.

However, facing problems and conflict are not only a part of life; it is often what causes growth and gives meaning to our lives. I have had one of my favorite quotes about this from Dr. Peck's *The Road Less Traveled* framed and hanging on the wall in my office for many years:

> Yet it is in this whole process of meeting and solving problems that life has its meaning. Problems are the cutting edge that distinguish between success and failure. Problems call forth our courage and our wisdom; indeed, they create our courage and wisdom. It is only because of problems that we grow mentally and spiritually. When we desire to encourage the growth of the human spirit, we challenge and encourage the human capacity to solve problems, just as in school we deliberately set problems for our children to solve. It is through the pain of confronting and resolving problems that we learn.

Let's face it. Conflict is a part of life and conflict management and problem resolution are part of how all great leaders and their relationships and teams are defined. As Dr. Peck suggests, it can mean the difference between success or failure. At moderate levels, anxiety is actually the motivator of a lot of behavior, development, and accomplishment. Many are familiar with the Yerkes-Dodson law. Originally developed by famed psychologists, Robert M. Yerkes and John D. Dodson in 1908, the law states that performance increases with physiological or mental arousal, but only up to a point. 'Arousal' in this context can also be thought of as stress. With little or no arousal or stress, we're just not that motivated to do anything. As arousal or stress increase, we eventually arrive at a level of optimal performance. Too much, and performance deteriorates.

Figure 9. The Yerkes-Dodson Law

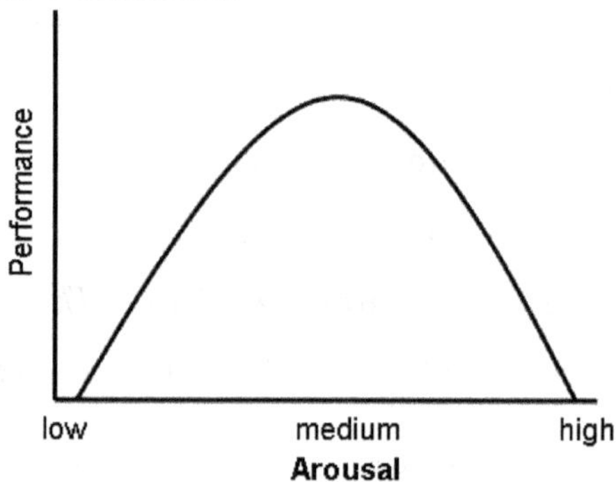

Research has found that different tasks require different levels of arousal for optimal performance. For example, difficult or intellectually demanding tasks require lower levels of stress or arousal to promote concentration, whereas tasks demanding stamina or persistence may be performed better with higher levels of arousal in order to increase motivation. As psychologist David H. Barlow has so famously summarized, "Without anxiety, little would be accomplished."

However, many of us avoid the anxiety of conflict. We don't want to hurt someone else's feeling and we certainly don't want to be hurt, either. Sometimes, the leader or a team member during a meeting that's starting to escalate will ask members to take their issues "off-line" or will divert the discussion in an attempt to 'rescue' the meeting from getting nasty. Others withdraw and bury their heads pretending to take notes or check their phone or computer. Other times, someone, often the leader, is openly domineering and manipulative imposing his or her solution on someone else or the group. Some call this win-lose. The boss wins. The employee loses. But, in reality, everyone loses as a suboptimal relationship is established creating a downward spiral for just about everything else. When conflict is avoided and open discussion, even heated debate, is repressed (either passively or directly), needed growth and/or change is denied, dangerous hidden tensions ensue, and real issues are buried only to resurface later, often with explosive and destructive results.

The best leaders have the courage to engage in and encourage their teams to engage in productive conflict and problem-solving for several reasons.

The best leaders have the courage to engage in and encourage their teams to engage in productive conflict and problem-solving for several reasons. First and foremost, it's the best way to find the best possible solution to a problem. Members define the problem/conflict, banter out the facts and feelings, brainstorm possible options, evaluate those options, negotiate, and arrive at the best possible solution with much better 'buy-in' than if it were rammed down their throats or simply settled on out of fear or apathy. Teams that engage in productive conflict management have more sound commitment to decisions and solutions. Second, when allowed to openly process a problem in this way, the likelihood of residual, negative feelings coming back to haunt the leader and/or the team is

Some negativity is *required* for healthy relationships and teams.

greatly reduced. Because of that, it is also less time-consuming in the long run. Finally, when team members begin to learn that they can be vulnerable with each other and openly confront issues and problems, they build trust. As Barbara Pachter said in her marvelous book, *The Power of Positive Confrontation*, "Positive confrontation skills benefit everyone – brain surgeons have trouble handling conflict on the job and at home. So do sales people, homemakers, airline pilots, administrative assistants, husbands, PTA presidents, Cub Scout leaders, wives, and significant others."

The most compelling evidence to reinforce the need for conflict comes from Gottman's marital research and Fredrickson and Losada's research with business teams and others. Their conclusions? Some negativity is *required* for healthy relationships and teams. But, it must be appropriate and relative to the amount of positivity. For example, Gottman found that criticism, contempt, defensiveness and withdrawal, and loneliness and isolation were destructive. However, anger was not! It was only when anger was coupled with criticism or contempt or became defensive, that it had any negative impact on the relationship. He wrote, "Even happily married couples can have screaming matches – loud arguments don't necessarily harm a marriage." And, "In fact, occasional discontent, especially in the early years, seems to be good for the union in the long run." While he admits that active listening may come in handy and recommends it as a way to show and demonstrate positivity on a more day-to-day basis, when it comes to conflict resolution, it is not how stable, long-lasting couples resolve problems.

In their sophisticated nonlinear dynamics model, Losada and

Heaphy demonstrate that negativity is required for the high performance business teams; it just has to be outweighed by a factor of 5.614 of positivity. They state, "In our model, positivity and negativity operate as powerful feedback systems: negativity dampens deviations from some standard, whereas positivity acts as amplifying or reinforcing feedback that expands behavior." In later research investigating mental health, Fredrickson and Losada replicate and expand the model. They established that the "critical" positivity ratio or ultimate dividing line between flourishing and languishing, whether for individuals, marriages, or business teams, is 2.9 – with or without conflict. This evidence suggests that whatever conflict management style we have or technique we choose to use, as long as we avoid criticism, contempt, or defensiveness *and* maintain at least a positivity/negativity ratio of around 3, we will be cultivating healthy and stable, long term relationships, whether in our personal or professional lives. Barbara Pachter presents her 'Don't Attack 'em, WAC'em' model in her book, *The Power of Positive Confrontation.* She emphasizes the positive by being "Polite and Powerful." She presents a very practical process that help us emphasize the positive and to develop more productive conflict management skills. I highly recommend her book if you want a more in-depth, systematic process of productive conflict management that is beyond the scope of this book.

The leader plays a pivotal role in directing and allowing productive conflict and conflict management. We are responsible for checking criticism, contempt, and defensiveness and fostering a positive environment. Lencioni

The leader plays a pivotal role in directing and allowing productive conflict and conflict management.

recommends that leaders avoid protecting members by letting them engage in conflict in order to allow them to learn and develop their own coping skills and personally model productive conflict management.

Is there an upper positivity limit? Some may interpret all of this to be a Pollyanna approach to leadership. That is neither the message here nor what the research implies. In fact, Fredrickson and Losada's model, predicts that when there is too much positivity, approaching 12 or higher, the model or 'structure' begins to break down. Too much or fake positivity is as damaging as too much negativity. There must be a certain tension between the poles of positive and negative in order for there to be success – with the bend towards the positive at a level of at least 3:1 in order for there to be long-lasting success.

Remember, empathic listening, the magic ratio, and productive conflict resolution are tools we use on Relationship Road. They are not the only tools in the chest – they just happen to be some of the 'major players.' The goal is to create connectedness, respect and value, to foster appreciation and trust, to allow self-discovery, and to encourage growth and learning. You could say that we are empowering others to do their best and to be their best. It takes more patience and work, but in the end, it is more effective and enduring. It reminds me of a fortune that paraphrases the Tao Te Ching that I once received when I opened a Chinese fortune cookie:

A leader is powerful to the degree he empowers others.

Leadership Travel Tips Chapter 7: Take the Relationship Road

- The need to belong – the need to form and maintain strong, stable relationships – is both an innate and universal human need.
- Much of what a leader does involves listening and communication. Our ability to communicate, the Communication Expedition, is one of the most important tools of leadership.
- People don't quit jobs, they quit bad bosses.
- When we choose to actively, empathically listen, we give concrete evidence that we respect and value someone.
- *Silent* is the anagram of the word *listen.* Learn to discipline yourself to silence your inner thoughts, judgments, and distractions about what's being said and about who is saying them. Practicing mindful meditation, contemplation (as was described in Chapter 3), yoga, or other meditation practices will enhance your executive function of inhibition.
- Get the story by trying to understand the inner world of another.
- Be real and genuine.
- Use validation statements.
- Encourage others to derive their own solutions. Avoid advice-giving.
- Understand and use the Magic Ratio. Foster interactions and moments that have a positivity ratio between 3-5 in all of your relationships.
- Don't be afraid of stress and conflict. Have the courage to engage in and encourage your teams to engage in productive conflict and problem-solving. Remember, some appropriate negativity is *required* for healthy flourishing.
- Set the goal in your relationships to create connectedness, respect and value, to foster appreciation and trust, to allow self-discovery, and to encourage growth and learning. In other words, love.

CHAPTER 8

The Trust Trek

Whenever you lead people, it's as if they consent to take a journey with you. The way that trip is going to turn out is predicted by your character.
~ John C. Maxwell ~

I once had a short stint as the Executive Director of a small, privately owned EMS company. The owner who brought me on board was overworked, over stressed, and was dealing with some serious anger management problems. My initial responsibility was to help him and the company realign the leadership model and operations to a point where he could transition away from the day to day involvement in every detail of operations. He wanted to transition to a more 'hands-off' role and get back to enjoying his life. Understandably, it wasn't easy for him to let go of managing his dream business that he had started from scratch – but his life depended on it. Stress was taking its toll on his health and his personal and professional relationships were falling apart.

While the reorganization was still being planned and some first steps initiated, a call came into our dispatch center during Friday evening rush hour for an unconscious man at a nursing home way across town. Seconds counted. This man's life was at stake and our unit in the area was

As enigmatic as trust, character, and integrity may sometimes seem to be, they are the heart and foundation of the leadership journey and of high-functioning teams.

already busy transporting another patient to the hospital. The only EMS unit we had available would take close to an hour to get through downtown and then further to the outskirts of the city through rush hour traffic – even running "hot" (lights and sirens). I instructed our dispatcher to contact 911 and have the city's fire department EMS handle this emergency. They would have an EMS unit much closer and get this man the help he needed much quicker. The owner heard the radio messages while eating dinner at a nearby restaurant. Hungry for the few hundred dollars or more this call could generate, he jumped into his car and rushed over to the office livid that I would turn over a sure money-making call. I couldn't believe my ears. This man, my new boss and the owner, was telling me to rescind my instructions, send our unit from the other side of town, and risk a man's life for a few hundred dollars – not that the amount mattered. I urgently and emphatically explained the ethical and possible legal ramifications. He didn't care and said as much; actually screamed it at the top of his lungs. Any hopes and dreams I had of implementing our new leadership model, growing the company, developing the employees, and giving this man his life back, vanished in an instant. Trust was completely and irreparably destroyed. In an eerie silence, I walked into my office, picked up my briefcase, walked back up to him, handed him my keys and radio, and told him, "I told you when you interviewed me and asked me about commitment, 'I will stand by you and your company through almost anything and I can endure almost anything. But, I cannot tolerate ethical or legal violations or requests to do so. Integrity issues are the only thing that I can foresee that would ever cause us to part ways… and I hope that never happens.' Well, this is that time." And I walked out.

As enigmatic as trust, character, and integrity may sometimes seem to be, they are the heart and foundation of the leadership journey and of high-functioning teams. John C. Maxwell wrote, "Trust is the foundation of leadership. To build trust, a leader must exemplify these qualities: competence, connection, and character." As we will see in the following pages, the research supports Maxwell's contention. Without trust and integrity – our character, if you will – our ability to influence and lead is severely undermined.

Patrick Lencioni, author of the bestseller, *The Five Dysfunctions of a Team*, carries this effect of leaders to the entire team. He wrote, "Trust lies at the heart of a functioning, cohesive team. Without it, teamwork is all but impossible." Trust and integrity delineates being a *boss* from being a *leader*. When we nurture trust in our relationships and teams, we transform ourselves from simply being a boss into being a leader. So, what is trust, why is it so important, and how do I nurture it?

What is Trust?

"The willingness to be vulnerable" and "the willingness to take risk" have been at the heart of an integrative model of organizational trust in relationships and organizations for over 15 years. Eminent trust researchers from Purdue University, the University of Akron, and the

When we nurture trust in our relationships and teams, we transform ourselves from simply being a boss into being a leader.

University of Notre Dame, developed a measurement of trust based on the ideas of vulnerability and risk-taking in relationships that has three important attributes: ability, benevolence, and integrity. Since its original publication, the model and its three attributes have appeared consistently in the literature and the original study has been cited over one thousand times.

Ability. The first attribute of trust is ability. When evaluating trust in a leader, ability is more than simply the capacity to get a job done. Rather, the kind of ability related to trust is the perception by the follower that the leader will use their discretion and have access to resources that enhance the leader's ability to have an influence on the follower and their work life. In other words, those we lead want to know "What can you do for me *and* will you do it?" In the literature, this attribute is "domain specific." For example, a leader might have the ability to facilitate solving an IT problem an employee has by making a call to the IT supervisor and encouraging her to work on their employee's problem (inter-departmental domain). However, that same leader has little influence adding new personnel to help overworked employees because of a corporate "hiring freeze" that has been initiated company-wide (corporate hiring domain). And again, that same leader might have some, but limited impact, on pay increases as corporate HR has given an upper limit to merit increases (pay raise domain).

Benevolence. The second attribute of trust is benevolence and it is central to the definition of trust. The word *benevolence* comes from combining the Latin *bene-* meaning *good* with *vol* meaning *will*; hence, goodwill. Benevolence is the goodwill and positive personal orientation of the leader toward the other. But there's a catch. It is the *perception* of the other – the team member, the partner, the direct

What can you do for me *and* will you do it?

report – of a leader's benevolence. It's how confident they are that we will behave in positive ways toward them. It's their perception of the magic ratio when applied to our goodwill. Does your benevolent behavior regularly meet or exceed the minimum 3:1 or even 5:1 ratio *from their perspective*? Benevolence is a companion to our earlier discussion on love. When those we lead sense and expect that we will go out of our way on their behalf, we nurture trust. Research shows that leaders who show consideration towards followers have higher levels of follower trust than those who did not.

Benevolence – love if you will – and trust aren't just idealistic, 'head in the clouds' thinking.

Benevolence – love if you will – and trust aren't just idealistic, 'head in the clouds' thinking. Take for example; two studies conducted three years apart at the same eight restaurants within a corporation reported in the *Strategic Management Journal*. The researchers compared the trust levels of over 750 employees in their general manager to sales, profit, and turnover. Restaurants that had higher employee trust in their general manager had higher sales and profit and lower turnover. The experience of the research and analysis led the investigators to conclude, "Thus, a GM who can garner higher trust from the firm's workforce gains a competitive advantage over rival firms. A manager can increase his/her perceived trustworthiness via behaviors and tactics which improve the workforce's perceptions of the three trustworthiness factors [ability, benevolence, and integrity]."

Integrity. The final attribute of trust is integrity. The word *integrity* comes from mathematics *integer* and originates from the Latin for *untouched* and *whole*, or in other words, pure and holy. The spiritual or

We chose to be leaders. By doing that, everything changed and we're now held to a higher level of accountability and integrity than ever before.

religious connections of integrity are apparent when understood from the more venerable roots of the word. Integrity as being pure and holy seems like a high aspiration. Are we now to conjure that to be a leader one must aspire to be a saint or sage? And yet, the definition of *saint* is "a person of great holiness, virtue, or benevolence" and the second attribute of trust mentioned above is benevolence. In addition, integrity and virtue are similar constructs. Philosophers even argue that integrity is itself a virtue, albeit a complex one.

We chose to be leaders. By doing that, everything changed and we're now held to a higher level of accountability and integrity than ever before. Regardless of what's written in our ethics code, code of conduct, compliance procedures, or taught in our trainings, what we do – whether right or wrong – is looked to and magnified by those around us as guidance for *their* behavior in our organizations. Are we saints or sages? Maybe, maybe not. But shouldn't we aspire to be? Religious and spiritual traditions, great thinkers on leadership, and the most current research, all point to the conclusion that being the most capable, authentic, virtuous, and most benevolent or loving person, also makes us the best leader.

Integrity: The Foundation of Trust

If trust is the foundation of leadership, then integrity is the foundation of trust. Unfortunately, many of us, maybe most of us, are not even close to being saints or sages – at least not yet. The plethora of examples of scandals and ethical violations in business, government, sports, education, and even religious organizations are far too common. It could be argued that the lack of integrity in modern leaders has severely eroded trust and fueled cynicism and suspicions of leaders in general.

Take for example what researchers from the University of Bergen in Norway uncovered. They revealed some surprising news about the prevalence of "destructive leadership." Destructive leadership is the "systematic and repeated behavior by a leader, supervisor, or manager that violates the legitimate interest of the organization by undermining and/or sabotaging the organization's goals, tasks, resources, and effectiveness and/or the motivation, wellbeing, or job satisfaction of subordinates." They analyzed over 2,500 employees' responses to questionnaires about their work and their leaders. As many as sixty-one percent of them reported that their immediate superiors had shown some kind of *consistent* and *frequent* destructive leadership during the last six months! Only forty percent of them reported no exposure whatsoever to such destructive leadership behavior.

As many as sixty-one percent of employees reported that their immediate superiors had shown some kind of *consistent* and *frequent* destructive leadership during the last six months!

Destructive leadership and its opposite, constructive leadership, are defined along two continuums. The first axis or dimension, how leaders treat subordinates, runs from the extreme of being anti-subordinate or abusive of direct reports to being pro-subordinate or supportive of their direct reports. Pro-subordinate behavior and constructive leadership are very much like our discussions on love, benevolence, and fostering employee engagement. For example, leaders strong in pro-subordinate behavior foster the motivation, well-being, and job satisfaction of subordinates. Anti-subordinate behavior is just the opposite. Leaders who display anti-subordinate behavior undermine or sabotage the motivation, well-being, or job satisfaction of subordinates, which could even include harassment, mistreatment, and abuse.

The second axis, how leaders support the organization, runs from one extreme of anti-organizational behavior to the other, pro-organizational behavior. Anti-organizational behavior violates the legitimate interest of the organization by working in opposition to the organization's goals, values, and optimal use of resources. These leaders may actually steal from the organization, sabotage tasks and goals, or even get involved in corruption. On the other end of this continuum, leaders strong in pro-organizational behavior actively work toward fulfilling the organization's goals, set clear objectives, make or support strategic decisions, and implement legitimate organizational change. The research supports the model's ensuing five leadership types:

- **The Constructive Leader.** Also known as transactional, transformational, charismatic, or empowering leadership, the constructive leader actively promotes both subordinates and the organization. It would include the attributes of the New Millennial Leader as described in Chapter 5. This leader epitomizes the good qualities and behaviors that inspire and encourage others *and* achieves results.
- **The Tyrannical Leader** (actively destructive). The tyrannical leader supports the organization's goals and tasks, but obtains her results at the expense of her subordinates. While the

tyrannical leader's superiors may see them as strong in task completion, their subordinates view this leader as abusive, manipulative, or even as a bully. It is important to note that any early gains made by this leader in task completion, diminish and eventually disappear over time.

- **The Derailed Leader** (actively destructive). The derailed leader is both anti-organizational and anti-subordinate. Such leaders may bully, humiliate, manipulate, or deceive their subordinates while simultaneously undermining the organization through absenteeism, fraud, or outright theft of resources. Derailed leaders may also use their charismatic qualities for their own narcissistic, personal gain while turning away from what is good for both their subordinates and the organization.
- **The Supportive-Disloyal Leader** (actively destructive). While this leader supports her subordinates, maybe even giving them benefits that they aren't entitled to or deserve, she may steal time, materials, and/or financial resources from the company and encourages unethical behavior and anti-organizational sentiment and behavior in her team. Supportive-disloyal destructive leadership behavior ranked #2 in prevalence of exposure as reported by employees in the study and may be under-reported because leaders may hide their anti-organizational behavior from their subordinates.
- **The Laissez-Faire Leader** (passively destructive). Laissez-faire leadership has also been called avoidant or passive leadership and could more accurately be described as a lack of leadership. This leader avoids decision-making, shows little

> concern for goal attainment, and seldom involve themselves with their subordinates, even when it's necessary. Interestingly, this type of destructive leadership behavior ranked #1 in prevalence of exposure as reported by employees in the study.

The researchers in this Norwegian study concluded in a 2009 article published in the *British Journal of Management*, "Destructive leadership is very common… [It] is not a low base-rate phenomenon, but something that most subordinates will probably experience during their working life."

In her book, *The Allure of Toxic Leaders*, Jean Lipman-Blumen, professor of public policy and organizational behavior at Claremont Graduate University in California, describes toxic leaders as "leaders who act without integrity by dissembling and engaging in various other dishonorable behaviors," including behaviors such as "corruption, hypocrisy, sabotage and manipulation, as well as other assorted unethical, illegal, and criminal acts." She concludes that destructive leadership has an uncanny ability to thrive even after its destructiveness has become apparent to nearly everyone. These toxic or destructive leaders are allowed and even encouraged to do so by their followers. You see, people turn to leaders to keep them safe, to give meaning to their lives, and to help maintain the illusion that life is manageable and under someone's control. But the price for this illusion with a toxic leader may be a loss of freedom and authentic experience.

A 2007 Florida State University study published in *Leadership Quarterly* revealed that forty percent of employees surveyed report working for a lousy or abusive boss. Their findings indicate that when people quit their job, most of the time they are leaving their boss, not their job. Thirty-nine percent of employees reported that their supervisor failed to keep promises, twenty-seven percent noted that their supervisor made negative comments about them to other employees or managers, twenty-four percent reported that their supervisor invaded their privacy, and twenty-three percent indicated that their supervisor blames others to cover up their own mistakes or to minimize embarrassment. This study and reports from Gallup highlighted in the bestseller, *First Break All the Rules: What the World's Greatest Managers Do Differently*, have popularized the saying: *People don't quit jobs, they quit bad bosses*.

It was tempting to add here a litany of recent scandals and ethical violations that seem to be constantly in the news and to even to add a few personal stories about destructive or toxic leaders from my own experiences. However, it should already be quite apparent that the experiences of most of those that we lead probably have a bad taste in their mouth when it comes to issues of their past leaders' trust and integrity. We leaders have a 'long row to hoe' when it comes to integrity and trust with those we lead, whether we deserve it or not.

Fairness. Fairness is an oft-cited element of integrity. Conventional wisdom may tell us that fairness means treating everyone the same and to follow the golden rule, "Do unto others as you would have done unto you." However, great leaders know that fairness does *not* mean treating everyone the same or necessarily treating others the way you want to be treated. Fairness is also about

Great leaders know that fairness does *not* mean treating everyone the same or necessarily treating others the way you want to be treated. Fairness is also about being just.

being just. Don't get me wrong, the Golden Rule is a great place to start when understanding and developing empathy and I encourage it often. As we mature in this knowledge and ability, however, we can learn from what Bryan K. Williams calls the "Platinum Rule" and the "Double-Platinum Rule" when talking about customer service. In our role as leaders, we can add his lessons into our leadership repertoire on fairness, integrity, and trust.

The Platinum Rule states "Treat others the way *they* want to be treated." If I exclusively follow the Golden Rule then, the way *I* want to be treated might offend or be inappropriate to someone else. As leaders, we must listen to and learn the individual nuances that motivate each member of our team. That way, we can customize our responses, rewards, and even punishments. For example, when I first started working as a training specialist in the corporate world, I often finished projects, reports, and newsletters late on Friday afternoons. Applying the Golden Rule, I thought our team would appreciate getting these things as soon as I was finished with them – until someone on the team privately approached me. "Our Inboxes are already plum full by the end of the week and then right before we close up, you send these things and they cause our Inboxes to reach their maximum limit. We can't send or receive a thing until we take care of your email first." When *I* thought they wanted and needed these things, was not when *they* wanted and needed them – and the weekend wouldn't make much difference with most of the stuff, anyway. I applied the Platinum rule and began waiting until the following Monday or later to send them these things. I am treating them the way *they* want to be treated.

The Double-Platinum rule states "Treat others the way they don't even know they want to be treated." As leaders, we may have information, tools, and guidance that those we lead just aren't aware exists. For example, a new manager needed to know the top clients who sent their patients to one of our sites for service. Discussions ensued among the managers about possible ways to find this out, including using the famous marketing and analytic company Buxton, the company we were using and companies like Starbucks use to help decide where to place new stores or facilities. I told her about a feature in one of our very own internal programs that could get her the top 10 clients using that facility in just a few minutes, that I would be happy to run it for her, and it would be free! She didn't even know this was available. She was thankful. There are endless opportunities for using the Double-Platinum Rule with those around us and those we lead. Fairness isn't about treating everyone the same. It's about having the consideration to know each individual member of the team; the situations they are involved in, what makes them 'tick,' what motivates them, their strengths and weaknesses, what their needs are, and what inspires and rewards them. Then, and only then, can a customized 'fairness' be employed. Fairness is doing the right thing for the right person in the right situation; not doing the same thing for all people in all situations.

Treat others the way they don't even know they want to be treated.

Ethical Leadership

While the dual-part definition of trust, 'the willingness to be vulnerable" and "the willingness to take risk," are both frequently cited and well-supported, other evidence that can affect our understanding of the trust trek and leadership does exist. A new leadership theory based in empirical social science, *ethical leadership*, makes ethics its central component. Researchers from Pennsylvania State University indicate that ethical leadership consists of two parts: the moral person and the moral manager.

- *The moral person*, which consists of: 1) Personal attributes such as honesty, integrity, and trustworthiness; 2) Ethical behavior such as concern for others, openness, and personal morality; and, 3) Ethical decision-making that is value-based and fair.
- *The moral manager* or the leader who fosters a culture and climate of ethical behavior in subordinates and work teams not only by serving as a role model, but by actively shaping and influencing subordinates' ethics through communicating an "ethics message," and holding people accountable.

Thus, the ethical leader not only possesses and demonstrates positive ethical qualities; she also makes ethics an explicit part of her leadership agenda and holds team members accountable for ethical behavior. In other words, not only do they have a reputation that they are an ethical, moral person; they have a reputation for setting ethical expectations and creating an ethical culture through their role as leaders, too. Brown and Trevino emphasize that ethical leadership is about *reputation*. Our behavior as ethical leaders must stand out in order for others to perceive our reputation as being truly ethical.

Simply having a code of ethics or a code of conduct does not have a strong influence on employees' ethical behavior – leaders do.

Simply having a code of ethics or a code of conduct does not have a strong influence on employees' ethical behavior – leaders do. When we decided to become leaders, we decided to become role models, whether consciously or not. So here is a moment of truth: If you are in any type of leadership position, which almost everyone is in some capacity or other, you are a role model. Social learning theory has well-established that people are influenced and learn from others – and those we emulate, like significant others, parents, celebrities, and leaders have the most influence of all. You are a light to the world. Leaders who demonstrate ethical behaviors provide examples for others to pattern. Similarly, leaders who demonstrate the opposite, unethical behaviors, are more likely to have employees or team members or partners who also engage in unethical activity.

So here is a moment of truth: If you are in any type of leadership position, which almost everyone is in some capacity or other, you are a role model.

Social exchange theory explains that when you do something beneficial for me, I will feel an obligation to reciprocate that action to you or someone else. When we engender trust, goodwill, integrity, and honesty, and treat people with fairness, they learn that they can count on us and want to return those favors – not just to us, but to others, as well. They are more likely to respond in ways that benefit the entire team and refrain from destructive actions.

Trying to determine if and how ethical leadership flows through an organization and affects employee behavior, researchers from the University of Central Florida, Southern Methodist University, and the University of Washington conducted a comprehensive study based on the ethical leadership model. They assessed over one thousand employees and supervisors from one hundred and sixty organizations. They discovered a cascading effect – a trickle down model – flowing from senior leadership and top management through supervisors down to employees.

All leadership in the organization influenced employees' ethical and organizational citizenship behavior (OCB) – for good or bad. Unethical leaders fostered unethical or deviant behavior and poor OCB. Ethical leaders, on the other hand, fostered ethical behavior and positive OCB with employees. As suspected, leaders not only serve as ethical role models; their use of rewards and punishments also reinforce ethical behavior and OCB. Employees learn from their leaders and their environment which ethical behavior is, and is not, expected. They also learn to reciprocate obligations because of the fair, ethical treatment from those leaders. What you do on the trust trek affects those you lead, your organization's culture, and beyond.

How to Nurture Integrity and Trust

An interesting finding of the ethical leadership study cited above was that it was only supervisors who had a direct effect on employees' ethical behavior and OCB. Top management and senior executives' influence was made indirectly *through* the supervisors. Supervisors look to higher management for ethical behavioral expectations and message cues within the organization. Through role modeling and interactions, they become an extension of top management. We can glean from the analysis that those at the top bear the important responsibility of making sure that their good ethical intentions do in fact trickle down throughout the organization. That can be accomplished through several methods.

Four Methods Top Management Can Employ to Foster Integrity

- Model ethical behavior – "walk the talk."
- Create, interpret, and enforce ethical policies
- Include assessments of integrity in the hiring process of management at all levels.

- Provide leadership-specific ethics training to both top management and supervisors (not just employees).

Supervisors interact with employees almost every day. They interpret and enforce ethical guidelines directly with employees. Therefore, supervisors influence of ethical leadership as the extension of senior leadership, takes on a different shape.

Seven Methods Supervisors Can Employ to Foster Integrity

- Model ethical behavior – "walk the talk."
- Use appropriate and early reinforcement for ethical and unethical behavior to establish norms or a positive ethical culture.
- Regularly and consistently use formal and informal rewards systems.
- Coach employees through ambiguous situations.
- Allow and encourage conversations about both the positive and negative consequences of others behaviors (within legal and policy privacy guidelines).
- Show concern for others and help others.
- Communicate the importance of helping each other for the good of the group.

Regular Contemplation. Marci Shimoff discovered that one of the guiding principles of the happiest people is "What you appreciate, appreciates." Buddha is often quoted to have said, "We are shaped by our thoughts. We become what we think." In order to nurture integrity and trust we must guard what we think and what we appreciate. We, therefore, regularly contemplate and aspire to adhere to a set of guiding principles. We discussed contemplation and guiding principles and mission statements in Chapter 4, GPS for Leaders.

Regularly contemplating and putting our guiding principles into action helps to create virtue and integrity. This practice creates consistency, restraint, discipline, and goodness. We must sometimes suspend what we initially think or desire for a higher cause and purpose. At first, our virtue and integrity are not so readily apparent to those around us and those we lead. It is something that they come to learn about us over time – the all-important reputation that Brown and Trevino talk about. It's like making regular, routine deposits into an integrity bank account that we can then later draw on when faced with ethical dilemmas and challenges. We come to know about ourselves that we will do the right thing and others come to rely on us to do the right thing, too. When that happens consistently over time, it leads to trust and influence; and that leads to the awareness that we can accomplish anything. The 59th verse of the Tao Te Ching captures this so beautifully:

> Restraint begins with giving up one's own ideas. This depends on virtue gathered in the past. If there is a good store of virtue, then nothing is impossible. If nothing is impossible, then there are no limits. If a man knows no limits, he is fit to lead.

So, we first begin to nurture trust and integrity by regularly contemplating our guiding principles.

Don't Be a Hypocrite. One of the quickest ways to destroy trust is to empty that store of virtue or bank account of integrity by even appearing hypocritical. When followers even think – whether accurate or not – that a leader has one set of rules for them and another for themselves, trust is lost. The leader becomes only a boss – an authority figure – and has lost his or her ability to influence, and therefore, his or her ability to lead.

For a simple example, let me tell you a short and simple story about a manager named 'Bill,' who faced something along these lines. Bill called in one of his supervisors, 'Jane,' to talk to her about email etiquette. Bill gave Jane some honest and careful coaching about corporate email branding and signature requirements, what he expected to be and not to be copied on, and other email etiquette rules. He cautioned Jane to be more sensitive to office politics and his position. Jane's pride was a little damaged, because she took great pride in her work and was very conscientious. However, Jane took the coaching very well and began to change her emails since she wanted to please Bill and she looked up to him.

At the time of the coaching, they had an important site audit coming up in a couple of weeks that was already on their calendar that would last a couple of days. A few days after the coaching meeting, Bill sent Jane an email informing her of an important strategic meeting that had been scheduled the first day of the audit and that he wouldn't be there until day two. When the first day of the audit rolled around, Jane was surprised to see her manager, Bill at the site. "I thought you had an important out of town meeting today?" she asked. "Oh yeah, that got cancelled," he said in passing and walked off to the audit. When Jane came to me, she was indignant, "How can he sit there and criticize my emails and 'office politics' when he can't even call or send an email informing me that his meeting was cancelled and that he'd be here for the audit? What a hypocrite!" She had lost a little faith and trust in her boss.

One of the quickest ways to destroy trust is to empty that store of virtue or bank account of integrity by even appearing hypocritical.

In the larger context of their work, it was a small thing and Bill was probably very busy and didn't even give it much thought. However, it doesn't have to be a man's life at stake, as it was in the situation with the owner of the EMS company I worked for, in order for integrity and trust to be damaged or even destroyed. As my story turns out, Bill had a pretty hefty 'integrity bank account' with Jane and the event didn't completely empty it. However, it took some time for Bill to replenish it and for Jane to feel a deeper level of trust again. Avoid being a hypocrite by being a consistent ethical role model.

Deliver on Your Promises. Failing to deliver on a promise is one of the most common ways integrity and trust are depreciated. For example, Greg is a supervisor who is sometimes late for his one-on-ones with his frontline employees or cancels them completely. He forgets to return telephone calls and emails from time to time, has trouble confronting employees and clients with issues that come up, and promises things that he can't deliver just to please people or avoid painful conversations. He often explains these things away saying that he "just got too busy" or "was overwhelmed with so many other issues." Those we lead *want* to trust us. People will forgive the occasional mistake or oversight, especially when you apologize. "But," as John Maxwell said in *Leadership 101*, "they won't trust someone who has slips in character." Consistently deliver on your promises and if you can't, apologize and make sure you communicate that to the person as early as possible. When you are a good person and fulfill your obligations, you develop renown and true power.

Failing to deliver on a promise is one of the most common ways integrity and trust are depreciated.

Take the Trust Trek. Look for ways to consistently demonstrate your ability, benevolence, and integrity. This builds trust. For example, while dealing with the effects of the Great Recession, our company would enforce intermittent hiring and supply-ordering freezes. It seemed like no one could predict when they would hit. After ordering some routine training supplies, I was informed by the supply supervisor that we were once again under a supply-ordering freeze. I buzzed off a quick email to my boss letting her know that I wouldn't have some of the routine supplies I needed for a training coming up in a few days. By that afternoon, the comptroller had received an appeal from my boss and he granted a special approval for the order. She had the ability to influence the comptroller and my world. It may seem like a small thing, but it's just that kind of thing that demonstrates not only that she has the ability to help; but that she cares enough to do so.

Our benevolence towards those we lead demonstrates care. When done again and again over time, this builds trust. People feel obligated and want to return the favor.

The Message. Communicating both positive and negative stories – and their consequences – about ethical and integrity issues in your organization helps cultivate an awareness of integrity issues and the organization's culture. It is the leader's responsibility to transmit culture and people learn vicariously through others. Sharing stories without divulging privacy, let's people know what is and what is not expected and what the consequences could be. The wording can make a difference. For example, there is a difference between "the technician signed the document for the patient" versus "the technician forged the patient's signature on the document." Use language that emphasizes the ethical nature of the story. Also, emphasize the 'why' and importance of ethical behavior. Do this often. Employees so often hear messages about the bottom line and other business metrics that can easily drown-out important ethical messages. Clear, frequent, and consistent messages about what is and isn't expected can go miles to reinforcing ethical behavior and creating an ethical culture. Ethics and trust must be a priority, too.

Use rewards and punishment. Incorporate ethics into evaluations and everyday coaching and rewards. Create rituals and celebrations around exemplary behavior. Most importantly, don't reward or tolerate unethical behavior. Discipline of unethical behavior should be swift and fair – at every level of the organization. Don't take the easy way out after disciplining by labeling someone as a 'bad apple,' either. Take responsibility as a leader and investigate and determine how leadership and culture may have contributed to the incident, too. Then, make necessary changes to prevent further episodes.

Building integrity and trust in relationships and organizations builds a sense of security, confidence, hope, and positiveness – all indispensible characteristics of healthy relationships and successful employees and leaders.

Kohlberg's Theory of Moral Development

One of the most provocative and well-known theories of moral development was engineered by psychologist Lawrence Kohlberg who served as a professor at both the University of Chicago and Harvard University. After twenty years of using a unique interviewing technique with children, he found that people develop sequentially through moral stages with each stage becoming more complex, sophisticated, and independent. He presented stories in which the characters had to face a moral dilemma. Depending on how someone answered a series of questions about the story and its dilemma, determined how advanced the individual's moral development was. The six stages are divided into three higher-order levels:

Stages of Kohlberg's Theory of Moral Development

Level 1: Preconventional Reasoning

Stage 1

Stage 2

Level 2: Conventional Reasoning

Stage 3

Stage 4

Level 3: Postconventional Reasoning

Stage 5

Stage 6

Level 1: Preconventional Reasoning. The lowest level is characterized by responses to external rewards and punishment. The individual has no internalized moral values or guiding principles. In stage 1, moral thinking is tied to punishment. Children obey their parents because they are told to. As moral development continues, what is right involves being nice to others so that they'll be nice in return (stage 2) – a *quid pro quo* basis of what is right and wrong.

Level 2: Conventional Reasoning. At this stage of moral development, the standards of parents and society are internalized. In stage 3, individuals conform to their familial or parental norms seeking to be a "good boy" or "good girl." When this conformity begins to broaden to organizations and the larger society, the value of rules and laws are understood, valued, and internalized (stage 4). Still, at this level, moral reasoning comes from outside the self because it's good for the group or good for society.

Level 3: Postconventional Reasoning. At the highest level of moral development, morality is completely internalized with a personal moral code or guiding principles and is not based on other's external standards. The individual understands that values, rights, and principles undergird or can even transcend the rules or law. The individual can now use this moral code or guiding principles to evaluate the validity of rules and laws (stage 5). At the final and highest level of Kohlberg's moral development hierarchy, stage 6, the individual has developed a moral code or guiding principles based on universal human rights. When faced with a conflict between one's conscience and the law, the individual at this level will follow their conscience, even though it might put them at personal risk.

In a 2004 article in the *Academy of Management Executive*, Linda Trevino and Michael Brown of Pennsylvania State University report that less than twenty percent of adults ever reach the principled and autonomous postconventional level. What does that mean to us as leaders? It means that the vast majority of those we lead are still looking outside of themselves for answers to ethical dilemmas. They need to know the rules and laws and may turn to significant others, peers, and leaders for guidance. Most people need sound, ethical leaders for continued guidance. As Eric Harvey and Al Lucia from *Walk the Talk* famously said, "People hear what we say but they see what we do. And seeing is believing."

Leadership Travel Tips Chapter 8: The Trust Trek

- Trust, character, and integrity are the heart and foundation of the leadership journey and of high-functioning teams.
- Higher employee/follower trust in their leader is correlated to higher sales and profit and lower turnover.
- Use the three attributes of trust: ability, benevolence, and integrity.
- If trust is the foundation of leadership, then integrity is the foundation of trust.
- Remember, destructive leadership is very common. Most subordinates will probably experience destructive leadership during their working life.
- Use the Golden Rule, the Platinum Rule, and the Double-Platinum Rule to foster fairness with those you lead.
- It is not enough to be an ethical, moral person. You must develop a reputation for setting ethical expectations and creating an ethical culture, too.
- If you're in top management, use the Four Methods Top Management Can Employ to Foster Integrity.
- If you're a supervisor, use the Seven Methods Supervisors Can Employ to Foster Integrity.
- Remember, both methods start with "walking the talk."
- Regularly contemplating and putting our guiding principles into action helps to create virtue and integrity.
- Avoid being a hypocrite by being a consistent ethical role model.
- Consistently deliver on your promises. It is only when you are a good person and fulfill your obligations that you develop renown and true power.
- Use benevolence to engender in people feelings of obligation to return the favors.
- Use stories. It is the leader's responsibility to transmit culture. Clear, frequent, and consistent messages about what is and isn't expected engender an ethical culture. Ethics and trust must be a priority, just as other metrics are.
- Less than 20% of adults ever reach a principled and autonomous level of moral development. Most of those you lead need you to be a sound, ethical leader and look to you as a role model and for guidance.

CHAPTER 9

You Are Here

Remember then: there is only one time that is important – Now! It is the most important time because it is the only time when we have any power.
~ Leo Tolstoy ~

Remember the movie *Back to the Future*? Michael J. Fox got into a high-tech DeLorean and accidentally found himself in the 1950s and had to find a way to get back to the future. As much as we may sometimes want, it's impossible to get in our cars and take a drive down the highway and exit the present and drive into the past or the future – it's impossible to live anywhere but in the present moment. However, walk through any office or school and ask someone how they're doing and you'll hear things like:

"I just gotta get through this _____ [week, day, meeting, class....]"
"Only three more days 'til the weekend!"
"Thank God it's Friday! Almost the weekend!"

The renowned spiritual teacher and bestselling author, Eckhart Tolle, captures this attitude beautifully in his beautiful book, *The Power of Now*, "Most people treat the present moment as if it were an obstacle that they need to overcome. Since the present moment is Life itself, it is an

When our primary time orientation is anywhere other than the present moment, we are likely to miss the dangers – and the joys – on the journey right in front and all around us.

insane way to live." If we, or those we lead, are living for some future weekend Monday through Friday while *being* in Monday through Friday, what happens to Monday through Friday while our minds are on Saturday and Sunday? The traditional five workdays of a week represent about seventy percent of the week. Are we partially sacrificing the majority of our lives with lamentation and anticipation for the other thirty percent? Is our 'now' an obstacle?

And yet, as Leo Tolstoy observes in our opening quote, it is the only time we truly have any power. We do not have power in either the past or future. What we do *now* may affect the future, but the power, the influence, is in the present. We are human *beings*, here and now. What is the state of that *being*? Is it haunted by the past eating up the present moment energy and power with regret, guilt, or sadness? Or, is our state of being filled with worry, anxiety, or constant anticipation of the future or some future event?

Living in the present moment or as others have called it, 'being in the now,' is not saying that there isn't inherent value from learning lessons from the past or making practical plans and strategies for the future. These *are* healthy for us individually, for our families, for our work and business, and the larger society and world.

However, when our focus, influence, or state of being is overwhelmingly in the past or toward the future, we can lose sight of the moment and our power is reduced. The now becomes an obstacle. When our primary time orientation is anywhere other than the present moment, we are likely to miss the dangers – and the joys – on the journey right in front and all around us. On our leadership journey, it is important to look at our leadership GPS (our Life Mission Statement) from time to time and find the spot that says, "You Are Here."

Past-Orientation

The person with a past orientation is like someone trying to drive a car forward while only looking in the rearview mirror. In a car, this is dangerous. In life and leadership, it is self-defeating, ineffective, and energy-draining, not only to ourselves, but to those around us and to those we lead. We so often define and learn about ourselves by our past – what we've done and accomplished or not accomplished, who we've loved and lost, where we've been, etc. There's absolutely nothing wrong with that. Ruminating on the past, however, can breed feelings of vindictiveness, regret, self-pity, guilt, sorrow, or even anguish. Here are some examples of the inner mantras of those who have a past-orientation:

"If I (he, she, they) would have…"

"I (he, she, they) should have…"

"I (he, she, they) could have…"

It's difficult to forgive – whether it's forgiving ourselves or someone else – while living in the past. The opportunity for the offender to grow beyond their transgression and for healing to occur is blocked as long as we hold our past hurt and grudges ever in front of us. Instead of providing lessons learned, the past becomes a haunting obsession that blocks our ability to be fully present in the moment and move effectively forward. Remember this: No amount of present guilt, regret, anger, or sorrow will *ever* change something that has *already* taken place! Current negative thoughts, ruminations, and emotions will not change history.

No amount of present guilt, regret, anger, or sorrow will *ever* change something that has *already* taken place!

Period. They simply consume energy in the present. Differentiate that from the energy of contemplating and learning from your mistakes and successes. That *is* productive.

Another way that past orientation manifests is what Wayne Dyer, PhD calls self-defeating "I'ms" in *Your Erroneous Zones*. He said that self-defeating "I am" statements are founded in four neurotic sentences. You've probably heard them before and maybe even said them yourself:

"That's just me."
"I've always been that way."
"I can't help it."
"It's just my nature."

In organizations, you hear this past-oriented labeling manifested with another such phrase: "We've always done it that way." It reminds me of the story of Grandma's Cooking Secret. A young bride is trying to cook her first ham for her husband. He watches her cut off both ends of the ham before putting it in the oven. "Why'd you cut off both ends?" he asked. "That's the way mother always did it," she replied. Not fully understanding this family cooking secret, they decide to call up mother and find out the answer. "That's the way my mother always did it," she replied. With curiosity eating them up, they decide to make a three-way conference call to grandmother. "Grandmother, why did you always cut the ends off a ham before putting it in the oven?" they asked. Grandmother promptly replied, "That's the only way it would fit into my small roasting pan!" When we are doing something simply because that's the "way it's always been done" or the way "grandmother did it," we risk missing the *whys* of our rituals, procedures, feelings, and thought patterns.

Statements like "I've always been that way" are rooted in – and attempt to lock you into – the past. Most of this type of thinking and behaviors were probably ingrained during childhood and reinforced as we grew up. When we say them, we are trying to avoid growth and change – for whatever reason. Dr. Dyer adeptly points out the important unstated implication connected to each of these past-oriented statements is just that: "And I intend to continue being the way I've (we've) always been." This is self-defeating because the statements, and the intention behind them, are trying to slam the door shut to present energy, circumstances, growth, and change.

These statements are then translated into repetitive excuses and beliefs or, what Dr. Dyer calls, "I'ms." Here are a few examples:

"I'm poor at math, tennis, remembering names, etc."

"I'm shy, nervous, jealous, clumsy, etc."

"I'm ugly, fat, sloppy, too tall, too short, etc."

Each of these statements creates a vicious cycle of non-change, immobilization, and self-defeating behaviors that result in deep-rooted beliefs about ourselves and the world.

In *The Biology of Belief*, Bruce Lipton, PhD wrote about the effects of placebos and the placebo effect (the power of positive beliefs) and nocebos and the nocebo effect (the power of negative beliefs) on our genes, health, and wellbeing. Our culture has led many of us to believe that our genes control who we are and that we are simply victims of our heredity – some kind of 'generational curse.' "That's my nature." "I get it from my father (or mother, uncle, grandfather, etc.)."

In his book, he lays out a very solid case demonstrating that there is something else controlling our genes –epigenetics. It turns out that it is the environment and our perception of the environment – our beliefs – that

Cells, as it turns out, are programmable. It is not necessarily our nature, but what we believe and what we choose in our environment that determines how nature will express or manifest.

actually change and influence the expression or readout of our DNA. You see, DNA is not programmed to turn out only one type of outcome. It's not a final blueprint, but one dependent upon the environment and the environment of our mind or what some call our *state of being*. There are as many as 30,000 possible variations from the blueprint. Cells, as it turns out, are programmable. It is not necessarily our nature (genes, DNA, heredity), but what we believe and what we choose in our environment that determines *how* nature (genes, DNA, heredity) will express or manifest. We can no longer use the excuse "It's my nature." We have a choice. Dr. Lipton said, "Our positive and negative beliefs not only impact our health but also every aspect of our life."

For me, what some call "leaving the past behind" really means reframing and learning from the past so that I can let go of avoiding the *present* – the excuses – and the negative thoughts and emotions so that I can now take the risk to change and grow in the now.

I dove head first into a past orientation after my divorce. I went down what Dr. Gottman calls "the downward spiral." When I looked back over my marriage, I started to focus on all of things that had gone wrong: the fights, the days of not speaking to each other, and on and on. Soon, it seemed liked *everything* had gone wrong. I felt hurt and betrayed and kept images that reinforced that foremost in my mind. I couldn't help but feel like a cartoon character with a dark cloud following me overhead all the time. Poor me! As long as I was 'the victim,' I could elicit pity from others and I didn't have to take the risks of working on my current situation and myself. It also transferred responsibility away from myself. "It was all *her* fault!" I could think. When I did start to take responsibility for my part in the dissolution, now I could wallow in guilt and shame – all the while, staying rooted in a negative past orientation. This was not only affecting me, but everyone around me, including my children.

I remember one day feeling particularly dark; I really wanted to ruminate. I dug out the old family videos and started watching. To my surprise, instead of seeing hurt, pain, wrongdoings, or betrayal, I saw love, laughter, and joy. It suddenly dawned on me that no matter what happened and how I chose to look at it, it was the past. It was done. Over. None of my lamenting about it now, was going to change a thing. I began to focus on the joys, love, and lessons from my marriage and family and turn the memories into gratitude. Even though the realization was sudden, my inner world didn't change overnight. It was a process. When I chose to be grateful for my past – to see that both the joys and pain brought me *here* – then I seemed to magically return to the here and now. I was radically and forever changed. I encourage you to go back through Chapter 6, the Bridge of Gratitude, and implement the travel tips of gratitude that seem right for you.

Business organizations and leaders can get caught up in past orientations that can distort the present. I can't tell you how many meetings I've attended in which year over year comparisons and results are the focus of the presentation. They become more important than current processes, strategies, and culture or analysis of how we can learn from them or plan effectively for the future. It's comparing the more distant past of how we did Q1 last year with how we did in Q1 this year while *being* in Q2 this year. If, for example, the comparison is limited to a presentation of how Q1 results this year are so much greater than Q1 results last year, it can create a false sense of security and optimism. If the comparison is limited to a presentation of how terrible Q1 results are this year compared to Q1 results last year, it can create feelings of pessimism and leave teams without answers. Those simple comparisons say nothing about what is happening *now* or how we got *here* or where we're going from *here*. Meetings that simply compare distant past figures with recent, yet still past figures that we just call 'current,' are a symptom that your organization is suffering from a past orientation and are sapping present moment energy. On the other hand, if those comparisons serve as a starting point and then turn the focus of the meeting to variation, statistically significant differences, trends, probable causation, lessons learned, past, present, and future strategies, etc., then a full integration of past, present, and future is being employed to make *this moment* something of value.

Future-Orientation

"I am an old man and have known a great many troubles, but most of them never happened." This famous quote from Mark Twain tells us something about the future-oriented person. The person with a future orientation is like someone trying to drive a car forward while looking down at a roadmap trying to avoid those "many troubles," even though most of them will never even happen. "What if…" becomes the inner mantra of the future-oriented person. Variations on the theme of the past-oriented person changes for the future orientated person to:

"What if..."

"I (he, she, they) should..."

"I (he, she, they) could..."

These are examples of predominant thinking patterns that get people stuck. Instead of *doing* in the now, the future oriented person is constantly thinking and rethinking. They may even be thought of as procrastinators. This pattern can generate feelings of worry, anxiety, fear, or even panic. The future-oriented person spends a great deal of their present moments worrying about things that they have little control over. They fret over every possibility of failure or catastrophe – no matter how remote. Then, they play the worst scenarios over and over in their head. A self-creating anxiety cycle develops that can spin out of control.

This isn't a healthy development of a plan or strategy, but a worrying rumination about 'what-ifs' – worrying about all of the things that *could* go wrong and allowing that to disturb them, and often others, in the *now.* Careful planning is a present-moment activity that helps contribute to and enrich our future present moments. It helps us to be more effective. Worrying is a negative emotion that saps the energy out of the now and no matter how much worrying we do, it will not prevent or prepare us effectively for what is to come.

Culture and custom teach us that we are supposed to worry and be anxious. We are enculturated to worry about the economy, the war, our children, our health – just about everything. We worry to prove our love: "I love you so; of course I'm worried about you." We question others' worry-levels: "Aren't you worried about him?" And we worry so we don't have to move forward: "I'm so worried I can't even think." The list is endless. We are taught that worrying is expected and that it is the

The future-oriented person spends a great deal of their present moments worrying about things that they have little control over.

right thing to do. The future-oriented person often has difficulty tolerating uncertainty. They just can't stand that there are some things in life that we simply don't have the answers to right now. They may not have confidence in their ability to solve problems or deal appropriately with situations and people.

The Christian tradition has words of wisdom about worrying and the future-oriented person. Jesus of Nazareth is quoted as saying, "Look at the birds of the air; they neither sow nor reap nor gather into barns, and yet your heavenly Father keeps feeding them. Are you not worth much more than they? And who of you by worrying and being anxious can add one unit of measure (cubit) to his stature or to the span of his life?" (Matthew 6:26-27). Buddha knew these secrets, too. He said, "The secret of health for both mind and body is not to mourn for the past, worry about the future, or anticipate troubles, but to live in the present moment wisely and earnestly."

Centuries later, research provides scientific evidence to support these spiritual, psychological, and philosophical insights. It is now well-accepted that approximately eighty percent of all diseases and illnesses are stress-related. Just as worry, fear, and stress are rampant in our culture, so too, are the stress-related diseases: coronary heart disease, cancer, hypertension, arthritis, back pain, headaches, ulcers, and the common cold, to name only a few. Although worry, anxiety, and stress are not the direct cause of these diseases, their influence weakens the body's physiological systems, thus rapidly advancing the disease process. Worry, anxiety, and stress do not add to

And who of you by worrying and being anxious can add one unit of measure to his stature or to the span of his life?

our lifespan. Rather, just the opposite; they weaken our health making us more vulnerable to disease. Worrying and ruminating about the 'what ifs' will not solve financial crises, war, prove your love, or enhance your health. A future-oriented focus that causes worrying, anxiety, and stress will eat up your time and energy now and solve absolutely nothing.

A future-oriented focus that causes worrying, anxiety, and stress will eat up your time and energy now and solve absolutely nothing.

Another characteristic of the future-oriented person is that they are constantly pursuing but never quite arriving. They live their lives always thinking that the next goal will finally bring them happiness. "Just as soon as I graduate, I can start living my life and be free." "Just as soon as I get that perfect job, I'll be happy." "Just as soon as I get married, everything will be great!" "Just as soon as I get that promotion, I can finally settle down, relax, and be happy." "When I can finally buy that new car, I'll know I'm successful and I'll be happy." "Just as soon as I get divorced, my life can finally go on." On and on the litanies go. Future-oriented people are in pursuit of happiness – they just never quite seem to get there.

I'm reminded of the words of President Abraham Lincoln, "The best thing about the future is that it comes one day at a time." There is only today, only this moment, only now. We've all heard the quote from the Roman poet, Horace, "Carpe diem" or "Seize the day." Well, the full line sheds a little more insight, "Carpe diem, quam minimum credula postero" or "Seize the day, putting as little trust as possible in the future."

Perfectionism and Catastrophic Thinking

A common irrational thought process that both the past and future-oriented person uses is called *catastrophizing* or *catastrophic thinking* (you'll also see this called *magnification*) – especially perfectionists, which many leaders are. We were introduced to this concept in Chapter 2 when discussing ANTs. Catastrophizing is an exaggerated and irrational way of thinking. It is believing that something was or is going to be far worse than it actually was or will be. A person overreacts and then let's their thoughts and feelings run away. Catastrophic thinking can proceed like a chain of events.

For example, let's say I tend to be a perfectionist – something that usually helps me in my tasks and career. I start to ruminate and catastrophize about a job task that I did last week. "What will my boss think? I could've analyzed that one section much better. I wish I could rewrite that other section. It wasn't the best I could've done. I should have had more time." I start to wonder if *all* my past work performance was subpar. The rethinking, regret, lamentations, and guilt builds. Next, I start thinking that not only was all of my work possibly subpar; *I* am a subpar and a failure. Next thing you know, *present* moment guilt and other negative feelings and thoughts that are consuming *present* energy about a *past* event begin to transform into predictions and feelings about my future performance. One 'what if' leads to another until that leads me to worry that my boss will call me into her office, I'll be fired, and become broke and homeless. Next thing you know, I'm depressed. Seem farfetched?

In a longitudinal study published in the *Journal of Counseling Psychology* in 2010, links between perfectionistic concerns, catastrophic thinking, and depression were well-established. The researchers concluded that perfectionists are prone to depressive symptoms because they engage in automatic, catastrophic thinking patterns and experience profound difficulty in accepting the past.

Living in the Now

It is our power – our ability to influence ourselves and others and to get things done – that often defines us as leaders. Leo Tolstoy reminds us of this in the opening quote of this chapter. Being fully present in *this* moment – living in the now – is the only time we really have any power. Living in the now allows us to live each moment in our lives more fully than if we live through some past memory or future fantasy. No matter how far the journey and how many steps we must take, the only step I have any influence over is the step I am taking *right now.* As Lao Tzu wrote over 2500 years ago, "A journey of a thousand miles begins with a single step." Although this quote is usually used as encouragement for someone who is about to begin a major project or life mission, when you read the full 64th verse of the Tao Te Ching, it is apparent that Lao Tzu is giving far more wisdom than just a kick-off spurt of encouragement. Later in the verse he said, "People usually fail when they are on the verge of success. So give as much care at the end as at the beginning, then there will be no failure." It is through attentiveness to *each and every* step, each *now*, from beginning to end, that we achieve success and a fully-lived life.

Eckart Tolle argues that time is an illusion we create in our minds. He wrote:

> What you perceive as precious is not time but the one point that is out of time: the Now. That is precious indeed. The more you are focused on time – past and future – the more you miss the Now, the most precious thing there is. Why is it the most precious thing? Firstly, because it is the only thing. It's all there is. The eternal present is the space within which your whole life unfolds, the one factor that remains constant. Life is now. There was never a time when your life was not now, nor will there ever be.

We are on a journey – a leadership journey. We spoke of how important it is to have a mission, guiding principles, goals, and objectives – to know where we're headed. And it is. But what Tolle is reminding us is that "the only thing that is ultimately real about your journey is the step that you are taking at this moment. That's all there ever is."

He explains that our life journey has an inner purpose and an outer purpose. The outer purpose is our personal mission, life goal, or calling and guiding principles. It can also include the mission, strategies, and goals and objectives of our work, business, or team. That journey may have a million steps. It is about *where* we're going and *what* we're doing to get there. The inner journey, however, is all about the moment and the single step we are taking now – it is about the *how.* It is about the quality of our consciousness or state of being right now, here and now. It's about the single step you are taking *now.*

Being fully present means that we can attend to the situation of the moment without letting regrets of the past or worries of the future interfere; our minds do not wander. It means we can be fully aware of our own needs and take care of ourselves more fully. It further means that at work and in our relationships, we can fully attend to our significant others, students, patients, clients, team members, and coworkers with laser attention and awareness – fully being in service. It is a consciousness of our state of being.

State of Being and the Great I AM

We are human *beings*, here and now. As such, we are constantly in a dynamic state of being or 'state of mind' – what psychologists call the *stream of consciousness.* What is your state of *being*? We usually talk about our state of being by saying, "I am…" and then fill in the blank with some descriptor of how we feel. One of the most mysterious passages in the Old Testament is known as the "Great I AM." It is the heart of the story of Moses and the burning bush. When Moses asks God's name, God replies, "I AM WHO I AM and WHAT I AM, and I WILL BE WHAT I WILL BE. You shall say this to the Israelites: I AM has sent me to you!" (Exodus 3:14). In ancient Israel, it was vital to know a name, especially of a god. It was believed that a name had power, vitality, and represented the innermost self or personality/identity. If you knew someone's name, you *really knew them.* It's because of this belief that the naming ceremonies for children were, therefore, very important events.

The special name of the Israelite God is *Yahweh*, which means, "He is." For thousands of years, these ancient biblical stories – or traditions – were handed down orally from generation to generation. When they were finally written down, the Hebrew was written without vowels. They only used consonants. So when the passage above where God gives his name was originally written down, it was written as *hyh* or with the vowels *'ehyeh* – "I am" – the first person. The third person singular, "He is" was originally written *yhwh* or with the vowels *Yahweh* – the special name of God. So *Yahweh* means, "He is" and *'ehyeh* means "I AM." The full statement that God made in the Hebrew is "'ehyeh 'asher 'ehyeh" or "I am who I am." Jesus of Nazareth later makes reference to this when he is quoted in the Gospel of John, "I assure you, most solemnly I tell you, before Abraham was born, I AM" (John 8:58).

In the late 1990s I attended training in yoga and Hindu breathing meditation techniques that were unveiled by the now world-famous Sri Sri Ravi Shankar, founder of the Art of Living Foundation. It was during these teachings that I learned about the ancient "OM" or "AUM" sound, familiar to many who practice meditation. It is considered the original name of God and by repeating the sound as a mantra during meditation, can achieve higher levels of consciousness and power of manifestation. Hindus believe that at the creation of the universe, the divine, all-encompassing consciousness took the form of the first and original vibration, manifesting as a powerful sound "AUM." Many also believe that it is the first and oldest sound of human beings – being that Sanskrit is one of the oldest human languages.

"AUM" from the ancient Sanskrit is pronounced in three sounds – A (*ahh*), U (*ooo*), and M (*mmm*) and the vibration of "AUM" symbolizes the manifestation of God in form – absolute reality without beginning or end. Each of the three sounds have meaning and significance. The A (*ahh*) sound is the sound of creation and form. I immediately recognized the similarities between the sound of "AUM" and the sounds from many religious and spiritual traditions for the name of the creating force or Being of the universe: Allah, Alpha and Omega, I AM, Buddha, God, Krishna, Ra, Tao, Yahweh, for example. The sound of "ahh" is common in all of these names. Dr. Wayne Dyer said about this sound, "…you begin to manifest without the use of the mind. It is done through the power of sound… It is the first sound of creation."

The U (*ooo*) sound is the sound and essence of the formless, like water or air, and is a sustaining or maintenance sound. Finally, the M (*mmm*) sound is neither form or formless – yet still exists – and is similar to the dark energy, Zero Point Field (ZPF), or Akashic field mentioned earlier. Some have said the M (*mmm*) sound is also the sound of completion, death, or cycling back. Dyer said that these two sounds together are "the sounds of peace and harmony and joy in your life. It is the sound of serenity that you want to go off to sleep to every night." The "AUM" sound is used to bring us to a beautiful and near perfect state of consciousness or state of being – what the Hindu tradition calls *sidi consciousness*. The great I AM, no matter our religious or spiritual belief, is a universal and a powerful sound and tool for contemplation, meditation, manifesting, and bringing us to a higher state of being.

State of being is not just a powerful spiritual idea. It has recently been described as "the master competency" for leaders and organizations in a 2009 article published in the *Organization Development Journal*. A great deal of leadership development strategies and hiring are based on models of competencies. They are primarily behavioral, cognitive, and emotional competencies like decision-making, organization, delegating, interpersonal communication, influencing others, building talent, and compassion. Others competencies are based in personality traits, motives, attitudes, and values. Psychologist Craig Polsfuss and Alexandre Ardichvili, associate professor at the department of Work and Human Resource Education at the University of Minnesota, make the case that there is a single master competency that is the executor of all other competencies. The authors conclude that State of-Mind is *the* master competency. Their description reminds me a lot of what Abraham Maslow termed *self-actualization* or Csikszentmihalyi called *flow*. The higher one's State-of-Mind they say, "the more one experiences being present and undistracted, calm, capable, at ease and free-flowing while feeling a freshness or zest for life." A strong State-of-Mind allows leaders to constantly absorb the experiences and information life provides

The great I AM, no matter our religious or spiritual belief, is a universal and a powerful sound and tool for contemplation, meditation, manifesting, and bringing us to a higher state of being.

for them, and to continue to evolve their abilities to creatively express newfound knowledge.

Achieving or maintaining this higher state of being is not usually easy in the corporate, educational, and other modern institutional environments. For most people it takes persistent efforts through frequent readings, self-awareness exercises, being open to feedback from others, contemplation, meditations, etc. It's what some people call "returning to your center." You can begin right now. As you move through your day, start noticing where your attention is. Use your Life Mission Statement, guiding principles, love, and gratitude as foundations. When you notice that your awareness is not in the present moment, notice where it is and change your focus. You don't have to live your life waiting or yearning for the future or regretting the past. Life happens to us when *we* happen to life in the now. I leave this chapter with a quote from the famous Roman, stoic philosopher, Epictetus (emphasis in the original):

> Caretake *this* moment. Immerse yourself in its particulars. Respond to *this* person, *this* challenge, *this* deed. Quit the evasions. Stop giving yourself needless trouble. It is time to really live; to fully inhabit the situation you happen to be in now. You are not some disinterested bystander. Participate. Exert yourself.

Leadership Travel Tips Chapter 9: You Are Here

- You do not have power in either the past or future.
- Begin to notice if you or others treat the present moment as if it were an obstacle that needs to be overcome.
- No amount of present guilt, regret, anger, or sorrow will *ever* change something that has *already* taken place. Be aware of past orientations. On your leadership journey, don't drive while mainly looking in the rearview mirror.
- Worrying is a negative emotion that saps the energy out of the now and no matter how much worrying we do, it will not prevent or prepare us effectively for what is to come. Be aware of future orientations. On your leadership journey, don't drive while mainly looking down at the map.
- Be aware of perfectionism and catastrophic thinking. Perfectionistic concerns and catastrophic thinking will only lead to depression and defeat present moment activities.
- Live in the now. No matter how far the journey and how many steps you must take, the only step you have any influence over is the step you are taking *right now.*
- Learn to use the Great I AM, "OM," or "AUM" in your contemplation.
- Constructively integrate your past, present, and future so that they are being used to make *this* moment something of value.

CHAPTER 10

Conducting the Tour

The first step to take is to become aware that love is an art, just as living is an art; if we want to learn how to love we must proceed in the same way we have to proceed if we want to learn any other art, say music, painting, carpentry, or the art of medicine or engineering.

~ Eric Fromm ~

I'd like to share with you a personal story that relates to the opening quote, which comes from a penetrating and practical book, *The Art of Loving*, by the renowned psychologist and social philosopher, Eric Fromm. When I was nine years old, my mother enrolled me in private piano lessons. My older sister was already playing very well, so I had an idea of what playing the piano was like. At first, I didn't want to (it just seemed girlish to the only boy of five children) but my mother promised that if I applied myself for a year and I still didn't want to take piano lessons, I would be free to make my own choice after that. Learning piano and music was difficult, at first. It was like learning a new language – all those black dots and squiggly lines on the paper. After a few weeks, some of it began to make sense and I was able to play a few very simple, beginner tunes. After a few months, I was improvising and expanding on what was actually written in the piano lesson books. I was playing the piano! I actually enjoyed it and could get lost in the nuances of variations and melodies.

After a year, I decided not to continue. Years later, when I picked up the clarinet in junior high school, those lessons really paid off. Although I never became a life-long master of the piano, I, at least for a short while, became one of the better clarinet players in our high school. That practice of the art of music influenced me – and eventually my children – for the rest of our lives in profound ways. It certainly gives me an appreciation for what 'the art of something' is. I now have great respect and admiration for those that *are* truly masters of the art of music (and other arts) and I still dabble around with a synthesizer. Because music has been and still is a part of our home, all three of my children have become amazing singers and performers – one of them professionally.

In the opening quote of this final chapter, Eric Fromm is telling us that love is an art and that our first step on the journey is to become aware of that. The art of leadership is no different. To become New Millennial Leaders, or NMLs, we must first sit with the awareness that *we are on a journey* – a leadership journey – and that leadership is an art.

Dr. Fromm further explains that learning *any* art requires discipline, concentration, and patience. At first, the many elements, tasks, and nuances of any art seem disconnected. It takes discipline, concentration, and patience for them to come together. Like my learning the piano – learning notes and musical notation, finger placement, posture, performing scales, and routine practice – doesn't seem to make sense, at first. Slowly, and seemingly imperceptibly, the various parts begin to integrate on a path toward mastery – and the master of any art soon realizes that continual practice and learning is required to remain a master. There is a sense of humility that stems from that because we soon also realize that there are those further along the path we can learn from and others who follow behind who need us to mentor them.

The art of leadership and the art of loving are beautifully interwoven and we can't truly have one without the other. Leadership without love becomes a transitory, oppressive, and coercive form of narcissism and ethnocentrism. Love without leadership is really not love at all; but a temporary, neurotic dependency. When love and leadership are interwoven, they are not transitory or temporary; they become abiding and resilient – they become a state of being. Our world is now in desperate need of NMLs to lead in government, industry, on the playground and in our homes. This New Millennial Leader (NML) is aware that love and leadership are interwoven and that they are arts to be nurtured, learned, and practiced – and that it is a life-long journey.

What then, are some of the key, seemingly disconnected, elements of the art of leadership that come together for the NML? How does the NML put these elements into a disciplined practice in order to be happy and successful and add value to their work or organization, others, and the world? What does an NML look like day to day? In other words, on the leadership journey, how does an NML conduct the tour? In the final pages, we're going to examine some answers to those questions and look at a portrait of an NML.

To become New Millennial Leaders we must first sit with the awareness that *we are on a journey* – a leadership journey – and that leadership is an art.

In the classic, *The Strangest Secret: How to Live the Life You Desire*, Earl Nightingale gives us a big hint about how to begin to conduct the tour, "If someone is working toward a predetermined goal, and knows where he or she is going, that person is a success. If they are not doing that, they are failures. Success is the progressive realization of a worthy ideal."

Take Time to Define and Align

First and foremost, the NML takes time to define and align. Her Leadership GPS is on. She has awareness – an awareness that she is on a powerful and meaningful journey and mission. She has discovered and regularly contemplates and affirms her vision, mission, and purpose – and that is primarily concerned with serving others. Sure, she has her personal goals, but her Life Mission is primarily about adding value to others in her special way, to something bigger than herself, and to the world. She knows that a recurrent theme from the spiritual masters to modern science is that if she serves others, not only does she add value to others lives, she will also be personally more successful and more authentically happy.

The NML has clearly stated the meaning and direction of her life and set personal and professional goals that manifest that vision. Most mornings, she pulls out her Life Mission Statement and contemplates those parts that seem to speak to her that day. Some days, she reads and re-reads the entire thing. She then gets out her Blackberry, opens Outlook, or gets out her "To Do" list and schedules activities that support her mission. She notices how even the tasks assigned by others, those required by career, mundane tasks, and day to day stuff are actually serving her mission.

The NML has clearly stated the meaning and direction of her life and set personal and professional goals that manifest that vision – she is defined and aligned.

Because her vision, mission, and purpose are central to her life, the NML is more than simply being aware of them; she wakes up each day and contemplates them. She finds a quiet place to sit undisturbed and sometimes she does this in bed before she even gets up or as she falls asleep. She examines it from different angles, often incorporating recent lessons learned from reading or interactions with others. As she contemplates an element, she doesn't just think about it, she *feels* it.

There is an emotional fire that burns with each value, goal, and objective. She visualizes the manifestation of them, what it looks like, and how that feels. Often, she visualizes the acts of service and giving – everything from preparing a meal to the most challenging work she will do that day. The NML understands that the end of the journey and other intermediary milestones are only half the equation. She equally – sometimes even more so – contemplates the steps or tasks of the day and how those serve the ultimate goal. While her vision is far-reaching, she remains diligent to the now and the tasks at hand. She isn't simply fantasizing and allowing her mind to wander. She is contemplating and that's harder, more focused mental work.

The NML frequently remembers and contemplates how *she* has been served, nurtured, and blessed. This generates feelings of gratefulness that she holds in her being. She is particularly nurturing of the positive feelings of joy, gratitude, trust, confidence, creativity, goodness, connectedness, abundance, service, and freedom that flow out of this contemplation.

When she notices that she is getting out of alignment, such as when less productive feelings arise (e.g., fear, anxiety, lack of confidence, anger), she recognizes that ANTs may be around, and actively works to realign. She doesn't fuel them, push them away, or bury them. She chooses from a list of techniques and strategies that might include:

- The Sedona Method
- The Freeze-Frame Technique
- Reframing ANTs
- The 100% Test
- Binaural Entrainment
- Any number of gratitude-generating techniques
- Seeking counsel

She seeks to replace negative, self-defeating emotions with powerful, positive ones. She knows it's not easy to do, but she asks herself, "How will feeling angry or anxious (or other negative emotions) serve me or anyone else in *any* way?" "Do I *want* to feel this way or something more positive and productive?" She doesn't ignore or sweep them under the rug or make excuses. She acts on them. She incorporates goals, objectives, and action items into her mission that lead her down a path of improvement. But her primary focus is on the positive, especially her vision, mission, and purpose. She concentrates her energy like a laser.

In addition, her life mission and her organization's mission are aligned. Being aligned doesn't necessarily mean that the two missions are exactly the same – they just serve each other well. Because her Leadership GPS is on, she notices and communicates messages congruent with the organization's mission and values to her direct reports and others. Her work team is aware of their role in making the mission real and each of them knows what is expected – what their specifics tasks and targets are and precisely when they are due – and how they are connected to the greater good, not just for the organization, but those they serve. She is inspired and inspiring.

She also possesses an amazing patience with and trust of herself that spills out to others around her. She is tranquil, but alert and aware that she is not finished; she's on a journey – and so are others. One step, then another. Growing, learning, becoming. She has a deep-rooted confidence in those she leads. Some say it stems from a deep, personal faith. Because her Leadership GPS is always on, she is defined and aligned.

She has a deep-rooted confidence in those she leads. Some say it stems from a deep, personal faith.

Loving Leader

Because the NML's life mission is aligned with her organization's mission and she contemplates them almost every day, she loves her work. Most days she is excited, enthusiastic, and frequently enjoys personal rewards and fulfillment from what she does. That excitement is contagious to those around her.

Not only that, she loves the people around her. Her work team has high group cohesion, productivity, job performance, and they are happy. It's very seldom that anyone quits this high-performing and connected team. And that's because, in addition to regularly communicating the mission, goals, and targets, she *listens to them.* She takes time to regularly touch base with each of her team members and direct reports. Not only is she skilled with empathic listening techniques, you can tell she's not simply using them because they're a technique to get her something; the NML listens because *she genuinely cares and responds* to the needs of those she leads.

She also makes sure they have the proper tools, equipment, and support – and will fight for them 'behind the scenes' to get them, if necessary. When she does occasionally lose a battle to get them what they

She sees her role as being in service to those she leads, caring about them and their work, and then lets them go.

need or it's simply not possible, she doesn't blame; she takes responsibility, apologizes, and works with her team towards the best alternative solutions or remedies.

She sees her role as being in service to those she leads, caring about them and their work, and then lets them go. While the NML is clear about goals and timelines, she doesn't micro-manage. She knows that when her team is connected to the mission and goals, feels cared for and respected by her, and have what they legitimately need, her team is going to 'bust their butts' for her and each other. She nurtures the natural tendency that people want to do a good job and contribute to something larger than themselves.

Validation

The NML is particularly skilled at using validation statements. When discussing a problem, trying to resolve a conflict, or coaching a team member, she clearly states the issue and its importance. Then, instead of launching into her thoughts, feelings, and expectations, she first tries to understand the other's experience, thought process, and feelings. She is a master at validating that experience without necessarily agreeing or condoning. She can then follow validation with expectations or coaching, if necessary, but she first enters the other's world for a while and affirms that. This makes those who are on her team feel respected and valued – even if the boss doesn't always agree or condone what was done.

The NML does simple little caring things, like setting birthday and hire date anniversary reminders about each team member. She knows personally important stuff about each of her team members; like, who they love, their hobbies, and what they dream of. She's interested in what motivates each individual and cares about their day to day state of being.

Genuine

One of the NML's qualities that you often hear about from her team is that she is *real*. She's never fake and is rarely defensive. She is a very positive person, but not Pollyannaish. It's not that she doesn't sometimes have and display emotions such as dissatisfaction or frustration; it's just that when the NML does have challenging or even negative emotions, she's not out to 'get' you or anyone else because of them – and knowing that about her makes you feel safe. She's simply genuine. That's different from someone who wears their heart out on their sleeve and lets every emotion come gushing out. No, the NML is aware of and regulates her emotional response and the thoughts that go with them in order to serve others and herself more effectively. She doesn't have a secret agenda. She's real.

Gratitude

One of the NML's shining attributes is her gratitude. She is a grateful person in every aspect of her life. She nurtures gratitude by keeping a gratitude journal. She looks for things to be grateful for throughout the day – even in challenging and disappointing situations.

She regularly rewards her team members with an appropriate level of gratitude for corresponding good work. She's not limited to how she shows her gratitude. She does it all. She likes to give them credit where and when credit is due. Because she knows that the quicker the reward, the more powerful the reinforcement, she uses a simple "Thank

> One of the New Millennial Leader's shining attributes is her gratitude.

you" what seems like all the time. She writes thank you emails, notes, and cards, but the NML prefers to come to you in person or in front of the team, shake your hand, and say, "Thank you! You did a great job!" And she names specifically what that is.

She also uses the Tell Your Boss Technique and the two of them collaborate on gratitude and rewards for some of the more outstanding work. She also encourages those that supervise others on her team to use it with her, too. Of course, she uses the formal reward program at her organization in those cases, too, but that's not the primary or most frequent way she expresses gratitude. She remembers the words of President Harry Truman, "It is amazing what you can accomplish if you do not care who gets the credit." She is humble about her efforts and praises her team for theirs.

Integrity

Undergirding every aspect of the NML's life is integrity. The NML 'walks the talk' with a sense of humility. She is not condescending and at the same time holds herself and her team to the highest of standards. She not only hires people who are capable and caring, she hires people with strong character and integrity. She regularly communicates to her team about ethical issues and incorporates the language of ethics, character, and integrity into daily conversations. She doesn't tolerate unethical behavior while realizing that sometimes, ethics is not always black and white, so she is aware of and coaches through ambiguous situations and quickly enforces correction, including termination

Undergirding every aspect of the NML's life is integrity. The NML 'walks the talk' with a sense of humility.

(when necessary), when it *is* clear. She also understands that most people look outside of themselves to leaders and team members for the rules and guidelines of behavior so she is a model of integrity and cultivates an ethical culture. She isn't afraid of conflict, knowing that when it is resolved openly and positively, her team will be more cohesive and determined in their agreed strategies.

Her joy and happiness originates from a connectedness and gratitude for everyone and everything – even if she may not fully understand.

Now

The NML lives in the now. Although powered by a powerful mission, she is not always looking at the map or in the rearview mirror. These serve her as tools, but by being present to the tasks and people of the moment, she connects more fully, gets more done, and enjoys life more. She forgives both herself and others. That doesn't mean she forgets. She learns from past mistakes; she just doesn't brood over them or use them as weapons on others. While goals and targets are important, she knows that they are only achieved by taking each step attentively and if she allows herself or the team to be caught up in worry, they will only be wasting valuable energy. She can be comfortable with uncertainty; she knows that she possesses the skill, character, flexibility, creativity, and team that can deal with anything.

Happy

The one quality that everyone seems to agree on about the NML is that she is happy. She's not manically ecstatic; she has a real deep joy about her. She genuinely smiles at anyone and everyone – from the CEO to the janitor. It's as if she were in that classroom from the urban legend about

The New Millennial Leader's joy and happiness originate from a connectedness and gratitude for everyone and everything – even if she may not fully understand.

the final exam. Have you heard it? It's final exam time at a prestigious University. A professor in an advanced Philosophy course is about to administer his final exam. He walks up to the chalkboard that's covered by a film screen. As he retracts the screen, he explains, "To understand philosophy, you must understand people, to understand people you must know them. To that end, this one question will comprise your course grade: *Write the name of the janitor who cleans this room and hallway and this floor every day so you can attend this fine institution and receive an advanced degree from it:* _________________. You see, pass, interact, and rely upon this 'silent,' humble, yet dependable stalwart, who day in and day out performs his task with dignity and pride. We should *all* know these individuals in our lives. They demonstrate leadership at its essence." She passed that final exam. She respects and honors everyone.

Her joy and happiness originates from a connectedness and gratitude for everyone and everything – even if she may not fully understand. Because she is genuinely happy, people gravitate to her and enjoy her company. She is less concerned about herself and seems to be naturally curious about the other person. You just feel better when you're around her. She is a focused, grateful, respectful, strong, happy, servant who lives in the now. These attributes, which she regularly cultivates and nurtures, are what makes her and those she leads successful.

The famous words of Lao-tzu ring true about her:

With the greatest leaders above them,
people barely know one exists.
Next comes one whom they love and praise.
Next comes one whom they fear.

When a leader trusts no one,
no one trusts him.

The great leader speaks little.
He never speaks carelessly.
He works without self-interest and leaves no trace.
When all is finished, the people say,
"We did it ourselves."
17th Verse of the Tao Te Ching

I urge you to become a New Millennial Leader. The people of the new millennium are expecting – and need – a new type of leader that focuses on love, service, and people – as well as results. Begin a new and powerful journey of transforming – of leading – yourself and others. May your journey be filled with an active and vibrant passion for adding value and love and for nurturing growth in yourself, others, and our world.

About the Author

Alan A. Mikolaj, MA is a professional, positive, and powerful speaker, the author of three books, and the founder and Executive Director of Lædan Enterprises, LLC. Alan holds his Master of Arts degree in Clinical Psychology from Sam Houston State University. He has taught at San Antonio College, the North Harris County Community College District, the University of Texas Health Science Center at San Antonio, Sam Houston State University, and the Bradford School of Business. He has served volunteer critical incident stress management organizations for over eleven years. He was the founding president of the Southwest Texas CISM team in San Antonio and is currently a clinical member of the Bluebonnet CISM team that serves the greater Houston area emergency services. He has been a frontline emergency paramedic and has served the emergency services and healthcare communities as a trainer, educator, and author for over twenty-five years. He has also served as the Director of Youth Ministry for a church in Texas.

Website: www.alanmikolaj.com

Email: alan@laedanenterprises.com

NOTES:

NOTES:

NOTES:

Bibliography

Aasland, M. S., Skogstad, A., Notelaers, G., Nielsen, M. B., & Einarsen, S. (2009). The prevalence of destructive leadership behaviour. *British Journal of Management , 21*, 438-452.

Aknin, L. B., Norton, M. I., & Dunn, E. W. (2009). From wealth to well-being? Money matters, but less than people think. *The Journal of Positive Psychology, 4* (6), 523-527.

Anderson, B. W. (1975). *Understanding the Old Testament* (Third ed.). Eglewood Cliffs, NJ: Prentice-Hall.

Anthony, K. (2002). *EEG and Your Brainwaves - Binaural Beats*. Retrieved July 16, 2010, from Scientific Audio Resources: http://www.rainfall.com/cdroms/brainwave.htm

Ashkanasy, N. M., & Daus, C. S. (2002). Emotion in the workplace: The new challenge for managers. *Academy of Management Executive , 16* (1), 79-86.

Atkinson, W. (1906). *Thought Vibration.* Chicago, IL: The New Thought Publishing Company.

Baldoni, J. (2011, July 16). *Women in Leadership*. Retrieved July 16, 2011, from Australian Centre for Leadership for Women: http://www.leadershipforwomen.com.au/quotes.htm

Barlow, D. H. (1988). *Anxiety and Its Disorders.* New York: Guilford Press.

Barrios-Choplin, B. M. (1997). An inner quality approach to reducing stress and improving physical and emotional wellbeing at work. *Stress Medicine , 13*, 193-201.

Bass, B. M. (1990). From transactional to transformational leadership: Learning to share the vision. *Organizational Dynamics , 18* (3), 19-32.

Baumeister, R. F., & Leary, M. R. (1995). The need to belong: Desire for interpersonal attachments as a fundamental human motivation. *Psychological Bulletin , 117* (3), 497-529.

Baumeister, R. F., Bratslavsky, E., Finkenauer, C., & Vohs, K. D. (2001). Bad Is stronger than good. *Review of General Psychology , 5* (4), 323-370.

benevolent. (n.d.). *Dictionary.com Unabridged*. Retrieved May 2, 2011, from from Dictionary.com website:: http://dictionary.reference.com/browse/benevolent

Bennis, W. (1994). *On Becoming a Leader.* Cambridge, MA: Perseus Books.

Bible, T. A. (1987). *Amplified Bible*. La Habra, CA: The Lockman Foundation.

Blanchard, K., & Spencer, J. (1981). *The One Minute Manager.* New York: HarperCollins Publishers.

BlessingWhite. (2008). *The State of Employee Engagement 2008.* Princeton: BlessingWhite, Inc.

Boehm, J. K., & Lyubomirsky, S. (2008). Does happiness promote career success? *Journal of Career Assessment , 16*, 101-116.

Bono, G., Emmons, R. A., & McCullough, M. E. (2004). Gratitude in practice and the practice of gratitude. In P. A. Linley, & S. Joseph (Eds.), *Positive Psychology in Practice* (pp. 464-481). Hoboken, NJ: John Wiley & Sons.

Braden, G. (2008). *The Spontaneous Healing of Belief.* New York: Hay House, Inc.

BrainyMedia. (2010). *Tony Robbins Quotes*. Retrieved July 8, 2010, from BrainyQuote: http://www.brainyquote.com/quotes/authors/t/tony_robbins.html

Brava, J. (2010, April 12). *How's Your Vision?* Retrieved July 17, 2010, from FrontlineLeadership.com: http://www.frontlineleadership.com/2010/04/hows-your-vision/

Brehm, S. S. (1992). *Intimate Relationships.* New York: McGraw-Hill.

Brower, L. (n.d.). *The Gratitude Rock*. Retrieved November 9, 2010, from leebrower.com: http://www.leebrower.com/the_gratitude_rock.htm

Brown, M. E., & Trevino, L. K. (2006). Ethical leadership: A review and future directions. *The Leadership Quarterly , 17*, 595-616.

Buckingham, M., & Coffman, C. (1999). *First Break All the Rules: What the World's Greatest Managers Do Differently.* New York: Simon & Schuster.

Buscaglia, L. F. (1992). *Born for Love: Reflections on Loving.* Thorofare, NJ: SLACK Incorporated.

Canfield, J. (2010, August 14). *Daily Disciplines for Effortless Success: Six Steps for Activating "The Secret" in Your Life*. Retrieved August 14, 2010, from Article North: http://www.articlenorth.com/templates/JackCanfield_Articles1.html

Carnegie, D. (1936). *How to Win Friends and Influence People.* New York: Simon & Schuster.

Charles, S. (2004). *Frequency of Brain Waves*. (G. Elert, Editor) Retrieved July 16, 2010, from The Physics Factbook: http://hypertextbook.com/facts/2004/SamanthaCharles.shtml

Childre, D., & Cryer, B. (2004). *From Chaos to Coherence: The Power to Change Performance.* Boulder Creek, CA: HeartMath LLC.

Clark, J. (2010, January 7). *The Biggest Financial Deception and Scam of the Decade*. (Market Oracle Ltd) Retrieved February 12, 2011, from The Market Oracle: http://www.marketoracle.co.uk/index.php?name=News&file=article&sid=16281

Coolidge, F. L., & Wynn, T. (2001). Executive functions of the frontal lobes and the evolutionary ascendancy of Homo Sapiens. *Cambridge Archeological Journal , 11* (2), 255-60.

Covey, S. R. (2004). *The 8th Habit: From Effectiveness to Greatness.* New York: Free Press.

Cox, D., La Caze, M., & Levine, M. (2005, Fall). *Integrity*. Retrieved April 28, 2009, from Stanford Encyclopedia of Philosophy: http://plato.stanford.edu/archives/fall2005/entries/integrity/

Crawford, C. (2003, July). Exploring the relationship between knowledge management and transformational leadership. *Paper presented at the ALE 2003 Conference.* Anchorage: Paper presented at the ALE 2003 Conference.

Crum, A. J., & Langer, E. J. (2007). Mind-set matters: Exercise and the placebo effect. *Psychological Science , 18* (2), 165-171.

Czinkota, M. R. (2005). *Loosening the Shackles: The Future of Global Higher Education.* Georgetown University. Geneva: McDonough School of Business.

Davis, J. H., Schoorman, F. D., Mayer, R. C., & Tan, H. H. (2000). The trusted general manager and business unit performance: Empirical evidence of a competitive advantage. *Strategic Management Journal , 21*, 563-579.

Deci, E. L., & Ryan, R. M. (2000). The "what" and "why" of goal pursuits: Human needs and the self-determination of behavior. *Psychological Inquiry , 11*, 227-268.

diem, C. (2011). *Carpe diem.* Retrieved July 9, 2011, from Wikipedia, The Free Encyclopedia: http://en.wikipedia.org/wiki/Carpe_diem

Diener, E., & Christie, S. (2003). Subjective well-being is desirble, but not the summum bonum. *Minnesota Interdisciplinary Workshop on Well-Being.* Minneapolis.

Diener, E., & Lucas, R. E. (1999). Personality and subjective well-being. In D. Kahneman, E. Diener, & N. Schwarz (Eds.), *Well-being: The Foundations of Hedonic Psychology* (pp. 213-229). New York: Russell Sage Foundation.

Diener, E., & Seligman, M. E. (2004). Beyond money. *Psychological Science in the Public Interest, 5* (1), 1-31. Washington, DC: Sage Publications.

Dobbs, D. (2006, April). A revealing reflection. *Scientific American* . New York: Nature Publishing Group.

Dooley, M. (2011). *Leveraging the Universe: 7 Steps to Engaging Life's Magic.* New York: Atria Books.

Drucker, P. F. (1999). *Management Challenges for the 21st Century.* New York: Harper Business.

Drucker, P. (1993). *Post-Capatilist Society.* New York: Harper Business.

Dunn, J. R., & Schweitzer, M. E. (2005). Feeling and believing: The influence of emotion on trust. *Journal of Personality and Social Psychology , 88* (5), 736-748.

Dwoskin, H. (2003). *The Sedona Method: You Key to Lasting Happines, Success, Peace and Emotional Well-being.* Sedona, AZ: Sedona Press.

Dyer, W. (Composer). (1995). [W. Dyer, Performer] On *Meditations for Manifesting*. Carlsbad, CA, USA.

Dyer, W. (2009). *Excuses Be Gone! How to Change Lifelong, Self-Defeating Thinking Habits.* New York: Hay House.

Dyer, W. (2009). [W. Dyer, Performer] On *Excuses Be Gone! Excuses Begone! 7-CD set. How to Change Lifelong, Self-Defeating Thinking Habits.* . Audio CD. New York: Hay House.

Dyer, W. (2004). *The Power of Intention: Learning to Co-Create Your World Your Way.* Carlsbad, CA: Hay House.

Dyer, W. W. (2008). *Living the Wisdom of the Tao: The Complete Tao Te Ching and Affirmations.* New York: Hay House.

Dyer, W. (1976). *Your Erroneous Zones.* New York: Harper Perennial.

Dyer, W. (1995). *Your Erroneous Zones.* New York: Avon Books.

Einarsen, S., Aasland, M., & Skogstad, A. (2007). Destructive leadership behaviour: A definition and conceptual model. *The Leadership Quarterly , 18* (3), 207-216.

Emmons, R. A., & McCullough, M. E. (2003). Conting blessings versus burdens: An experimental investigation of gratitude and subjective well-being in daily life. *Journal of Personality and Social Psychology , 84* (2), 377-389.

Emmons, R. A., & Shelton, C. M. (2002). Gratitude and the science of positive psychology. In C. Snyder, & S. Lopez, *Handbook of Positive Psychology* (pp. 459-471). New York: Oxford University Press.

Epictetus. (1995). *The Art of Living: The Classic Manual on Virtue, Happiness, and Effectiveness.* (S. Lebell, Trans.) New York: Harper Collins.

Felmlee, D., & Sprecher, S. (2006). Love. In J. Stets, & J. Turner (Eds.), *Handbook of the Sociology of Emotions.* New York: Springer.

Fournier, J. C., DeRubeis, R. J., Hollon, S. D., Dimidjian, S., Amsterdam, J. D., Shelton, R. C., et al. (2010). Antidepressant drug effects and depression severity: A patient-level meta-analysis. *The Journal of the American Medical Association , 303* (1), 47-53.

Fowler, J. H., & Christakis, N. A. (2008). Dynamic spread of happiness in a large social network: Longitudinal analysis over 20 years in the Framingham Heart Study. *British Medical Journal , 337* (a2338), 1-9.

Frankl, V. (1984). *Man's Search for Meaning.* Boston, MA: Beacon Press.

Fredrickson, B. L., & Losada, M. F. (2005). Postive affect and the complex dynamics of human flourishing. *American Psychologist , 60* (7), 678-686.

Fredrickson, B., Tugade, M. M., Waugh, C. E., & Larkin, G. R. (2003). What good are positive emotions in crises? A prospective study of resilience and emotions following the terrorist attacks on the United States on September 11, 2001. *Journal of Personality and Social Psychology* , 365-376.

Fromm, E. (1956). *The Art of Loving.* New York: HaperCollins Publishers.

Fulghum, R. (1997). *True Love.* New York: Harper Collins.

Gerber, M. E. (2008, June 24). *Invention, creation, contagion, growth and possession.* Retrieved January 8, 2011, from Times Online: http://business.timesonline.co.uk/tol/business/entrepreneur/article4205979.ece

Glickman, R. (2002). *Optimal Thinking: How to be Your Best Self.* New York: John Wiley & Sons.

Goleman, D. (1997). *Emotional Intelligence: Why It Can Matter More Than IQ.* New York: Bantam Books.

Gottman, J. M., & Levenson, R. W. (2000). The timing of divorce: Predicting when a couple will divorce over a 14-year period. *Journal of Marriage and the Family , 62*, 737-745.

Gottman, J. M., & Silver, N. (1999). *The Seven Principles for Making Marriage Work.* New York: Three Rivers Press.

Gottman, J. (1994). *Why Marriages Succeed or Fail... and How You Can Make Yours Last.* New York: Fireside.

Graham, A. R., Sherry, S. B., Stewart, S. H., Sherry, D. L., McGrath, D. S., Fossum, K. M., et al. (2010). The existential model of perfectionism and depressive symptoms: A short-term, four wave longitudinal study. *Journal of Counseling Psychology , 57* (4), 423-438.

Lucas, G. (Director). (1977). *Star Wars* [Motion Picture].

Haanel, C. F. (1912). *The Master Key System.* In the public domain.

Haisch, B. (Ed.). (2010). *Calphysics Institute.* Retrieved January 11, 2010, from Calphysics Institute: Introduction to Zero-Point Energy: http://www.calphysics.org/zpe.html

Haisch, B. (2006). *The God Theory.* San Francisco, CA: Red Wheel/Weiser.

Harter, J. K., Schmidt, F. L., & Keyes, C. L. (2002). Well-being in the workplace and its relationship to business outcomes: A review of the Gallup studies. In C. Keyes, & J. Haidt (Eds.), *Flourishing: Positive Psychology and the Life Well-Lived* (pp. 205-224). Washington, D.C.: American Psychological Association.

Harvey, E., & Ventura, S. (2008). *Leadership Lessons.* Flower Mound, TX: Walk the Talk.

Harvey, P., Stoner, J., Hochwarter, W., & Kacmar, C. (2007). Dealing with bad bosses. The neutralizing effects of self-presentation and positve affect on the negative consequences of abusive supervision. *Leadership Quarterly , 18*, 264-280.

Hays, J. M., & Kim, C. Y. (2008). Renaissance leadership: Transforming leadership for the 21st century. *Asia Pacific Expert Seminar.* Sydney, Australia: Asia Pacific International College.

Hazan, C., & Shaver, P. R. (1994). Attachment as an organizational framework for research on close relationships. *Psychological Inquiry , 5* (1), 1-22.

Byrne, R. (Producer), & Heriot, D. (Director). (2006). *The Secret* [Motion Picture].

Herring, J. (2005, September 2). *Stress Management: Have To vs. Get To*. Retrieved November 20, 2010, from EzineArticles: http://ezinearticles.com/?Stress-Management:-Have-To-Vs.-Get-To&id=66579

Hill, K., Hoffman, D., & Rex, T. R. (2005). *The Value of Higher Education: Individual and Societal Benefits.* Arizona State University's W. P. Carey School of Business, L. William Seidman Research Institute. Tempe: Arizona State University.

Hill, N. (1938). *Think and Grow Rich.* Meriden, CT: The Ralston Society.

Holden, R. (2005). *Success Intelligence: Essential Lessons and Practices form the World's Leading Coaching Program on Authentic Success.* New York: Hay House.

Hopper, W. (2011). [Gratitude] Your Guidance System. *Daily Gratitude: Using the Power of Gratitude for Health, Wealth, and Happiness.* (personal communication, April 11, 2011). www.dailygratitude.com

Hunter, J. C. (1998). *The Servant: A Simple Story About the True Essence of Leadership.* New York: Crown Business.

integer. (n.d.). *Online Etymology Dictionary*. Retrieved May 2, 2011, from from Dictionary.com website:: http://dictionary.reference.com/browse/integer

James, W. (1902). *The Varieties of Religious Experience: A Study in Human Nature.* New York: The Modern Library.

Kahneman, D. (2003, August 17). Toward a science of wellbeing. *All In the Mind.* (N. Mitchell, Interviewer) ABC Radio National.

Kahneman, D., & Krueger, A. B. (2006). Developments in the measurement of subjective well-being. *Journal of Economic Perspectives , 20* (1), 3-24.

Kamhawi, R., & Grabe, M. E. (2008). Engaging the female audience: An evolutionary psyhchology perspective on gendered responses to news valence frames. *Journal of Broadcasting and Electronic Media , 52* (1), 33-51.

Kelloway, E. K., Inness, M., Barling, J., Francis, L., & Turner, N. (2010). Loving one's job: Construct development and implications for individual well-being. In P. L. Perrewe, & D. C. Ganster (Eds.), *New Developments in Theoretical and Conceptual Approaches to Job Stress* (pp. 109-136). Bingley, UK: Emerald Group Publishing Limited.

King, J. M. (2011, January 17). *Martin Luther King, Jr: A Time to Break Silence (Declaration Against the Vietnam War)*. Retrieved January 18, 2011, from American Rhetoric: http://www.americanrhetoric.com/speeches/mlkatimetobreaksilence2.htm

King, L. A., Eells, J. E., & Burton, C. M. (2004). The good life, broadly and narrowly considered. In P. A. Linley, & S. Joseph (Eds.). Hoboken, NJ: John Wiley and Sons.

Kornfield, J. (1993). *A Path With Heart: A Guide Through the Perils and Promises of Spiritual Life.* New York: Bantam Books.

Laff, M. (2007, March). *The Myth of Multitasking.* Retrieved March 19, 2011, from T+D: Training + Development, American Society for Training and Development: http://www.astd.org/NR/rdonlyres/F667EFB0-058C-4369-B9B4-04E1DBEE91AC/0/Mar2007_research_free.pdf

Laszlo, E. (2004). *Science and the Akashic Field: An Integral Theory of Everything.* Rochester, VT: Inner Traditions. www.InnerTraditions.com

lead. (n.d.). *Online Etymology Dictionary*. Retrieved December 31, 2009, from http://dictionary.reference.com/browse/lead

Lencioni, P. (2002). *The Five Dysfunctions of a Team.* San Francisco, CA: Jossey-Bass.

Lipman-Blumen, J. (2005). *The Allure of Toxic Leaders: Why We Follow Destructive Bosses and Corrupt Politicians-and How We Can Survive Them.* New York: Oxford University Press.

Lipton, B. (2008). *The Biology of Belief.* New York: Hay House.

Lohmann, U. G. (2001). Learning leadership. (R. I. Lester, & A. G. Morton, Eds.) *Concepts for Air Force Leadership* , pp. 139-142.

Losada, M., & Heaphy, E. (2004). The role of positivity and connectivity in the performance of business teams: A nonlinear dynamics model. *American Behavioral Scientist , 47* (6), 740-765.

Lyubomirsky, S., King, L., & Diener, E. (2005). The benefits of frequent positive affect: Does happiness lead to success? *Psychological Bulletin* , 803-855.

Marieb, E. N. (1989). *Human Anatomy and Physiology.* Redwood City, CA: The Benjamin/Cummings Publishing Company.

Maxwell, J. C. (2002). *Leadership 101: What Every Leader Needs to Know.* Nashville, TN: Thomas Nelson Publishers.

Maxwell, J. C. (1998). *The 21 Irrefutable Laws of Leadership.* Nashville, TN: Thomas Nelson Publishers.

Mayer, D. M., Kuenzi, M., Greenbaum, R., Bardes, M., & Salvador, R. (2009). How low eoes ethical leadership flow? Test of a trickle-down model. *Organizational Behavior and Human Decision Processes , 108*, 1-13.

Mayer, R. C., Davis, J. H., & Schoorman, F. D. (1995). An integrative model of organizational trust. *Academy of Management Review , 20*, 709-734.

McCraty, R., Atkinson, M., & Tomasino, D. (2001). *Science of the Heart: Exploring the Role of the Heart in Human Performance.* Boulder Creek: Institute of HeartMath.

McTaggart, L. (2009, March 22). *Living the Field-The Scientific Study of Spirituality*. Retrieved March 22, 2009, from Personal communication: A thought for the day from Living the Field: http://www.livingthefield.com/

McTaggart, L. (2002). *The Field.* New York: HarperCollins Publishers, Inc.

Media, B. (2010). *Albet Einstein Quotes*. Retrieved July 31, 2010, from BrainyQuote: http://www.brainyquote.com/quotes/quotes/a/alberteins133991.html

Meyer, J. P., Stanley, D. J., Herscovitch, L., & Topolnytsky, L. (2002). Affective, continuance, and normative commitment to the organization: A meta-analysis of antecedents, corrleates, and consequences. *Journal of Vocational Behavior , 61*, 20-52.

Mikolaj, A. A. (2004). *Stress Management for the Emergency Care Provider.* Saddle River, NJ: Brady/Prentice Hall Health.

Mindell, A. (2000). *Quantum Mind: The Edge Between Physics and Psychology.* Portland, OR: Las Tse Press.

Moseley, J. B., O'Malley, K., Petersen, N. J., Menke, T., J., B. B., Kuyendall, D. H., et al. (2002). A controlled trial of arthroscopic surgery for osteoarthritis of the knee. *The New England Journal of Medicine , 347* (2), 81-88.

Myers, D. G. (2004). Human connections and the good life: Balancing individuality and community in public policy. In P. A. Linley, & S. Joseph (Eds.), *Positive Psychology in Practice* (pp. 641-657). Hoboken, NJ: John Wiley and Sons.

Newquist, K. (2010, Decemeber 9). *The Great Fullness of Life*. Retrieved June 25, 2011, from Sacrament Coaches Association: http://www.sacramentocoaches.org/the-great-fullness-of-life/fulfillment/

Nightingale, E. (2005). *The Strangest Secret: How to Live the Life You Desire.* Naperville, IL: Simple Truths/Nightingale Conant.

Olshansky, B. (2007). Placebo and nocebo in cardiovascular health: Implications for healthcare, research, and the doctor-patient relationship. *Journal of the American College of Cardiology , 49* (4), 415-421.

Organisation for Economic Cooperation and Development (OECD). (2009). *Average Annual Hours Actually Worked Per Worker*. Retrieved December 31, 2010, from Organisation for Economic Cooperation and Development (OECD): http://stats.oecd.org/Index.aspx?DataSetCode=ANHRS

Pachter, B. (2000). *The Power of Positive Confrontation: The Skills You Need to Know to Handle Conflicts at Work, Home, and in Life.* New York: Marlowe and Company.

Parker, S. & Anderson, M. (2006). *212° The Extra Degree.* Aurora, Illinois: Simple Truths.

Patterson, K., Grenny, J., McMillan, R., & Switzler, A. (2002). *Crucial Conversations: Tools for Talking When Stakes Are High.* New York: McGraw-Hill.

Peck, M. S. (1978). *The Road Less Traveled.* New York: Simon and Schuster.

Perrone, K. M., Webb, L. K., & Jackson, Z. V. (2007). Relationships between parental attachment, work and family roles, and life satisfaction. *Career Development Quarterly , 55* (3), 237-248.

Polfuss, C., & Ardichvili, A. (2009). State-of-mind as the master competency for high-performance leadership. *Organization Development Journal , 27* (3), 23.

Post, S., & Neimark, J. (2007). *Why Good Things Happen to Good People: How to Live a Longer, Healthier, Happier Life by the Simple Act of Giving.* New York: Broadway Books.

Quinn, R. E. (2011, July 17). *Change Quotes*. Retrieved July 17, 2011, from Leading Thoughts-Leadership Now.com: http://www.leadershipnow.com/changequotes.html

Rath, T., & Clifton, D. O. (2004). *How Full is Your Bucket?* New York: The Gallup Organization.

respect. (n.d.). *Dictionary.com*. Retrieved March 24, 2011, from Dictionary.com Unabridged: http://dictionary.reference.com/browse/respect

Rieber, L. P. (1995). A historical review of visualization in human cognition. *Educational Technology Research and Development , 43* (1), 45-56.

Rizzolatti, G., & Craighero, L. (2005). Mirror neuron: a neurological approach to empathy. In J.-P. Changeux, A. R. Damasio, W. Singer, & Y. Christen (Eds.), *Neurobiology of Human Values* (pp. 107-123). Berlin: Springer Berlin Heidelberg.

Robyn, S. (2005). *Go Gratitude!* Ashland, OR: Pass Along Concepts.

Rogers, C. (1975). Empathic: An unappreciated way of being. *The Counseling Psychologist , 5* (2), 2-10.

Ryan, M. J. (2007). *Giving Thanks: The Gifts of Gratitude.* San Francisco, CA: Red Wheel/Weiser Books and Conari Press.

Ryan, R. M., & Deci, E. L. (2001). On happiness and human potentials: A review of research on hedonic and eudaimonic well-being. *Annual Review of Psychology , 52*, 141-166.

saint. (n.d.). *Dictionary.com Unabridged*. Retrieved May 7, 2011, from from Dictionary.com website:: http://dictionary.reference.com/browse/saint

Salovey, P., Caruso, D., & Mayer, J. D. (2004). Emotional intelligence in practice. In P. A. Linley, & S. Joseph (Eds.), *Positive Psychology in Practice* (pp. 447-463). Hoboken, NJ: John Wiley & Sons.

Santrock, J. W. (2002). *Life-Span Development.* New York: McGraw-Hill.

Schneider, B. D. (2008). *Energy Leadership: Transforming Your Workplace and Your Life from the Core* . Hoboken, NJ: John Wiley & Sons, Inc.

Schoorman, F. D., Mayer, R. C., & Davis, J. H. (2007). An integrative model of organizatonal trust: Past, present, and future. *Academy of Managment Review* , *32*, 344-354.

Schwartz, B., & Ward, A. (2004). Doing better but feeling worse: The paradox of choice. In P. A. Linley, & S. Joseph (Eds.), *Positive Psychology in Practice* (pp. 86-104). Hoboken, NJ: John Wiley & Sons.

Seaward, B. L. (1994). *Managing Stress: Principles and Strategies for Health and Wellbeing.* Boston: Jones and Bartlett Publishers.

Seligman, M. E. (n.d.). *Positive Psychology Center*. (University of Pennsylvania) Retrieved December 28, 2009, from http://www.ppc.sas.upenn.edu/

Seligman, M. E., Stern, T. A., Park, N., & Peterson, C. (2005). Positive psychology progress. *American Psychologist* , 410-421.

Seligman, M., & Csikszentmihalyi, M. (2000). Positive psychology. *American Psychologist* , 5-14.

service. (n.d.). *Dictionary.com Unabridged.* Retrieved January 18, 2011, from Dictionary.com website: http://dictionary.reference.com/browse/service

Sheldon, K. M., & Houser-Marko, L. (2001). Self-concordance, goal attainment, and the pursuit of happiess: Can there be an upward spiral? *Journal of Personality and Social Psychology* , *80* (1), 152-165.

Sheldon, K., & Lyubomirsky, S. (2004). Achieving sustainable new happiness: Prospects, practices, and prescriptions. In P. A. Linley, & S. Joseph (Eds.), *Positive Psychology in Practice* (pp. 127-145). Hoboken, NJ: John Wiley & Sons.

Shimoff, M. (2008). *Happy for No Reason.* New York: Simon & Schuster, Inc.

Siddharta, G. (n.d.). *Buddha Quotes*. Retrieved July 15, 2010, from ThinkExist.com Quotations: http://thinkexist.com/quotation/all_that_we_are_is_the_result_of_what_we_have/250612.html

Siddhartha Gautama, B. (n.d.). *Buddha Quotes Part 1*. Retrieved October 2010, 2010, from Yoga Mind Control: http://www.yoga-mind-control.com/buddha-quotes-1.html

Sivanathan, N., Arnold, K. A., Turner, N., & Barling, J. (2004). Leading well: Transformational leadership and well-being. In P. A. Linley, & S. Joseph (Eds.), *Positive Psychology in Practice* (pp. 241-255). Hoboken, NJ: John Wiley and Sons.

Smith, H. (1991). *The World's Religions:* . San Francisco, CA: Harper Collins.

Sott, B. A., Colquitt, J. A., Paddock, E. L., & Judge, T. A. (2010). A daily investigation of the role of manager empathy on employee well-being. *Organizational Behavior and Human Decision Processes* , *113*, 127-140.

Spendlove, M. (2007). Competencies for effective leadership in higher education. *International Journal of Educational Management* , *21* (5), 407-417.

Sternberg, R. J. (1986). A triangular theory of love. *Psychological Review* , *93* (2), 119-135.

success. (n.d.). *The American Heritage® Dictionary of the English Language, Fourth Edition*. Retrieved January 1, 2010, from from Dictionary.com website: http://dictionary.reference.com/browse/succeed

Sweetland, B. (1962). *Grow Rich While You Sleep.* Englewood Cliffs, NJ: Prentice-Hall.

Talbot, M. (1991). *The Holographic Universe.* New York: HarperCollins Publishers.

Tanner, J. (2009, July 10). *What is Executive Function?* Retrieved March 19, 2011, from Persuing Psychology: Current ideas and research in psychology and neuroscience: http://www.brainybehavior.com/blog/2009/07/what-is-executive-function/

Teilhard de Chardin, P. (1959). *The Phenomenon of Man.* New York: Harper and Row.

Tolle, E. (1999). *The Power of Now: A Guide to Spiritual Enlightenment.* Novato, CA: New World Library.

Tolstoy, L. (1907). *Twenty-Three Tales.* (A. Maude, & L. Maude, Trans.) New York: Funk and Wagnalls Company.

Trevino, L. K., & Brown, M. E. (2004). Managing to be ethical: Debunking five business myths. *Academy of Management Executive , 18* (2), 69-81.

Troward, T. (1909). *The Edinburgh Lectures on Mental Science.* In the public domain.

Vivekananda, S. (1896, June 26). *Vivekananda.net.* (F. P. Jr., Editor) Retrieved July 15, 2010, from The Real and Apparent Man: http://www.vivekananda.net/BooksBySwami/JnanaYoga/16_RealApparentMan.html

Watson, T. (2010). Leader ethics and organizational commitment. *Undergraduate Leadership Review , 3* (1), 16-26.

Wattles, W. D. (1911). *The Science of Being Great.* In the public domain.

Wattles, W. (1910). *The Science of Getting Rich.* In the public domain.

Weissman, D. R. (2005). *The Power of Infinite Love and Gratitude: An Evolutionary Journey to Awakening Your Spirit.* New York: Hay House.

Wilcox, E. W. (1919). The Winds of Fate. In David Price (Ed.), *Poems of Optimism.* Retrieved January 2, 2012, from Project Gutenberg: http://www.gutenberg.org/dirs/etext05/pmop10h.htm

Williams, B. K. (2008, February 3). *Three Universal Rules of Service Excellence.* Retrieved May 7, 2011, from ezinearticles.com: http://ezinearticles.com/?Three-Universal-Rules-of-Service-Excellence&id=964010

Williams, R. (2010, February 3). Science for Life. *The Perception Effect.* (D. Parks, Interviewer) Seattle, WA.

Woodbury, T. (2010). Leadership: What's love got to do with it? *Oxford Leadership Journal , 1* (3), 1-6.

www.ingramcontent.com/pod-product-compliance
Lightning Source LLC
Chambersburg PA
CBHW051943090426
42741CB00008B/1254

9780985228613